Stock & Options Trading for Life

By:
Russ Mathews

Copyright © 2019 by Russ Matthews

ISBN: 978-1-54397-546-8

Russ Mathews' social media addresses:
- **Twitter: Russ Mathews (@RussMathewsUSA)**
  https://twitter.com/RussMathewsUSA
- **Email:** Russ@MathewsCapitalManagement.com
- **Facebook (Business):** @MathewsCapitalManagement.com

Stock & Options Trading for Life

The most effective stock & option trading strategies for individual investors to profit safely in all market conditions

TABLE OF CONTENTS

Introduction: My Story – Financial Freedom Through Stocks & Options Trading for Life 1

Chapter 1: What to Do Before You Start Trading – Build Your Plan 13

Chapter 2: Develop Your Top Down Economic Worldview and Select Your Basket of Stocks and ETF's 44

Chapter 3: Fundamental Stock Analysis – What to Buy 66

Chapter 4: Technical Analysis – When To Buy 78

Chapter 5: Developing Your Personal Trading Process 92

Chapter 6: My Favorite Trading Strategies & Rules 112

Chapter 7: Trade Selection, Progression and the "Greeks" 174

Chapter 8: Trade Adjustments - What to Do When Trades Go Wrong 206

Chapter 9: Risk Management Rules – Portfolio & Trade Level 235

Chapter 10: Using Leverage and Portfolio Margin Effectively 269

Appendix A: Book Outline – Expanded Table of Contents........... 281

Appendix B: Trading Websites & Resources 290

Introduction

My Story: Financial Freedom Through Stock & Options Trading for Life

What You Will Get Out of This Book

- You will learn how to use the stock market, paired with related options, to generate a substantial consistent income for the rest of your life.

- You will learn how to identify and enter trades and longer-term investments with the strongest likelihood of winning.

- You will be able to determine the strongest stocks and related options to trade and which strategies best match each of your stocks.

- You will learn my favorite stock and options strategies for individual investors to use to transform their financial situation (after 25+ years of research & thousands of traders, markets and situations).

- You will learn how to effectively manage your downside risk in all market conditions.

- You will learn how to protect yourself and make adjustments if a trade goes wrong.

"If you want to have better performance than the crowd, you must do things differently from the crowd."
- Sir John Templeton

Welcome!

This book can change your financial life. It can turbo-charge your
investment and trading accounts, your taxable accounts, your IRA,
ROTH IRA and other qualified retirement accounts, and help you
build your savings. It may change how you think about how you
make a living, secure your retirement and pay for life's big-ticket
items.

Take this journey with me and I will show you that there are ways to
be intentional about securing your financial future. Ways to produce
a consistent income other than through a traditional job. You are not
taught the strategies covered in this book in any business school.
Nor are they taught by the vast majority of financial advisors, wealth
planning professionals, CPA's, or the educational videos or tools
available within online brokerage platforms. I will also help you
make distinctions between the ever-growing group of online trading
'coaches and educators,' also known as the 'follow my trades'
educators.

If you learn to execute the strategies and rules in this book, you will
be able to redirect most of your waking hours into more meaningful
things than going to your current job. Imagine focusing quality time
during each week on your family, church, charity, friends, helping
others and travel ... *for the rest of your life*.

Learning and practicing the stock and option strategies inside this
book will take time and practice. No skill worth mastering comes
without work and dedication. If you are disciplined and consistently
take action, you can use stock and options trading to create the life
you have always wanted. But have no illusion, the strategies inside
are *not* the same old advice of 'buy and hold and reinvest the
dividends.' It is not what 95% of financial advisors preach, which is
to build a 60% stocks / 40% fixed income portfolio, diversify, buy
and hold forever and hope for the best. That is the old way of
investing. The strategies taught here do not involve only holding a
portfolio of different diversified ETF's and mutual funds (or worse
yet, an annuity) that is so prevalent in investment literature and
professed as the only 'reasonable' investment vehicles by most
financial advisors and brokerage firms.

Instead you will learn the modern, sophisticated strategies of investing – using the news, digital tools, stocks paired with options and many other trade adjustment techniques that are infrequently taught nor used by the majority of investors.

My Story

Changing your financial life is a bold claim. I don't make such a grand claim flippantly. I can say it because I have lived it and personally taught these techniques to over 1,000 clients and students on a one on one basis. I used a small base of personal capital, a financial plan and the strategies and practices explained in this book to change my own life for the better.

I have been studying the stock market in earnest since 1988 and providing management consulting services to the financial services industry around the world since 1997. My consulting clients have included investment banks, broker-dealers, commercial banks, life insurance companies, hedge funds and mutual funds and high net worth individuals. I hold the MBA degree from a top school and was a senior financial advisor to high net worth clients for many years. This book is the distillation of all that I have learned from how the largest professional firms, universities, institutional investors and high net worth individuals invest capital and manage risk, boiled down for use and maximum impact for the individual investor no matter your starting capital.

For the record, I have made every mistake you can think of over my quarter-century of investing. Look up the 'Trading School of Hard Knocks' in the dictionary and there is a large picture of *Yours Truly*. But today, it has all paid off. I am a consistently profitable trader. I typically earn returns of anywhere from 10% to 50% annually. I had some down years as well (two to be exact) but have not had a down year since the financial crisis of 2008 when the stock market indexes lost over 50% of their value from the peak to the bottom.

Through the struggles, I developed the internal strength and character needed to win in the markets consistently. I have learned the lessons. I have learned how to consistently make substantial double-digit gains, without becoming a full-time trader, glued to the computer screen each day. I always felt, deep inside, that I was born to invest, using the stock market and related options and to help others learn to do the same. Even when I lost money, this internal calling kept me from surrendering and going back to the standard buy and hold (or more accurately the 'buy and hope') strategy. I knew there had to be a better way.

Prior to focusing full time on investing education and managing money for others, I had a significant corporate career. For nearly two decades, I was privileged to work at some of the most elite management consulting and financial services firms in the world. Firms which included Deloitte, EY, Experian, TD Ameritrade, Principal Financial Group and Wells Fargo Securities. While these are great companies and I respect them all tremendously, for me working 60-70 hours a week in a management consulting or in a broker dealer financial advisor role was not my highest calling.

Like many of you, I worked at a job as I was taught by society to do. I primarily worked in corporate to learn skills, pay the bills and raise my family. But over time I realized that I was not truly happy. I was constantly traveling. I wasn't giving back to my community, church, or helping individuals grow and protect their wealth with the freedom that I felt that I should be.

Using the techniques in this book, I was able to bid a fond farewell to my 18-year management-consulting career and seven-year senior financial advisor career. Using the strategies that you will learn here, I was able to become free from a corporate job, in a way that had seemed perpetually out of reach. I was able to become a financial knowledge broker, trainer, coach and asset manager to generate excess cash and use it to acquire assets that generated still more cash flow. These assets soon produced enough excess income to support my family and then some. I now spend most of my time with family, educating investors through speaking, writing and coaching and running my financial advisory & portfolio management firm.

The Book to Really Grow Wealth Quickly & Safely Did Not Exist – So I Wrote It

The book I needed to learn how to trade and invest in the financial markets in new and more powerful ways did not exist – or at least I had not found it after 25+ years of searching and reading more than 500 of them. The online supposed trading guru's and 'follow my hot trade alerts' services are also mostly garbage. I have studied many of them and my conclusion is that they will not make you substantial money. There are a few online services that are the real deal but most are services using stock screeners and technical indicators and touting these as can't miss trades. Buyer beware.

You see, despite majoring in Finance in a top US University, obtaining my MBA with an emphasis in Finance, getting jobs in finance and financial services consulting at top firms after University, and obtaining several securities and insurance licenses and working as a senior financial advisor, I did not learn how to invest and trade with any compelling strategies.

It seems the collective wisdom taught in Universities and investment-oriented firms consists solely of ONE broadly defined strategy. That strategy can be loosely summarized as follows:
- **Diversify** – by buying at least 25-30 different stocks and bonds (or more likely stock & bond mutual funds or ETFs)
- **Buy and hold for decades and never sell** – since no one can reliably time large upswings in the markets, the only prudent strategy is to stay continually invested in these securities for the long term, and
- **Focus only on asset allocation, not individual stocks**– meaning concentrate not on individual securities but rather the percentages you hold between stocks bonds and alternatives (given your age and risk tolerance), and
- **Rebalance your portfolio annually**.

That's it. That is the collective wisdom and a summary of hundreds of finance textbooks, PhD dissertations, financial advisor's advice and most mutual fund and advisor portfolio manager's strategies. The latest wrinkle to the strategy for portfolio's over $1M is to add a small percentage of your assets into mutual funds or now ETFs (Exchange Traded Funds) that focus on 'non-correlated' asset classes (known as alternative assets). This alternative asset class includes such assets as hedge funds, real estate investment trusts, venture capital and master limited partnerships, etc. These funds focus on absolute returns, not beating an index – more on these later. Alternatives do not change the overall strategy. They simply augment the same strategy of diversification and buy and hold, with a new category to choose from for a small percentage of your assets.

To be clear, the traditional four principles of investing (listed in the bullet points above) are good ideas and proven... *if you are already rich and working with a large portfolio or if you have 30+ years before you need the money.*

I needed something faster, something to help me quickly build from a small amount to a large amount in five to ten years. Buying and holding mutual funds and annual rebalancing was not going to do it for me.

I then turned to authors outside of academia and financial institutions. I read over 500 books on stock and option trading, ETF strategies and insurance investing strategies. I investigated bonds but quickly ruled them out for me. Part of the reason was that I was in my mid-30's (i.e. too young to have a significant allocation to bonds / fixed income assets) but also I knew buying and holding bonds earning 5% or less and collecting their interest payments would take years. For me this also was too slow to be effective, so I concentrated my studies away from bonds and other fixed income securities (though bond ETFs work well with my trading strategies as you will see in in later chapters). I subscribed to countless investment and stock market newsletters. I followed online trading rooms and guru services. All searching for the best strategies and *real* breakthroughs.

I realized over time that I was searching for the right investment *strategies,* not attempting to identify a specific highflying company stock or a specific options trade or two. The key, I discovered, was developing repeatable formulas and risk management rules to generate monthly cash flow and build wealth quickly.

After years of searching and frustration, I realized that the single comprehensive book on the best strategies and rules teaching how to invest in stocks and options to change my life did not exist – so I wrote it here.

The End Result Is This Book

To create this book, I used experiential learning. I traded with different strategies. I took the best ideas from all the books, my formal MBA and finance training, my 25+ years of assessments and consulting to professional institutional investment firms, advising high net worth clients and personal experience trading thousands of times. Along the way, I refined, adjusted and developed my own rules and formulas. The culmination of my work is aggregated in this book.

It is not full of whimsical stories or grandfatherly reflections on a life spent trading the markets. It is a how to do this, practical guide. It is a rule-based guide, a toolkit to help you get rich and get free, for life while hedging downside risks at various levels.

This book will un-pack the secrets of the best moneymaking strategies available today for the individual investor. It will teach you the tools and rules used by successful stock and options traders as well as some of the leading hedge funds and investment banks in the world.

These strategies are powerful because they enable you to take control and do things yourself. You will be able to tailor your trading and longer term investing to your own unique timeframe, situation, starting capital and risk profile. Using a combination of strategy, discipline and your own creativity in selecting stocks and vehicles to fit the strategies to, you can create exactly the portfolio and the returns that you need to transform your financial situation.

Who This Book Is Written For?

This book is written for individual retail traders and investors. Investors who are not trading professionals but who do have some basic stock trading knowledge and experience. It is for the person who has worked for several years and saved up some capital but to date, you have likely invested primarily in mutual funds, ETFs and a few stocks. The key qualifier – individuals who are not satisfied with the returns that their mutual funds (or ETFs) and the standard 'buy and hold' strategy have generated for them in the past. As I write this, 2018 just ended with the average US stock market index

(S&P500) returning -4.38% for the year. This is not good performance – a year wasted if you are invested in the buy and hold way the experts tell you to. Yes, the indexes recovered (to 0% by the end of April 2019), but is this type of performance moving the needle for you? I will show you how to gain even in down market years and trounce the performance of actively traded mutual funds.

This book is not specifically geared for the university student or the young person who is just starting to save (though you can paper trade my strategies and practice for free on most online brokerage sites with no risk). Nor is it geared for the mid to late retiree, as most of the strategies here are too aggressive for someone already in retirement and living on a fixed income (unless you are starting with a large amount or you do so with a small percentage of your account that you can afford to lose – just in case).

In short, this book is written for people who are savvy enough to have made and saved some money, opened an IRA (or ROTH IRA) and possibly a second taxable brokerage account outside of an IRA but want to move to the next level with their investments.

It all starts with the right context. That context means creating a financial plan, selecting and mastering the right strategies and learning the tools and techniques to manage your risk if investments or trades go wrong.

Though this book is written from the perspective of a US individual investor trading in the US stock and option market instruments, the techniques you will learn in this book will work in almost any stock and options market in the developed world. The trading setups, rules and strategies in this book are also powerful because of their flexibility to match many different styles of investors and for their ability for aggressive but safe compounding ability.
They say it takes 10,000 hours to master a skillset. I have done the hard work for you. Over my 25 years of trading and investing, I have learned a lot. I have made a lot of mistakes as well. Use the information in this book to profit and dramatically shorten your learning curve. After two and a half decades of hands-on trading experience and working with clients, I have filtered through the hundreds of available trading and investing strategies out there and narrowed them down to the best six investment techniques in the

world for the individual investor. That's right- just six strategies (with my added risk management rules and experienced based edges) are all you, the non-professional need to learn for a lifetime of successful investing.

The strategies are not simplistic, but they are simple enough for any diligent investor to learn. No advanced math skills or super computer algorithms are needed. The strategies taught in this book put the odds of winning in your favor before you enter trades. I teach you the mechanics of how to enter mange and exit trades for consistent profits.

This book focuses on equity-based (stock based) trading strategies. There are bonds, and real estate investment trust securities (known by their abbreviation, 'REIT') traded on the major exchanges that also have related options (calls & puts). These securities can be traded the same way as equities with the same rules in this book and I encourage you to do so. I, however, will focus on equities throughout for simplicity. These equity instruments include individual only stocks and exchange traded funds (ETFs), and their related options (derivative securities). Every one of these securities is available to the average retail investor in a regular brokerage account or individual retirement account (IRA) or ROTH IRA of any size. They cannot be done in a 401K, 403B, 457 plan or other workplace retirement vehicles (unless the workplace retirement plan has a brokerage account option – which some now do).

There are no esoteric techniques or complicated financial instruments. There is nothing overly exotic in this book, only time-tested strategies that are not widely known but any motivated investor can master – with my rules and enhancements to reduce risk. Most investors are simply not aware of these strategies or how to use them. Through study and application, you will know how to approach the markets and may substantially change your returns for the better.

The Typical Investor

If you are an average middle to upper middle-class individual living in the USA, the following situation is typical:

- You have been taught that investing and proper diversification means to hold a variety of actively traded *mutual funds* or passively traded ETF's with different investment objectives (examples include: target date funds, growth funds, income funds, bond funds, emerging market funds, etc.). This is the advice that you were given for all of your long-term savings, including:
  - o Your employer-based retirement accounts (such as your 401k or 403b plan) and
  - o Your individual retirement account (either a traditional IRA, or a Roth IRA) outside of a work, and
  - o Potentially a taxable brokerage account (typically titled as an individual, or joint, or trust brokerage account).
- You know your mutual funds and ETFs have not consistently performed well for you (like the lost decade from the year 2000 to 2009, again in 2015 and the beginning of 2016 and in 2018, where you have lost money) but you found yourself too busy with your job and your life to actively take control of your investments or look for a better way. You simply went with the advice you were given early on, bought several mutual funds and never questioned it.
- Every few months, you check your account balances. You're frustrated at the slow increases in your portfolio, and the high fees that you are paying to get those paltry returns.
- When you have attempted to focus on your investments and look at the various choices beyond these mutual funds, you look at the many thousands of individual stocks, ETFs and other financial instruments and services saying they can help you and become overwhelmed.
- Occasionally, you took the plunge anyway. You traded some individual stocks and maybe even some options. But your results were very hit or miss. Even following the trade

alerts of an online educator didn't help. You struggle to make meaningful progress with your overall investment portfolio.

If this sounds like you, you have come to the right place. I understand the above scenario, because for many years it described me and the majority of my financial advisory clients perfectly. I didn't have time to sort through a myriad of investment strategies, but I wanted to take my investments to the next level. Somehow, I just knew that there had to be a better way.

I was willing to learn strategies, work hard and take some risk, but I didn't want to take unnecessary risks or take risks caused by inexperience or lack of knowledge. I didn't have time to sort through hundreds of stocks and read thousands of research reports. I was very wary about "get rich quick" trading schemes and stock tip trading services that flooded my email inbox. What I needed when I was in your position, was just simple, repeatable strategies that worked.

That's what this book is all about. It teaches the essential homework and investing strategies that every serious individual investor and trader must know to be consistently successful. Financial transformation can be yours.

The Bottom Line

This book will teach you why you should always continue investing. When you take control of your finances, you effectively take control of much of your life. You will not win on every trade or investment. But as Bernard Baruch (a famous investor, financier and political advisor) said, "If a speculator is correct half of the time, he is hitting a good average. Even being right three or four times out of ten should yield a person a fortune if he has the sense to cut his losses quickly."

To be clear, no one needs to master all six strategies and variations taught inside this book to be successful and make money. You can do just fine mastering two or three of the strategies. I believe learning all six strategies helps when you have a large portfolio and / or want to trade in all market conditions. They are six different tools in the toolbox and much like when building a house or fixing a car, different tools are needed at different times and in different market conditions.

This book is designed to be read in order. After you have read it all, it is ok to jump around and revisit various parts. Use it as an ongoing reference. Please, however, avoid the temptation to jump ahead straight to the six strategies and example trades in Chapter 6 and skip the homework that comes beforehand. You need the context and risk management rules covered in the chapters on financial planning, stock selection, portfolio building and analysis that precede the specific strategies themselves. Think of the strategies taught in this book as driving a high-performance Porsche sports car. If you knew little about the car or how to drive, you would not just jump in behind the wheel and try to drive it on the expressway. With proper training and risk management rules, driving that Porsche is the best experience out there. Without the training and risk management, it can kill you.

Trading with leverage and options are similar. What is taught in this book is a system, with each step building and refining the decisions that come later, while always managing and minimizing risk. Use this book to avoid the losses and lessons I learned the hard way. Learn from me and avoid years of frustration and pain. Use what works consistently to protect and grow your hard-earned nest egg.

Successful stock and options trading is one of the main ways that people have changed their lives. Does the process for investment success take hard work and study? Absolutely…. but this book will help you focus and shave years off of your learning curve and cut down the frustration and losses. Good luck to you and may your trades yield many happy returns.

Read, learn, and profit.

Chapter 1

What to Do Before You Start Trading & Investing

BEFORE YOU START TRADING, BUILD A FINANCIAL PLAN WITH A SET OF TRADING GOALS WITH TIMEFRAMES

LEARNING OBJECTIVES

- Complete your goal based financial plan before you trade

- Organize your financial plan into timeframes (short term, medium term, long term) and into the BASE portion of the portfolio & the BOOST portion of the portfolio

- Basic financial planning rules everyone should follow

- Understand the psychological aspects of trading

"Let him that would move the world, first move himself."
- Socrates

The great Chinese military strategist, Sun Tzu, said "The battle is won or lost before it is ever fought." So it is with your investment and trading strategy as well.

You want to get started trading right away. I get that. But it is important first to take a step back and build an overall goal based financial plan and then decide how to invest each section of your portfolio appropriately based on a plan.

I've learned over my years of advising clients that creating your overall financial plan organizes, or 'buckets,' portions of your investable assets into different portfolio sections or categories. This is the key first step in risk management before launching into your trading and investment program. I have seen clients skip this step and then six months later their entire portfolio is in options trades… which is far too risky.

Completing Your Goal Based Financial Plan

All of the trading strategies in this book should rest upon the framework of first building a proper goal based financial plan. In other words, your trading plan for growing your money in stocks and options should be for only a portion of your portfolio and should be part of an overall goal based financial plan.

The investment plan can be created on your own or you can work with an investment professional with strong experience in this area. Either way it should cover your decisions on current assets, goals, timing, asset allocation and risk tolerance.

It also is recommended to 'bucket,' or divide up your money into the amounts you believe you need by timeframes. This is important because you can take different amounts of risk and it is prudent to deploy different investment strategies within each timeframe. A good rule of thumb is as follows:
- Short-term (generally 18 months or less),
- Medium-term (19 months to seven years) and
- Long-term (seven years +).

There are two popular software packages for helping create your written and thoughtful financial plan – MoneyGuidePro by PIEtech (details at www.moneyguidepro.com) & eMoney (details at www.emoneyadvisor.com). There are others but these two are the most widely used by financial advisors and financial planners. You do not need to purchase such software as many of the brokerage houses (such as TD Ameritrade and Schwab) have it and can help you build a goal based financial plan at no charge as long as you are a customer or large enough prospective customer (generally over $100K).

Your financial plan will help you strategically and intentionally set the right percentage of your available money into the safe bucket, and a percentage to invest and trade to grow more aggressively. In this chapter, I only intend to give you the highlights of creating a basic financial plan. This chapter is by no means designed to replace the value of meeting with a qualified financial advisor nor to comprehensively help you to develop your own specific financial plan.

In building a goal based financial plan, asset allocation is the key outcome – not deciding on the individual securities & trades.

The outcome to focus on in building your goal based financial plan is the decision on proper asset allocation strategy, not which specific securities to buy. Decisions around specific strategies and securities come later when you get to the tactical implementation of the plan. The outcome to focus on in building a goal based financial plan is asset allocation and how much risk should you take in your overall portfolio to achieve your goals. You want to take the least risk possible to still reach your goals.

What is asset allocation? Asset allocation simply means not putting all your eggs in one basket. It refers to the idea that different asset classes offer results that are uncorrelated (or at least not perfectly correlated with each other). The argument for making the asset allocation decision first says that because certain asset classes are not correlated, by diversifying across different asset classes one can better optimize risk-adjusted returns.

As a practical matter, asset allocation means what percentage of your investable assets should you put in each of the following 4

categories:
- **Equities (& related options)** – stocks and stock funds
- **Fixed Income** – corporate bonds, CD's, Gov't Bonds, Muni bonds. Some put preferred stocks in this category as well.
- **Cash** – cash, money market sweeps, money market funds.
- **Alternatives** – hedge funds, venture capital, etc.,

One famous study, by Brinson & Beebower done in 1986, determined that an estimated 93%+ of the variation in portfolio results are determined by the asset allocation decision and not by the individual security selection. Yet all everyone wants to discuss is 'which hot stock should I buy.'

The other key input to help you determine your proper final asset allocation is your risk tolerance (driven primarily by your age and / or the number of years before you anticipate you need the money). The five general risk ratings that most financial advisors and planners use are as follows:
- **Aggressive Growth:** (defined as 90% equities or equity funds / 9% fixed income / 1% cash)
- **Growth:** (defined as 70% equities or equity funds / 29% fixed income / 1% cash)
- **Moderate Growth:** (defined as 50% equities or equity funds / 48% fixed income / 2% cash)
- **Moderate:** (defined as 35% equities or equity funds / 60% fixed income / 5% cash)
- **Conservative:** (defined as 10% equities or equity funds / 85% fixed income / 5% cash)

You can estimate your risk tolerance but it is likely better to build your financial plan and let this process and the software help you determine which category you fall into (and how it changes over time as you get older).

Your financial plan will help you determine, with a percentage likelihood of success, different scenarios and market return outcomes to see how much risk you should take in your portfolio to best meet your goals and timeframes.

What can you allocate your assets into? There are many categories. The table below captures the asset classes that most individual investors should focus on. The key asset allocation decisions you will want to make are:

- Which of these asset classes fit with my goals and plan?
- What percent of our portfolio should we allocate to safer choices and what percent should be allocated to riskier strategies? Essentially what percentage of your investable assets should you allocate to stocks vs. fixed income vs. cash?
- Which accounts should take more risk and which less risk (if you have multiple accounts, such as taxable, ROTH IRA, traditional IRA, 401K, etc.)?

Safe / Secure Asset Choices:	Riskier / Growth Asset Choices:
1. Cash & Cash Equivalents (money market ETFs & funds, etc.)	1. Owning your own business
2. Life insurance (permanent life insurance with an investment / savings component)	2. Equities & Options on Equities – this is the focus of this book
3. CDs, Step-up CDs	3. ETFs & Mutual Funds (Stock, commodity and bond funds)
4. Treasury Bills, Notes & Bonds	4. High yield ("Junk") Bonds
5. Municipal Bonds & Investment grade Corporate Bonds	5. REITS – Real Estate Investment Trusts
6. Annuities – for retirement savings & longevity insurance Structured Notes from banks	6. Commodities – Gold, Coffee, etc.
7. Pension plan from work (if applicable – these are getting rarer)	7. Real Estate – besides your primary home
8. Income producing real estate	8. Collectables – art, wine, antique cars, etc.

As an example, here is my personal asset allocation. At the time of this writing, I am 47 years old married man with one child and my wife works part time. My asset allocation strategy today is as follows:

- 45% of my portfolio in safe and secure long-term investments and
- 55% of my portfolio in growth and trading investments.

I am currently invested at the following allocation percentages:
- o   40% in USA (domestic) equities & options on these equities.
- o   10% in international equities & options on these equities.
- o   5% in REITS (Real Estate Investment Trusts). Most publicly traded REITS trade just like stocks.
- o   20% in real estate (one primary residence and income property).
- o   15% in US Treasuries (intermediate and long term) and corporate bonds.
- o   10% Life Insurance – indexed universal life (with the investment component invested for growth in the S&P500).

There is a handy rule of thumb when it comes to your asset allocation model. You should invest your age as the percentage for the safe side of the asset allocation spectrum. For me, as a 47-year-old, this would mean investing 47% in safer assets and 53% in growth assets.

Be sure to work with your financial advisor and tax professional and do semi-annual rebalancing to ensure the ratios of your asset allocation stay in the correct proportions for your financial plan, and do so in a tax efficient manner. You do not need to be an expert in all of the asset classes listed here, nor all of the tax laws and strategies – just get a good fee-based advisor for these areas.

A Few Notes on Selecting a Financial Advisor

You can build a financial plan and trade these strategies with or without the help of a licensed financial advisor. It can be a minefield selecting and meeting with a financial advisor so be careful. Many of the less skilled financial advisors don't really understand stock and options trading strategies and will just try to talk you out of it and back into a 'buy and hold' mutual funds / ETF strategy. If you find one of these, thank them for their time and move on. They just don't get it and do not have the training or experience to advise you for the active trading portion of your portfolio effectively.

That said, some of you will feel more comfortable taking a cut at drafting your financial plan using this book but then getting a second opinion from a licensed financial advisor. That is encouraged. If you do the later, remember that there are many great financial advisors who will help you create a financial plan for just a few hundred dollars (or even free if you do other business with them).

How do you find a good one? Start by asking your friends whom they use. Ask them if they are merely satisfied, or if they are genuinely happy with the performance of their financial advisor. Make a short list of the advisors with satisfied clients – these are usually the best referrals.

It's imperative that your financial advisor be licensed by the state in which they do business. I recommend using fee-only investment advisors (firms know as RIAs, or Registered Investment Advisors) that are legally required to act on your behalf as a 'fiduciary' vs. a commission-based broker or agent (please refer to a more detailed discussion as to why below).

Beyond that, it is encouraged that you also look for an investment advisor who also has the optional advanced certifications such as a certified financial planner (CFP) or a chartered life underwriter (CLU) for more expertise in life insurance and estate planning if this is a need. These will help prove which financial advisors have more advanced training and usually are the true professionals. Many people call themselves financial advisors, but too often they are just commissioned salesman with limited investment training and knowledge. They are tasked with sales (gathering assets) without a lot of real investing expertise, portfolio management or trading experience. Remember, financial advisors at brokerage houses are not paid to make you money; they are paid to gather assets and sell managed account products.

An experienced financial advisor has deep financial knowledge as well as typically a fiduciary duty to act in the best interests of the client. On the other hand, commissioned based "advisors" who are merely asset gatherers and salesmen, are incentivized to consolidate your accounts with them and push a few specific managed account products. The products are generally actively traded mutual funds, ETFs or annuities with limited selection and are sold in different combinations to virtually all clients. This is true regardless of the client's financial situation as long as they meet a 'suitability' standard.

According to the US Consumer Financial Protection Bureau, financial advisors in the US are using more than 50 different titles today. Some of these credentials are very good, such as the CFP (Certified Financial Planner), CLU (Chartered Life Underwriter) and CFA (Chartered Financial Analyst). These credentials take rigorous study, commitment to high ethical standards and require the advisor to be effectively monitored by their supervisors. On the other hand, many of the other titles used by advisors today are little more than credentials that can be purchased, not earned through rigor, study and experience. In short, you need to research the credentials of your financial adviser are legitimate and that they are truly qualified.

Remember, you should distinguish between the two ways financial advisors are paid:
- COMMISSION BASED FINANCIAL ADVISORS (Sub-Optimal)- Advisors who work on pure asset gathering sales basis or based on pushing managed accounts rather than a flat annual fee. These commission-based sales agents can be good people but these advisors are product and transaction driven. They typically only represent a small number of 'house products,' whether managed mutual funds, ETFs or annuity products. Often, they are only paid when you move accounts from outside into their firm or when you buy managed accounts, regardless of the outcome of how the investment performs for you. Many commission-only advisors use questionable credentials such as: Senior Specialist, Retirement Advisor, or Certified Senior Specialist. Avoid these, because the potential for a conflict of interest is not just high, it's virtually guaranteed.

Unfortunately, 75% of financial advisors in the US today fall in this category – they are just sales reps there to gather assets and sell financial products with little real-world strategic experience. Vs.

- FEE ONLY FINANCIAL ADVISORS (Optimal)– financial advisors in this category charge their clients a flat fee per quarter or year. These firms are also known as Registered Investment Advisors (RIAs). They are fiduciaries and charge a flat fee. This fee is generally calculated as a small percentage of the total assets under management the advisor is managing for the client (example .8%-1.5% of assets per year). This type of advisor is usually superior for you as the client for several reasons. The first is that they have a fiduciary duty to do what is best for you. Secondly, they don't get paid extra by product or for individual investment recommendations or for "churning" your account through lots of trades or recommending house products that are not ideal for you. Finally, these advisors are able to access a wide variety of investment products from many different companies. They are not tied down to the proprietary products offered by their own firm, and they can find what is suitable for you regardless of who the product is offered by. Only about 25% of financial advisors fall into the fee-only category, but this is the group that you should strive to find.

Once you have located a number of promising fee-only planners, you should interview each one of them and select the one you are most comfortable with.

Building Your Financial Plan: An overview of the key activities in setting up your financial plan
Begin with mapping out your current life stage and financial goals. Make a best guess – it does not have to be perfect. Assess and record a current state analysis of the stage of life you are in and the issues surrounding it. These involve your age, number of children, future expenses, the number of years you are from retirement, and other factors. You can then contemplate and document your goals and dreams. Use these inputs to help create a set of financial goals

(long term and short term). Setting these goals and where you want to go will be the key framework for building a good financial plan.

At first, your analysis may result in a big-picture goal. That's okay. Your overall goal could be as general as
"Protect my family financially if I die, save 10% of my take home pay, and make a 12% average annual return in a growth-oriented retirement account, so that I can retire at age 65."

Once you have this high-level overview, you should drill down into it a level or two. How do you do this?

Ask yourself good questions about your future financial needs. You should assess your current financial situation by asking yourself good questions. This process can also take place under the guidance of your financial advisor or good online financial planning and investing website. For example, ask yourself:

- Do you need your investments to produce current income to live off of, or can you reinvest all of your earnings to create even more income in the future? What annual percentage gains are you aiming for? In dollar terms, how much dividend income to you require each year and when?

- How high is your risk tolerance? What is the maximum amount that your current portfolio could decline without you losing sleep over it, or panicking out to cash? It's important to be very frank with yourself on this subject. Many investors believe that they have a higher risk tolerance than they actually do. Realize that 10% pullbacks in the US stock market happen on average one time every year. 20% pullbacks happen on average once every five years. Make sure the percentage of your portfolio you place in the stock market can ride through such pullbacks if needed (though the strategies in this book should help you cut down such losses meaningfully).

- What level of investment experience do you currently have? (Are you a Beginner, Intermediate, or Expert)?

- How much money do you need each month to pay your bills? Do you know about any "obligatory" upcoming expenses, such as health care bills, college tuition payments for children, or assisted living expenses for your parents? What about discretionary upcoming expenses, such as that vacation that you've always wanted to take? Or that sports car that you've always wanted to buy?

- What is your current income from your present job? After you've met your monthly expenses, how much is left over for you to channel into your investment portfolio each month? Should you be saving more? Can you?

- Do you know your current tax bracket and likely tax liability this year and next?

- Do you have a proper estate-planning package? This typically includes a pour-over will, a revocable living trust, an advanced health care directive (for health care decisions) and a durable power of attorney (for financial decisions)?

- Do you have adequate life and disability insurance coverage to prevent a catastrophic loss?

- Do you have a strategy to not outlive your savings? (Note: The subject of insurance will be explained in further detail below).

This list of questions is just a start. There are many more questions like this that you should think through. The more you think about them, and the more accurately you answer them, the better your financial situation in the future will be.

It is critical to undertake this exercise. Thinking hard about your current financial situation, and answering the questions about your future needs honestly, will allow you to create a plan to set your financial life on a firm foundation.

Build Your Trading Goals with Timeframes
Congratulations! If you followed the rules above, you have now built

an initial financial plan and completed your asset allocation strategy. The next step is to take the amounts you've allocated to investing and organize your portfolio goals over estimated timeframes. This means that you should set your goals and targets for each timeframe of your trading program before selecting any specific securities or even strategies. Why is this the case? It's because there are many trading and investment strategies that you could choose from. Each one is designed to meet different investment goals, time frames, and risk tolerances. If you have not defined these beforehand, it is not possible to intelligently select between the multitudes of investment strategies available to you. Define your goals, targets, and timing first.

Remember the definition of our three timeframes to group your assets into:
- Short term (generally 18 months or less),
- Medium term (19 months to seven years) and
- Long term (seven years +).

Use the following exercise to help you focus on uncovering the answer to what you will need, when you will need it, and perhaps most importantly, a compelling "why" for your trading. The "why" is what will help sustain you emotionally and keep you on track when you have a streak of bad luck in your trading program (which happens eventually to every investor).

- Define how much money you can start investing and trading with,
- Determine how much money you need to generate to fund your commitments, needs and retirement goals, and
- Determine when you will need the money for each.

Using these inputs, design a trading plan that can achieve your growth goals within the framework of your overall financial plan.

After you bucket your investable assets into short, medium & long-term timeframes, there is one more division to make. For the **medium** & **long-term** investable amounts in your portfolio, divide this total further into two parts – the **BASE** portion of the portfolio & the **BOOST** part of your portfolio.

The short-term bucket is in the financial plan but does not really need a robust investment strategy as it is money needed in the next 18 months, so it is the most limited (investments in the short term should be limited to cash, money market funds, US Treasuries and very short-term CD's). The medium-term and long-term buckets however are the investable assets and where we attempt to make the real money.

What does the *BASE* of the portfolio and the *BOOST* parts of the portfolio mean?

THE BASE OF YOUR PORTFOLIO: The Base portion of the portfolio is the core of the portfolio. It means the serious, retirement-oriented money that needs to grow but cannot take as much risk of loss. This means that one of the first decisions you will want to make is to decide what percentage of your money should be allocated as your base portfolio (defined as the serious money for your retirement and your future that should not be risked in individual stock and options strategies). For most people in their 40s, 50s and early 60s, this is ~50% - 70% of their MEDIUM TERM & LONG-TERM investable assets. That money (the BASE portfolio money) should be placed in diversified low-cost baskets of stock & fixed income ETFs and should not be actively traded. You can perhaps set a trailing stop loss order on each ETF in the BASE portfolio (down 5% or so) to prevent catastrophe if the market crashes, but otherwise leave it alone and let it work. This portion of the portfolio follows modern portfolio theory, diversification and is the long-term hold portion of the portfolio. In the base portfolio we try to match the market returns with super low fees.
THE BOOST SECTION OF YOUR PORTFOLIO: The other ~15% - 40% of your money (depending on your age and risk tolerance) is the BOOST portion of the portfolio. That part is where this book and the six active management strategies within primarily come into play. The BOOST part of your portfolio is where you try to substantially beat the market. This portion is where you buy individual stocks, trade options, and do other strategies to generate some alpha. 'Alpha' means the returns generated in excess of the benchmark indexes – what you can earn through superior strategies and trading over just buying and holding the indexes such as the S&P500. In short this is where we try to substantially beat the

market and boost our portfolio returns.

So… do not place 100% of your investable assets in the six trading strategies taught in this book!

We are not gambling or actively trading with all of our money. We are being strategic and intentional with growing and protecting our limited resources by only trading the BOOST portion of your money in active stock & options strategies.

How do you layer the three timeframes with grouping into BASE & BOOST?

The following framework will illustrate:

TIMEFRAMES:	BASE Section of the Portfolio:	BOOST Section of the portfolio:
Long term (Seven+ years)	**The BASE of the portfolio will mostly be long term in nature (if you are over seven years from retirement)**	*Note: some of your long-term money can be in the Boost section of your portfolio if you are younger or have a higher risk tolerance (more on this later).*
Medium term (19 mo. – seven years)	*Some of your medium-term money should be in fixed income and ETFs which would be part of the BASE (more on this later).*	**The BOOST portion of the portfolio will mostly cover money you plan to use in the next two to seven-year timeframe.**
Short term (<18 months)	**Cash. High yield money market funds and maybe some short-term US Treasuries.**	*None*

Defining goals with targets and timeframes does not mean you will automatically achieve them. They are the targets to shoot for. Remember – the plan will not be perfect and will change over time. That is O.K. Just get started and make your best guesses today and as life happens you can adjust each year along the way. It is much like dieting. You should first set a diet or fitness goal. Next, you set the target weight you want to achieve to meet the goal. Finally, you set a time frame over which you wish to achieve it and milestones along the way. The timeframe and target determine how aggressive your diet and exercise program need to be in order to achieve your goals and targets. The goals, targets and timeframes are not guarantees, but they help you select between trading strategies and strategically create your trading plan.

As an example, your investment goals, targets and time frames might look like this:

Sample Investment / Trading Goals:	Targets to Achieve Goals:	Time Frames:
1.) **GROWTH for RETIREMENT:** Beat the S&P500 (net of fees) each year with the trading / investing portion of my portfolio – across my IRA, ROTH IRA and Taxable accounts.	1%+ above the returns of the S&P500 index (the key benchmark).	**LONG TERM** (Measured annually but monitored quarterly).
2.) **FUND COLLEGE IN TEN YEARS:** Save & Fund my child's college in ten years	Average 9%+ returns and save an additional $5K per year every year for ten years.	**LONG TERM** (Measured annually but monitored quarterly).

3.) **HEDGE/ MINIMIZE PROTFOLIO RISK:** Employ Proper risk management and hedge positions on every individual stock & ETF trade or on the portfolio overall.	Maximum loss of no more than 10% of trading / investing portfolio. Diversify across industries, timeframes, instruments and trading strategies to minimize losses when trades go wrong.	**MEDIUM TERM** (Measured semi-annually).

Setting goals and objectives for the growth portion of your portfolio is critical and the tactics and strategies for this portion of your portfolio is the focus of the strategies in this book.

Case Study: Bob & Mary are ages 48 & 43 respectively. They have two children ages 13 and 10. Their assets consist of the following:

- Bob's 401K at work = $95,000
- Mary's IRA Rollover from an old job = $150,000
- Joint Tenants Brokerage account = $72,000
- Bob's Pension (from an old job) = $58,000
- Bob's Variable Universal Life insurance policy (with a built-up cash value of $80,000)
- Home: (Market Value: $550,000 with a remaining mortgage of $300,000)
- Bank savings and checking accounts: $28,000
- 529 College savings plans for the two kids ($25,000 each) = $50,000

TOTAL ASSETS = $783,000

A typical 'bucketing' or timing for Bob & Mary would be:

Short Term (<18 months):	Medium Term (<19 months to seven years):	Long Term (seven years+):
• Bank Savings & Checking accounts ($28,000).	• Joint Tenants Brokerage account = $72,000. • 529 College savings plans for the two kids = $50,000 ($25,000 each).	• Bob's 401K at work = $95,000. • Mary's IRA Rollover from an old job = $150,000. • Home: (Market Value: $550,000 with a remaining mortgage of $300,000). • Bob's Pension (from an old job) = $58,000. • Bob's Variable Universal Life insurance policy (with a built-up cash value of $110,00).

As you can see – most of Bob & Mary's assets can be invested for the long term (more than seven years). If you are closer to retirement, you may have more assets fall into the Medium bucket. That is fine. The point is, you can take more risk and go for more returns in the longer-term bucket than in the short term (almost no risk) and the medium term (medium risk) buckets.

Tailor this example to fit your own situation and risk tolerance. If you have no children – you can take more risk. If you are still in your 30s (or younger) you can take a lot more risk. If you are age 62 and nearing retirement – then it depends on the size of your portfolio (with a larger portfolio of investable assets in the long-term bucket, the more risk you can take) otherwise you should take less risk.

Let's continue with the example. Next, we take Bob & Mary's medium-term & long-term buckets in BASE & BOOST. This would be typical given their ages, risk tolerance of say a seven, on a scale of one to ten and their current assets:

The BASE: Goal: Match the market with super low fees	The BOOST: Goal: Beat the market
• 50% of Mary's IRA Rollover from an old job = $75,000 • 30% of the Joint Tenants Brokerage account = $22,000 • Home: (Market Value: $550,000 with a remaining mortgage of $300,000) • Bob's Variable Universal Life insurance policy (with a built-up cash value of $110,00) • 529 College savings plans for the 2 kids ($25,000 each) • Bob's Pension (from an old job) = $58,000	• 70% of the Joint Tenants Brokerage account = $50,000 • 50% of Mary's IRA Rollover from an old job = $75,000

Let's continue with the example. Next, we take Bob & Mary's medium-term & long-term buckets in BASE & BOOST. This would be typical given their ages, risk tolerance of say a seven, on a scale of one to ten and their current assets:

In this example – Bob & Mary would put up to a maximum of $125K ($75K + $50K) into a combination of the six strategies taught in this book. Yes, they could potentially make more if they risked more in individual stock & options strategies taught here, but remember – risk management is more important than squeezing every potential dollar form the market.

Now you are ready to decide on the specific stocks, ETFs and strategies that will enable you to achieve these goals. If you are reading this and only have few assets or do not have a portfolio of cash to allocate – that is OK. I stated this process with $5,000. Don't give up. Start by investing in the base (a low-cost S&P500 index ETF for the first $10K is always a great place to start), and add a savings goal to build up your trading account. When you do start to build up your assets, you will do so with a well thought out trading plan already in place.

The rest of the book will go into the process to select and trade securities for the BASE & the BOOST portions of the portfolio. Before going there, I wanted to include a few more ideas to think through before you create your portfolio – some basic financial planning ideas and the psychology of trading as emotions are the hardest thing to battle when you trade and invest over various bull & bear market cycles.

Basic Financial Planning Rules Everyone Should Follow

If this book and the strategies taught are 'Level Two' in your financial development, the questions and the list below are the 'Level One' rules upon which your investment program will be grounded.

Here a few general best practices and financial planning rules of the road before you start trading. These may or may not apply to your particular financial situation and are not a comprehensive list of all pre-requisites to trading and investing – just a list of key items to review and make decisions on as you build out your financial plan and trading strategy:

Rule #1: Pay off your credit cards and other non-tax-deductible consumer debts before you trade

Pay off your consumer debts before investing in your trading portfolio. If you have consumer debt and credit cards with interest rates at 13%+, pay these down first before trading. You should still fund your retirement accounts such as a 401(k), 403b or other tax-advantaged pension program up to the amount of your company's matching contribution but after that focus on paying off the credit cards. Until you complete the payoff of high interest credit card debt, however, there should be no investing or trading outside of funding retirement accounts.

Rule #2: Pay yourself first & make it automatic

You should automatically save at least 10% to 20% of every dollar you make and invest it in your investment accounts. Put the maximum percentage into your 401(k) or other workplace retirement plan that your company matches some of your contributions, and have the rest auto deposited in your investment & trading account.

Your 401(k) account should only be invested in a low-cost S&P 500 and other index funds or ETFs, regardless of your age until you are age 50 (if you plan to retire at age 65 or later). The only time this should not be the case is if investment-grade bonds revert to yielding above 8%+, which does not appear to be a likely scenario any time soon.
One Note: You cannot do the stock and option strategies taught in this book inside a 401(k), Roth 401(k), 403B or 457 plan at work unless they have a brokerage account option within the plan (some now offer this). You can and should however do them in a self-directed Individual Retirement Account (IRA account or Roth IRA).

Rule #3: In the USA, use the Roth version of IRAs and 401(k)s if you qualify.

You may make too much in annual income to qualify for the ROTH versions of an IRA or 401(k). In 2019, the phase-out range for taxpayers making contributions to a Roth IRA is $193,000 - $203,000 for married couples filing jointly. For singles and heads of household, the annual income phase-out range is $122,000 to $137,000. If you qualify, however, the Roth is almost always worth selecting as your retirement vehicle. You can house an active trading account (including the ability to trade stocks and options) inside your Roth IRA in a tax-sheltered environment.

Remember, with tax deferred retirement savings vehicles such as a 401(K) and IRA, taxes are the single largest expense and threat, especially if tax rates rise in the future. All studies indicate that tax

rate increases in the future are likely. There is no income limitation to a Roth 401(k) but there is an annual income limit to be able to contribute to a Roth IRA. Note also if you start a small business, you can start a solo Roth 401(K) or a pension plan for your individual business qualified retirement plan.
These pension vehicles are great vehicles to hold brokerage accounts in. You can use the strategies in this book to trade stocks and options within these accounts to grow your retirement savings. Again, the nuances of these retirement plans are not the subject of this book, but you can discuss them in detail with your financial advisor.

Rule #4: Do not pay off your home mortgage if it has a low interest rate. Instead, invest that money for growth. Always carry a large mortgage when average mortgage rates are below 5%.

This is a controversial rule and differs from advice given by the Dave Ramsey's and Susie Orman's of the world (whom I respect but on the home mortgage issue, I disagree with them). Why would I recommend not paying off your home mortgage (and I mean never paying it off when mortgage interest rates are below 5%)? It's simple. The paid-in equity in your home is not an asset that earns you any income.

Your primary residence is an asset on the bank's balance sheet, but a liability to you. Every dollar of excess equity you think you are "investing" in your house by paying off your mortgage early is making you exactly $0 every year in income generation. Sure, your house may be appreciating in value; but that value does not put any cash in your pocket each month and you get that appreciation anyway. Only your investment portfolio can put income and dividends in your pocket. When you pay a large down payment, or make extra payments on your mortgage to pay it off early, who gets the benefit of earning income on those dollars? The answer is *the bank*, not you.

You will make zero in investment income or dividends on those extra dollars you pay into your mortgage. Think of it this way: every time you pay an extra dollar into your home equity, you are in effect saying to your mortgage provider, "here is some extra money and there is no need to pay me any interest on it – just keep it. Oh, and Uncle Sam? Please reduce my tax deductions while I am at it." Does that sound great to you? That is what happens when you pay extra on your mortgage trying to pay off your mortgage as quickly as possible.

There is a better use for that money. Instead of paying off your mortgage early, keep those dollars outside of your house. Don't let them get trapped- invest them and grow them. It's true that your home may appreciate over time (although this is not a given). You can tap that extra equity periodically by pulling it out through refinancing and invest that money in your trading account as well. Remember, whether or not you make a larger down payment or pay extra on your mortgage each month, you will receive that same home appreciation either way. You should always carry a mortgage – as large as the bank will allow you – and invest the extra money in your trading account when mortgage rates are below 5%. If you are prudent, these dollars will work harder and grow much faster than the interest you pay on your mortgage debt. They can certainly grow much faster than the trapped equity sitting dormant in your home earning you $0.

Consider the other side of the argument. Assume you did pay off your mortgage. Is the equity in your home liquid? The answer is no; you cannot use it all quickly. It is not safe from loss, either. Even if your house is insured, you may not recover its full value from the insurance company in the event of fire or flood. When you pull that money out of your house and keep it growing in your trading account, it is liquid. It is also much safer than being "invested" in something that Mother Nature can destroy (earthquakes in California, Hurricane Katrina in New Orleans anyone…). Those homeowners lost all of the value.

A large mortgage is your friend, not a burden. Real estate does not always go up. And should you encounter financial difficulty in paying your mortgage, guess which homes the lenders foreclose on first? The ones with the most paid-in equity.

"But what will I leave to my kids?" you may ask. Alternately, you may be concerned about what will happen if you lose your job and don't have a paid-off house with a large pool of equity to tap into to tide you over through the lean times. Both of these concerns are questions with the same answer: you should separate the equity from your house and grow it in a risk managed way in your investment accounts. Use the trading strategies taught here to grow those funds into a large pile of cash in your trading account that will cover all such emergency scenarios. Even if you put it in 3% CDs that are FDIC insured, that is 3% more than you will earn with extra paid in equity in your home.

If you want more guarantees, you can re-channel some of your extra equity payments into funding in a variable universal life insurance policy that earns more than your mortgage interest rate. The author and financial advisor Douglas R. Andrew provides a great explanation of the benefits of reallocating your home equity payments into tax-advantaged cash value life insurance policies in order to rapidly grow your wealth. You will have those investments to tap in case of emergency. There are some tax considerations with this strategy, but they are manageable. With the right advice, you may even be able to lower your tax bill by employing this technique.

I'm not referring to any investment properties that you may own. Those are assets that should earn you income and they are partially exempt from this rule. But for your primary residence, the interest on your mortgage is tax-deductible in the United States. Get with competent advisors in mortgages and taxes in this area.

The bottom line is that you should almost never pay off your mortgage and let your dollars sit idle. Instead, you should focus on generating income in order to grow your wealth faster.

Rule #5: Never buy an actively managed mutual fund ever again for the BASE part of your portfolio (only buy passively managed, low cost ETFs in this category of investment).

There are two kinds of mutual funds:
- Actively managed, and
- Passively managed (also known as 'index' funds).

In actively managed funds, the portfolio manager and their team researches and picks the various stocks or bonds that go into the mutual fund, hoping to beat the returns of the passively managed market indexes. In other words, in an actively managed mutual find you are paying experts to pick a basket of stocks or stocks and bonds to beat the market averages.

Passively managed funds (or Indexed mutual funds) mimic the performance of either a large stock index (US or International), such as the S&P 500 or the Dow Jones Industrial Average or they provide the investor exposure to a specific industry sector or strategy (such as the Technology sector, or gold, or REITS, etc.). These are very good; they provide exposure to the basket of securities that you want exposure too, but no active management or buying / selling / research is being done which can substantially drive up costs.

As you will see below, passive index ETFs and funds have in almost all cases done better than actively managed mutual funds and can be a good deal for investors. Low cost index ETFs are a good tool to grow your wealth, but you should never buy an 'actively managed' mutual fund ever again.

Why are actively managed mutual funds such a bad deal for most investors? There are a few reasons. Firstly, they charge high fees. These total fees average between 3% and 3.5% per annum when all of the fees and charges disclosed in the fine print are added together. Don't be fooled by the stated 'no-load' or '1% expense ratio' that most actively managed mutual funds advertise. This is not all you pay as the investor in an actively managed mutual fund. Actively managed funds do not call all of their many other charges, 'fees.' You need an PhD in finance to read the 30+ pages of fine print and disclosures for most actively managed mutual funds, which spell out the all of real fees you pay.

These 15+ other fees have confusing names like:
- 12B-1 expenses,
- Spread costs,
- Record keeping expense,
- Plan administrator charge,
- Brokerage commissions,
- Etc.

Don't be fooled, these administrative sounding names are all fees that most investors do not understand are passed along to you. You and your fellow investors are collectively paying all of these other hidden fees in actively managed funds. Actively managed mutual funds earn their fee revenue from you whether you win or lose. These funds are charging you a different price then advertised by their no load, or 1% expense ratio sales pitch. That's a huge drag on your portfolio. Some studies say it can be a 50% to 70% cumulative drag over time on how much money you will have in retirement. You cannot overcome a 50%+ hit in performance, no matter how well the actively managed fund performs.

Secondly, actively managed funds simply don't make large gains or outperform the market indexes as advertised – even without the excessive fees explained above. Remember, the only value to investing in actively managed mutual funds vs. holding a passive index fund is their promise to consistently beat the passive index funds and averages with better returns. The data does not support this conclusion. Historically, around 90% of actively managed mutual funds have not beaten their benchmark index or average in any given year. Of the 10% that do beat the index averages in a specific year, they can't repeat the performance for a second year. Out of a pool of 7,700 funds, only 100 of them will beat the index beyond two years in a row.

Rather than attempting to be a psychic and pick one of those 100 funds out of the vast universe of over fourteen thousand mutual funds on offer, you should just go with an index fund for the portions of your portfolio allocated to this type of investing. By owning a low fee, high return index fund, you will beat 98% of your peers with very little effort.

Thirdly, research has shown that over 60% plus of the portfolio managers of actively traded mutual funds, do not have any of their own money invested in the fund they manage. Think about that. The insiders managing the fund are not buying with their own money what they are selling to you to invest in. Most mutual fund managers are invested in hedge funds and other investments, which can consistently beat mutual funds.

If your 401(k) plan is currently invested in actively managed funds, you should change this today. Within most plans you can immediately switch your funds from actively managed funds to indexed funds at little to no cost. While index funds are available in most 401(k) plans, some still do not offer them. If that's the case with your plan, you should speak to your human resources department and ask them to make changes with the plan administrator to add index fund or lower cost ETF investment choices. If you have legacy 401(k) plans from a previous employer, you can transfer your service provider and roll your old 401(k) into a self-directed IRA.

Rule #6: Leverage the power of compounding your gains

The magic of compound interest is real, and it is amazing. Compound interest is in many ways the only free lunch when it comes to growing your wealth. This book will give you more tools as to how to do compounding exceptionally well. Maximizing compound interest is a great way to exponentially grow earnings aggressively yet with risk controls. Follow this book and you will have this rule covered and turbo charged. This is a topic that will be discussed in great detail in the pages that follow.

Rule #7: Buy key insurance policies to protect (and grow) wealth

There are many types of insurance policies and riders. You should work you're your financial planner to understand the details of each one. At a minimum, you must have:

- **Life insurance** – If you have a family to take care of, then you and/or your spouse simply must buy life insurance to protect your dependents if you are gone. You should select a death benefit that is a minimum of five times your annual income as a minimum in coverage, and eight to ten times is better. Your policy should be either:
    - A low-cost *Term Life policy.* This type of policy provides insurance only, with no savings or investment. It is less expensive than other types of insurance, and you should invest this cost difference in your trading account.
    - A *Universal Life policy.* This type of policy provides insurance protection as well as an investment savings vehicle that provides minimum guaranteed returns in

a tax-advantaged environment. There are even ways to withdraw the gains at retirement tax-free (even when you are not age 59 ½). I like the Indexed Universal Life version as most of these policies cut off all losses in the markets in down years but allow you to participate in the gains in good years (up to a capped amount – so get a policy with the highest cap you can find – all other things being equal). The protections and tax-free growth more than make up for the cost of insurance and fees.

- **Health insurance and long-term disability insurance.** You need to insure your ability to work and make a living or you will drain your savings and investments. This means having adequate coverage for health and if you become sick or disabled and cannot work. Healthcare expenses are among the leading causes of bankruptcies in America today. Not having proper health and disability insurance is a tremendous risk, and one that is avoidable. Get covered.

  o *Supplemental health insurance.* Many basic health insurance policies have numerous excluded illnesses and payment caps. You should purchase an additional supplemental health insurance policy to overcome these limitations.

- **Home insurance and auto insurance.** Outside of your trading account, your two most valuable possessions are likely to be your home and your car. Get both of them insured.

- **Professional liability insurance.** This is needed only if you are an independent professional with a business to protect.

- **Annuities.** I am not a big fan of annuities. They have incredibly high fees and are in many ways the equivalent of super high cost mutual funds. The one exception to this is if you are in good health and anticipate that you will live a long life in retirement. Because annuities pay out income for life, they can create a stream of income that you cannot outlive. If you are in good health and expect to outlive the average man or woman, I personally like the 'SPIA' or Single Premium Immediate Annuity when you reach retirement. In a SPIA you pay the insurance company a lump sum of money on day one and they term it into a stream of monthly income for the rest of your life. This is a way to create your own pension if you don't have one, or supplement the one you have. For example, at age 65 you could fund $250K into a SPIA, and the insurance company promises to pay you say $1,500 a month for life. They base the amount off of complex actuarial tables and calculations but the bottom line is it is based on the average man or woman's life span. If you live five, ten, fifteen years longer than the average lifespan (of approximately age 84 at the time of this writing) the SPIA still has to pay you. That is how you win and overcome the high fees, through collecting years and years of free money by living substantially longer than the average. You are advised to consult your independent financial advisor for more information on annuities as the details of this topic are beyond the scope of this book but suffice it to say that annuities can be a key component of a diversified financial plan if you have longevity and good health.

Rule #8: Make sure your will, living will, revocable living trust (and related items) are up to date

You should ensure that you have an up to date will. This includes a living will (a document that sets out your end-of-life decisions).

You should also establish a revocable living trust, in which you can place the legal title for your home, brokerage accounts, and other assets in order to protect these assets while you live and keep them out of probate when you die.

You should also have a durable healthcare power of attorney, which will state your wishes in the event that you may be incapacitated.

The details of these important instruments are beyond the scope of this book but they are a critical piece of your overall financial plan. You can work with your financial advisor and a good estate-planning attorney to create them. There are also online legal document websites if you want to try to complete the documents yourself (for example www.legalzoom.com & the "Must Have Documents" at www.suzeorman.com).

That is all for this general financial planning primer. I have presented these key financial planning rules here in high level, summary form. I encourage you to discuss each of these areas with your advisors to build your plan and determine what portion of your portfolio should be used to implement the more aggressive strategies in this book.

Understand the Psychological Aspects of Trading

One could write an entire book on the psychological aspects of trading and investing. Most unsuccessful stock and options investors fail not because they are using the wrong up-front planning, strategy or mechanics, but because they cannot handle it emotionally when markets move against them. They are not disciplined in entering and exiting the markets with the proper risk management and analytical mindset. Disciplined tactical trading requires a trading plan and proper risk management to guide entry and exit decisions before you enter trades. Most retail traders, however, do not create and follow a trading plan or risk management processes and are essentially "winging it." They trade on feelings and emotions, or blindly follow the trade alerts of a supposed online expert.

In trading and investing, the mental side is often is the most challenging part. The primary emotions of fear and greed often make very smart people do very dumb things with their money. We spend most of the time in this book on the strategies, the mechanics, the risk management techniques and adjustments that can help take the guesswork out of trading and reduce your fear levels. Despite this training, we must spend additional time on the mental side of trading. Spend time training and getting experience with your trades before going all in. This will help you build the right thoughts, habits, and actions. These attributes are what separate professionals from amateurs.

A key aspect of getting in the right mindset is in setting trading goals and objectives. Most retail traders do not do this. They simply buy mutual funds and maybe a few stocks, buy a call option or two, and hope for the best. However, hope is not a strategy. Relying on hope alone leads to inconsistency. You need to give much more thought to realistic trading goals and rules and make sure your actions follow rules and a plan. These rules and planned exits will then translate into proper actions and less indecision.

Most people believe that you must enter high-risk trades to achieve high returns. After trading for over 25 years, I can tell you that this is simply not true. You can very easily and realistically average gains of 1% **per week**. This translates into gains of 4% to 5% per month, or roughly 50% to more than 60% per year after commissions and margin interest are factored in.

Of course, you will not win every week of the year. You *will* have losses. But these are very achievable averages for your expected returns for stocks paired with options when you know the right strategies and risk management rules. Setting these types of risk managed, yet aggressive goals for the trading portion of your portfolio, is a potential life changer. You just need to adopt the strategies and tools that you may not yet be using and use risk management rules to hedge your downside. Buying and holding mutual funds will cut it – it is time to achieve more and compound your returns much more quickly.

Handling your emotions during trading is the single most difficult thing to do. It causes more losses than any other factor. A great deal of research all shows that people who are otherwise very smart are often bad traders because they let the emotions of fear and greed override even a well thought out trading plan. This leads them to make the opposite moves that they should.

While there is no quick fix for learning the proper mental approach to trading, my advice is to always remember the old Warren Buffett axiom: "Be greedy when others are fearful and be fearful when others are greedy." This is very difficult to do in the real world. It means that when you are in an overall long-term bullish market up trend and nothing has changed in the world, yet you wake up to see the stock market averages down 5% -10%, you buy the stocks your homework says to buy and you do so aggressively. And when the S&P and Dow Jones averages are making new highs and all looks fantastic, you should begin to sell, reducing risk and treading cautiously.

To manage your emotions effectively, you must learn to manage yourself. You must create an effective balance between being brave and being disciplined in the markets. Don't take small profits too quickly and don't let your losing trades run. Having a few losing trades is inevitable. It is just part of the business of trading. The key is to ensure that your winners make a lot for you and your losers are cut off early. That way, you will lose a lot less than you make on your winners. This all stems from your trading plan and rules, so you know how to react under market pressure. Learn from your mistakes and try hard not to repeat them.

I believe that almost anyone can learn the mechanics of trading – but the discipline to follow through and take action when your emotions are high, often separates those who break free financially and those that tread water.

My experience has shown that the best way to avoid fear and greed when trading is by having a financial plan, a trading plan, and by clearly defining your goals and risk tolerance and what you will do if your trades start to move against you. Then you must follow these plans, regardless of how you 'feel' at any given moment. Smart people often fail at investing by allowing their emotions to override their well thought out trading plan.

"Thoughts lead on to purpose; purposes go forth in action; actions form habits; habits decide character; and character fixes our destiny."
- Tryon Edwards

Chapter 2

Develop Your Top Down Economic Worldview and Select Your Basket of Stocks and ETFs

LEARNING OBJECTIVES

- Why should you actively trade a portion of your portfolio, instead of just buy and hold

- Creating your top down economic worldview using news and online resources

- Rank & prioritize your trade candidates by the key macro issues today and trade set-ups

- Develop & select a 'basket' of your favorite stocks to research, follow and trade

- Make selections across key sectors and sub-industry groups

- Rank and prioritize the stocks in your basket and your trade candidates (stocks & ETFs)

- Develop a short list of favorite ETFs to trade and use to hedge your portfolio

- My favorite ETFs

"I hated every minute of training, but I said, 'Don't quit.' Suffer now and live the rest of your life as a champion."
- Muhammad Ali

I love this quote from Muhammad Ali. It reminds us that for every worthwhile endeavor, training is required to be a champion. It's no different when you study and train to get your money to work harder for you.

The right financial and trading plan combined with hard work and discipline, creates results. It's exactly like getting in great physical shape. At times a difficult process and it does not occur overnight but having a plan and the disciple to follow-through achieves very rewarding results. Achieving a significant breakthrough, however, in your financial life is incredibly rewarding. Not just in term of the dollars but internally, in knowing you have developed a set of skills you can use to help yourself and your family for the rest of your life.

Chapter one covered the first step in this quest: the importance of creating an overall financial plan and dividing your investment capital into timeframes and BASE and BOOST sections (also known as 'sleeves'). The financial plan is the overall framework that the next chapters hang from. This chapter focuses on the next step in the process of narrowing down and selecting profitable stocks and ETFs to potentially trade. It also emphasizes the importance of related groupings of stocks in indexes and industry sectors, specifically called Exchange Traded Funds (or "ETFs") and how to diversify across the BASE and BOOST portions of your portfolio.

Why Should You Actively Trade a Portion of Your Portfolio, Instead of Just Buy and Hold (the BOOST portion of your portfolio)?

I used to be a buy and hold investor. I started out my career wholeheartedly subscribing to the Benjamin Graham/Warren Buffett style of 'value' investing. This approach can be loosely summarized as this: find a good business that has strong stable earnings, pays dividends and is trading at a deep value, buy it and hold it forever. I still like the value investing strategy, but only *AFTER* you are already rich. For the vast majority of people who are not already wealthy, following a long term buy and hold strategy has not worked. During the 2008 financial crisis, stocks crashed to their 1997 levels. That erased 11 years of gains for buy and hold investors. Subtract an additional 30% for inflation, fees and the declining value of the dollar, and you can come to only one conclusion- that buying and holding stocks won't get the job done for most individual investors. Even though stocks eventually recovered and formed new highs in 2016 and 2017, it is too slow and too much is out of your control. We need a new plan for growing some of our money more aggressively.

Why do I advocate an active trading strategy for retail investors instead of just buying and holding? It's because if you can sidestep many of the major declines in the stock market, you will in most cases at least double if not triple your long-term overall performance. You read that right – double or triple your long-term record compared to a buy and hold, or as it usually is executed, a "buy and forget" strategy.

This does not mean that you should become an active day trader or full-on market timer. Rather, it means when the market turns bearish and breaks through all of its major support levels, you can scale out some of your money and then scale it back in once a market turn is confirmed by multiple confirmation signals. You should not remain in all of your positions when major support levels are breaking to the downside. Adding the portfolio and individual trade hedging techniques taught in this book also greatly eliminate the catastrophic downside risks.

Creating your economic worldview using the news and online information resources.

After you have set up your financial plan, determined your asset allocation, and set your portfolio goals & targets, you are now ready to start the 'homework' that will enable you to select specific stocks and trades.

This section of the book will enable you to map out the steps for doing all of the necessary pre-investment research. Though the homework will at first feel a bit extensive and cumbersome, I have cut through the clutter of information to streamline it as much as possible. As you develop the new habits and process patterns in your research, it will begin to go much more quickly each week. I can now do the homework in about two or three hours a week.

Remember, there is no end to how much news and information you could potentially read and study. I advise to keep it simple and only do as much as is necessary to execute these strategies and processes. In other words, only do enough to form a good view based on the balance of information. Don't succumb to analysis paralysis.

The steps in my Stock & Options Trading for LIFE system follow the organization of the upcoming chapters (where the details on each step can be found). The system can be summarized as follows:

Step 1: DEVELOP A MACRO, TOP-DOWN ECONOMIC WORLDVIEW OF THE FACTORS AFFECTING THE ECONOMY AND YOUR STOCKS To create a top-down macroeconomic worldview, you should read and summarize key news developments in the world as they affect the overall stock market and the sectors. You should summarize this daily into a list of the top two to ten global issues affecting the stock markets you are trading at a macro level. The key issues will all be in the top world and business headlines. No more than ten issues on a given day should ever be significant enough on a daily basis to move stock markets. It will typically be two to five issues per day (details follow this table). *The method for doing this is covered in depth in this chapter.*
Step 2: BEGIN ORGANIZING TO TRADE BY SELECTING A BASKET OF THE TOP STOCKS IN EACH INDUSTRY. SELECT THE ONES THAT YOU BELIEVE HAVE THE BEST CHANCE OF RISING BASED ON YOUR RESEARCH & THEIR FUNDAMENTALS. ALSO SELECT A FEW KEY ETFs. Select a basket of your favorite stocks across the various 11 S&P industry sectors that you believe in and would like to follow. Research and select these stocks as well as a few sector ETFs. *The method for doing this is covered in depth in this chapter.*

Step 3: CONDUCT FUNDAMENTAL ANALYSIS ON THE STOCKS IN YOUR BASKET: Determine WHAT to buy based on a bottoms-up fundamental analysis and future projections.
The method for doing this will be discussed in depth in Chapter Three.

Step 4: CONDUCT TECHNICAL ANALYSIS ON THE STOCKS IN YOUR BASKET: Determine WHEN to buy or sell and how to match each trading strategy to various overall market conditions.
My favorite approach and technical indicators are covered in Chapter Four.

Step 5: DEVELOP YOUR HIGH-LEVEL TRADING PROCESS AND GENERAL TRADING RULES – Key rules to follow no matter which trading strategy you are using.
The method for doing this is covered in depth in Chapter Five.

Step 6: SELECT AND EXECUTE MY FAVORITE SPECIFIC TRADING STRATEGIES & TRADING RULES IN LINE WITH YOUR FINANCIAL PLAN: I will show you the most effective and risk-controlled stock and options trading strategies for both income trading and long-term portfolio growth.
My favorite strategies and rules are covered in detail in Chapter Six.

Step 7: MONITOR PERFORMANCE & MAKE ADJUSTMENTS
As your trades and investments develop, cut the losers short and let the winners run and perform.
The methods for doing this are covered in depth in Chapters Eight & Nine.

Details for Execution of Step 1: Develop a macro, top down economic worldview on the factors that can affect the stocks in your portfolio

Each business day, there are usually between two and ten global macro news events that can boost or put pressure on global stocks and the country specific stock market you are investing in. Most days I find two and five key news items. It is important to spend 30 minutes any day you plan to trade or put on new investments to conduct this top-down review of the news and world events.

Why is this macro top-down view homework necessary? Because years of stock market research indicate that a high percentage of stocks trade in lockstep with the overall market indices each day and month and quarter (such as the S&P 500 index). When you put money to work in the stock market, you will want to know if you are doing so on a day that the market is soaring, tanking or just treading water. This may influence when you put the new trade on, and how tightly you hedge it. The details of how to place trades and hedge them are covered later in the book.

Here is my daily process for developing a top-down macro worldview affecting stocks:

- Determine the top two to ten daily news events that can affect stocks. Pay special attention to any of the following:
    o Meetings of the U.S. Federal Reserve (also known as 'The FED")
    o Global conflicts or large US News items (for example, the BREXIT decision or the Mueller report release are examples)
    o Significant gains or declines overnight in major world stock markets such as Japan, China, Russia, and others.
    o Earnings announcements from major companies that have the potential to move markets (think Apple, Google, Amazon, Disney, Nike, etc.).
    o Other events that could impact stock markets that are temporary in nature but can have an effect today. Current examples would include a Presidential election cycle news item, or a natural disaster affecting a large country.
    o Options expiration days (the 3rd Friday of every month) or the days on which key ETF's are rebalanced.

- After you have written out one or two sentence summaries of each of these macro global issues / items for the day (that could affect markets), use your judgment to assign a "plus" or a "minus" to each item based on its likely impact on the markets as a whole. A plus sign means you feel it will likely have a bullish, or upward effect on stocks today, a negative sign means a bearish or downward effect.

- Finally, rank the day's macro issues in terms of priority using the stock market you are trading as the lens through which to view them. Place more importance on the top two items in influencing your trades for that day.

Make selections across key industry sectors and sub-industry groups, Rank the Top 10 and Bottom 10 Industry Sectors

After forming your macro view of world events affecting global stock markets, you should next see which industry sectors are currently being bought or sold. There are several online brokerage website resources that rank the relative strength of industry groups each day. The S&P 500 is broken into eleven industry sectors and twenty-four smaller industry groups. They rank the hottest sectors with heat maps as well as the weakest ones and rank them. This is important because research has shown that up to 50% of the movement in a stock price is determined not by the individual company but by the industry sector that it is in.

If you are trading for the short term this sector analysis is critical. If you are investing over a time horizon of six months or longer, it is less critical because sectors rotate in and out of favor over time.

In summary:

- A high percentage (between 65% to 75%) of stocks move *in the same direction as their related stock market indexes* on any given day, so develop your macro view in line with the momentum of major indices.

- Between 45% and 50% of stock price movement is in the same direction as their *industry sector*. Use the online tools available to determine the direction in which the sector is moving.

- Align your trades with the macro and sector trends first, and then analyze the individual stock itself. This will skew the percentages greatly in your favor and will greatly improve your trade entry prices and likelihood of following the trends correctly.

The bottom line is this: before trading in individual stocks, develop your trading strategy and a top-down macro view of the world to determine how it may affect the overall stock market.

Rank and prioritize your trade candidates by the key macro issues today and trade set-ups

As indicated above, after you have reviewed today's global news and selected the between 2 and 10 key items that could affect stocks it is critical to rank and prioritize these news items and industry sectors. Why is this so important? Because you want to determine if enough factors are aligning your way to put on new trades that day.

Remember, you are not an institution that is forced to put money to work every day. You can be very selective before trading. Only invest in the most compelling stocks and set-ups given current market conditions.

When in doubt – don't trade. Only trade when all or the vast majority of the macro and sector analysis lines up in your favor. Think on trade set-up's and price entries in terms of probabilities, and wait until as many factors as possible are aligned your way.

As an example, I would only put on a bullish trade if I see a day like the following:

I begin my daily work and am seeing a bullish market trend. In addition, I am looking to get long and put some money to work. This morning I have reviewed the following news sources: Investor's Business Daily, Briefing.com, the Wall Street Journal, Fox News, the BBC and CNN. The key news events potentially affecting stocks today are:

- The Fed indicates they won't raise interest rates until mid 2020 (My view: Bullish +)
- Europe and China add more quantitative easing (My view: Bullish +)
- Apple comes out with big earnings and raises guidance (My view: Bullish +)
- Russia and Ukraine sign a cease fire agreement (My view: Bullish +)
- ISIL terrorist group captures a mid-size city in northern Iraq (My view: Bearish -)

OVERALL DAILY MACRO VIEW / CONCLUSION: *Bullish*

That kind of a day gives me a green light to place bullish trades – if the next phases of our research line up (specifically the fundamental and technical analysis).

I next compare each name in my basket of stocks that I am seeking to add to against the daily top 10 and bottom 10 *industry sectors* for the day.

An example of my top and bottom industry sectors for a given day would look like this (note that this sample was taken from April 2019):

Today's Top 10 Industry Sectors:	Today's Bottom 10 Industry Sectors:
1. Technology – specifically search, cyber security and A.I. subsectors.	1. Financial Services – Banks – Foreign
2. Consumer Discretionary	2. Utilities – Gas Distribution
3. Semiconductors	3. Utilities – Water Supply
4. Media Diversified	4. Consumer Staples
5. Apparel – Shoes & Rel.	5. Food – Meat Products
6. Retail – Drug Stores	6. Utility – Electric Power
7. Media Radio / TV	7. Oil & Gas Integrated
8. Computer Software – Gaming	8. Auto Manufacturers
9. Telecommunications	9. Transportation – Rails
10. Internet – Network Solutions	10. Healthcare – Medical Diversified

If I want to place a bullish trade and the stock in my basket that I am considering is in one of today's top five industry sectors, paired with the above macro bullish outlook, then all the factors are lining up to give a positive signal for a bullish trade today.

For example, I was thinking about adding to my position in a semiconductor manufacturer I like from my basket of stocks (that I have already done the fundamental analysis on) named Advanced Micro Devices, ticker: AMD. As I see that Semiconductor manufacturing is #3 on the top ten industry sectors being accumulated today. That is a bullish sign. The fundamental homework has already been done and it checks out. If the technical analysis is positive, the trade has a green light.

Conversely, even though my fundamental analysis may have also given me a green light to trade an electric utility that is in my basket of stocks named American Electric Power (AEP), there is a red light on that industry sector. Even though the news of the day is positive for stocks in general, and even though my fundamental analysis is bullish on AEP, I can see that the Utility – Electric Power sector is the 6th worst industry sector today and is selling off.

I also notice that other utility sectors (water and gas) are also in the bottom ten daily industry sectors. This means that there is strong selling pressure on AEP and I would only consider it as a short candidate, generally by buying put options on it (more on this strategy in chapter six).

I then move to double-check my fundamental research summary and technical indicators before placing the trade (more on how to do this in chapters 4 and 5).

Develop a "basket" of your favorite stocks to research and follow

Let's start formulating the plan for the BOOST portion of your portfolio – with individual stocks.

What is a "basket "of stocks? It means selecting the companies that you like best by each industry group (or sector). You only want to follow and invest in the companies whose business models you understand and believe are the most compelling. Remember there are thousands of stocks that trade in the US. You can and should be *extremely* selective. Only follow the best of the best of the best. Ask yourself, what are the top 10-25 most compelling companies in the world right now? Be extremely selective.

I advise no more that 50 companies in your basket of stocks overall, if you have the time to be a full-time market participant. If you work or don't have the time or interest to follow that many companies, then select no more than12-15 stocks. Why so few? Because you have to do the research and homework on each one. These stocks should be your favorite one to three companies in each industry sector.

Investor's Business Daily – my favorite financial online newspaper- tracks 197 sub industry groups and ranks them by relative strength. This is a good place to begin making selections for the stocks in your basket.   To simplify things, you can also just choose from the S&P500 eleven Industry sectors (which is what I do most days). The eleven S&P 500 industry sectors are:
   1. Information Technology
   2. Utilities
   3. Financials
   4. Consumer Discretionary
   5. Energy
   6. Healthcare
   7. Industrials
   8. Materials
   9. Telecommunications
   10. Consumer Staples
   11. Real Estate

Make selections with a mix across key industry group and sectors

Multiple studies show that anywhere from one third to half of the price change in an individual stock is dependent upon the moves of the industry sector it is in. If the sector is rising rapidly, it is likely that the majority of all the stocks in the industry are rising.

The only exceptions I have observed where an individual stock will buck the trend and go in the opposite direction of the sector is when earnings on that specific company are announced or when there is an unexpected news event such as an accounting scandal that is discovered, the departure of a key executive, or a conflict breaking out in one of the company's key markets.

You will need to review and adjust your basket of stocks at least quarterly. This quarterly review is also the time to drop the underperformers whose story has changed and replace them with new names.

I advise not adding any company to your basket that is too small to be liquid and have options trading on it. A good rule of thumb is to not choose any company for your basket that has an average daily trading volume of less than 500,000 shares. I also like to look at the top mutual funds and hedge fund public quarterly filings to see what the big money is buying. I don't blindly add the names the institutional investors are buying into my basket, but this technique can uncover a few gems per year.

Bull markets are all about winning sectors; so, don't be afraid to swap a few names in your basket each quarter. Be opportunistic but still do the homework.

When the U.S. economy is weak, I like to rotate into stable consumer staple stocks like Procter & Gamble, Kimberly-Clark, and Johnson & Johnson. When the U.S. economy is strong, I like to focus more on growth and momentum names such as AMD, Apple, and Google.

As of the writing of this book in the first half of 2019, my current basket of stocks is as follows:

Each Company is presented as NAME (Ticker Symbol):

Information Technology: 1. Apple (AAPL) 2. Facebook (FB) 3. Alibaba Group (BABA) 4. Amazon.com (AMZN) 5. Workday, Inc. (WDAY) 6. Palo Alto Networks (PANW) 7. Salesforce.com, Inc. (CRM) 8. Adobe Systems (ADBE) 9. Microsoft (MSFT)	**Financial Services** (Banking & Capital Markets, Funds, Broker/ Dealers, etc.): 1. Goldman Sachs (GS) 2. Visa (V) 3. BlackRock Inc. (BLK) 4. MasterCard (MA) 5. JP Morgan (JPM) 6. TD Ameritrade (AMTD) 7. Square (SQ)	**Energy (Oil & Natural Gas) drilling, exploration & production:** 1. EOG Resources, Inc. (EOG) 2. Occidental Petroleum (OXY). 3. ConocoPhillips (COP) 4. Pioneer Natural Resources (PXD)
Semiconductors: 1. Nvidia (NVDA) 2. Advanced Micro Devices (AMD) 3. Cypress Semi (CY)	**Insurance (Life & Heath & General Insurance):** 1. Berkshire Hathaway – B shares (BRK-B)	**Oil Services & Pipeline:** 1. Schlumberger (SLB) 2. Kinder Morgan, Inc. (KMI)
Food & Restaurants: 1. McDonalds (MCD) 2. Starbucks (SBUX)	**Biotech:** 1. Bristol-Myers (BMY) (buying Celgene) 2. Alexion Pharmaceuticals (ALXN) 3. Exelixis, Inc. (EXEL) 4. BioMarin Pharmaceutical Inc. (BMRN)	**Healthcare (non-Biotech):** 1. HCA Holdings (HCA) 2. UnitedHealth Group Inc. (UNH)

Aerospace & Defense:	Airlines:	Transports:
1. The Boeing Company (BA) 2. Lockheed Martin Corporation (LMT) 3. Raytheon (RTN)	1. Delta Airlines (DAL) 2. Southwest (LUV)	1. FedEx Corporation (FDX)
Media / Entertainment:	Telecom:	Automotive:
1. The Walt Disney Company (DIS)	1. T-Mobile, Inc. (TMUS)	1. Tesla (TSLA) 2. General Motors (GM)
Retail / Apparel:	Vices (Gaming, Liquor, Tobacco, Cannabis):	Diversified Manufacturing & Chemicals:
1. The TJX Companies, Inc. (TJX) 2. V.F. Corp (VFC) 3. LuLu Lemon (LULU) 4. Walmart (WMT)	1. Las Vegas Sands Corp. (LVS) 2. Constellation Brands, Inc. (STZ)	1. The DOW Chemical Company (DOW) 2. Honeywell International Inc. (HON)
REITs / Real Estate:	Utilities:	Consumer cyclicals:
1. Ventas Inc. (VTR) 2. Apartment Investment and Management Co. ("Aimco") (AIV)	1. American Electric Power (AEP) 2. Duke Energy (DUK)	1. Procter & Gamble (PG) 2. Johnson & Johnson (JNJ) 3. Kimberly-Clark (KMB)

Rank the stocks in your basket

Once you have selected your basket of stocks, your homework from this chapter and chapter three ("Fundamental Analysis") will enable you to really get to know these companies. You will get a feel for them. You then will be able to use your knowledge and judgment to rank each stock and prioritize it within its industry sector for your potential investment. This ranking is not right or wrong – it is your view for your potential selections. So do the work and then use your gut to rank the stocks in your basket.

Remember to check each month the top industry sectors and relative industry group strength. You should only buy into the top five S&P500 industry sectors on the day you place a bullish trade. You can also go short or buy puts on the bottom-ranked five industry sectors.

Prioritizing the stocks on your 'shopping list'

After I have ranked each of the stocks in my basket within their industry sector (as in the table above), I like to take a step back. I then look across the top names in each industry column. About once a month, take the top name or two from each of the industry sectors in your basket – and try to prioritize them in the order of your personal conviction. This results in a list of what you believe are the top ten ranked stocks (regardless of industry). This list becomes your prioritized "shopping list" for when you are ready to put more capital to work.

Develop a short list of favorite ETFs to both trade and use to hedge

Trading individual stocks can be very profitable. In today's market, however, the fastest growing asset class in the world is the exchange-traded fund, (or "ETF" as they are referred to). Most of the popular ETFs also have options that trade on them, just like a stock. Therefore, you can substitute an industry sector ETF for an industry sector. You can even find ETFs for commodities like gold, bonds and oil, and trade options on them as well. The breadth of the ETF sector today is truly stunning, just like mutual funds.

Select a few ETF's that track your favorite industry sectors

Just like mutual funds, there are also now thousands of ETFs that track the performance of almost every industry sector, index and commodity. An ETF is essentially a custom constructed basket of stocks (or another asset class). ETFs are created to follow the movements of the asset class that it covers. Changes to the components (or company shares) making up the various ETF baskets are minimized, which keeps the transaction fees charged by each ETF to a minimum.

A further benefit is that you do not have to select individual stocks to gain exposure to a particular sector. For example, let's say you currently like the biotechnology industry and think it is a promising sector with above average growth prospects. You can either try to determine which biotechnology stocks you want to own, or you can minimize your homework and just buy the biotech ETF. For further leverage, you could also buy call options on such a biotech-focused ETF such as the ticker symbol IBB. The IBB is the ticker symbol for the iShares NASDAQ Biotechnology ETF.

The ETF market of today is so comprehensive that I know many traders who no longer trade individual stocks. Their argument is, why take the inherent single stock risk of trading an individual company, when you can trade the same strategies using sector-based ETFs. Using ETFs also reduces the need to do a great deal of company-specific fundamental analysis because each ETF has built-in diversification and low fees.

While these are all good arguments in favor of ETFs, I still like to do the research on individual stocks to try to outperform in the BOOST portion of the portfolio. That way, I really get to know individual companies. The process of fundamental analysis on individual companies gives me a higher level of conviction when making my trades. When trading ETFs alone, you can lose that feel for individual industries that you gain from individual company analysis. Studying companies directly makes me better able to stick with trades when they go against you. At the end of the day, it all comes down to personal preference.

Be careful using leveraged ETFs

Be careful (read don't use) leveraged ETFs and ETNs (Exchange Traded Notes). These products are fairly new and are potentially dangerous. This is because unlike regular ETF's that just buy a basket of underlying equities, leveraged ETFs buy the underlying stocks and then also further buy and sell futures, options and other exotic financial instruments to try to mimic exponential leveraged exposure (usually in the range of 2x or 3x) the underlying sector ETF. Even for a professional trader, 200% or 300% leverage is rarely employed. Until you are an experienced trader and investor, you should avoid these.

The upside to leveraged ETFs is that unlike regular margin in your brokerage account, leveraged ETFs require no margin tied up in your account. It is built into the product itself. This leverage can be very powerful when it works in your favor, but as every trader knows, "leverage works both ways." It can hurt you badly on the downside. I tell you about this good margin feature because you should be aware that this "baked in" leverage does have one potentially useful application. The use of leverage is generally not permitted in retirement accounts. However, because the leverage is incorporated into the leveraged ETF itself, these securities can be held in retirement accounts, creating a leveraged level of exposure without employing margin.

To be clear, I do use leveraged ETFs occasionally, though I typically sell them, not buy them. Sometimes they work well in the very short term to protect the overall portfolio when the market is crashing. Just remember that they are hard to understand and they do not move as you would expect. 3x Bullish ETFs rarely move three times the regular ETF as one example. If you are not experienced, I would avoid leveraged ETFs until you have lots of trading experience.

My Favorite ETFs
My favorite non-leveraged and leveraged ETFs are listed below. I do at times trade other ETFs, especially ones that have options trading on them as part of my options trading strategy. You can find the relative strength of an ETF by checking www.ETFscreen.com and going to the "RSf Trends" tab.

ETF Symbol:	Short Description:	Brief Description:
DIA	One times Bull DJIA	Also known as the 'Diamonds' – an ETF holding the Dow 30 industrial stocks
UDOW	Three times leveraged DJIA (long) *(Beginners should not use)*	The 3x (or three times leveraged) Dow index tracking ETF. It provides ~3 times the magnitude of moves in the DOW index.
DXD	Three times	The ultra-short 3X

	leveraged BEAR (short) DJIA *(Beginners should not use)*	leveraged DOW ETF
SPY or VOO	One times S&P 500 or Vanguard S&P500	This ETF mimics the movements and returns of the S&P 500 index
UPRO	Three times leveraged S&P 500 (long) *(Beginners should not use)*	The 3x (or three times leveraged) S&P 500 index tracking ETF. It provides ~three times the magnitude of moves in the S&P 500 index.
SDS	Three times leveraged S&P 500 (short) *(Beginners should not use)*	The ultra-short 3X leveraged S&P 500 ETF
QQQ	One times NASDAQ	This ETF generally correspond to the price and yield performance of the NASDAQ Index
TQQQ	Three times leveraged NASDAQ 100 (long) *(Beginners should not use)*	Mimics the daily investment results, equal to three times (3x) the daily performance of the NASDAQ-100 Index
QID	Three times leveraged NASDAQ 100 (short) *(Beginners should not use)*	The ultra-short 3X leveraged NASDAQ 100 ETF
IWM	One time the RUSSELL 2000	Mimics the Russell 2000 index
TNA	Three times leveraged RUSSELL 2000 (long) *(Beginners should not use)*	Mimics the daily investment results, equal to three times (3x) the daily performance of the Russell 2000 Index

TZA	Three times leveraged RUSSELL 2000 (short) *(Beginners should not use)*	This is the inverse (short) ETF mimics the inverse of daily investment results, equal to three times (3x) the daily performance of the Russell 2000 Index.
MDY	One time the Midcap 400	Corresponds to the performance tracking of the S&P Midcap 400 Index (the industrial midcaps).
OEX	One time the S&P 100	Mimics the performance of the largest members of the S&P, the S&P 100 index
VWO	Emerging Market Equities	Mimics the performance of a basket of emerging markets equities located in emerging market economies.
VNQ	High Income REITs	Mimics the high income (dividend payouts) and moderate long-term capital appreciation of a group of Real Estate Investment Trusts that are publicly traded.
VPU	Utilities Sector	Mimics a basket of top performing Utility companies. A good ETF in a bear market.
PEY	Mergent Dividend Yielders	Mimics the performance and income payout of the highest yielding Dividend paying stocks. In other words, the price and yield of the Mergent Dividend Achievers TM 50 Index
TLT	20 yr. Treasury	Mimics the 20 yr. US

	Bonds	Treasury Bond. This ETF seeks to track an index composed of Treasury bonds with maturities greater than twenty years.
BND	Vanguard Total Bond Market fund	Mimics a broad market-weighted index of bonds.
FXI	China – Large Cap Stocks	Mimics the performance of a basket of the 25 largest China Stocks.
CHNA	Powershares China A Shares ETF	Mimics the performance of the China Powershares index
DXJ	Japan – Large Cap Stocks	Mimics Japanese equity markets while at the same time neutralizing exposure to the Japanese yen relative to the U.S. dollar.
VGK	Vanguard – FTSE Europe ETF	Tracks an index of large companies located across Europe's major markets.
IBB	iShares Nasdaq Biotechnology	Mimics the index comprised of biotechnology and pharmaceutical equities listed on the NASDAQ.
XLF	Long Financial Sector	Mimics returns of equity securities of companies in the Financial Select Sector Index. Primarily large cap banks and insurance companies, payments (AMEX) etc.
FAS	Three times Financial sector (long) *(Beginners should not use)*	Three times leveraged ETF betting on bullish moves in the Financial sector.
FAZ	Three times Financial sector	Three times leveraged ETF betting on bearish

	(short) *(Beginners should not use)*	moves in the Financial sector.
MTK	SPDR Morgan Stanley Technology ETF	Tracks the performance of electronics-based technology companies. It tracks the Morgan Stanley Technology Index (the "index"). *Note that this fund employs a sampling strategy.*
GLD	Gold ETF	COMMODITIES – exposure to gold prices
OIL	OIL ETF	Mimics returns in the West Texas Intermediate (WTI) crude oil futures.
OIH	Oil Services ETF	Mimics the price and yield of the Market Vectors® US "Oil Services Index" for the equities of companies in the oil services sector.
JO	Coffee ETF	COMMODITIES – Mimics the Dow Jones-UBS Coffee Sub index, which tracks an unleveraged investment in the coffee futures contracts.
MOO	Agribusiness ETF	COMMODITIES – Agricultural companies (those in the Agribusiness Index) including companies supplying farm machines, livestock, agrichemicals, seeds, and trading of agricultural products.
HAP	Natural Resources	COMMODITIES –

	ETF	Mimics the Rogers^{TM}-Van Eck Natural Resources Index (RVEIT) comprised of companies in the mining, metals, water & alternative energy and forest products industries.

Remember, don't just look at the overall stock market averages each day and whether they are going up or down. It is also key to look at a few industry sectors and judge the overall breadth of the rise or sell-off. If the breadth across ETF sectors were narrow, I would not put much credence in the overall move in the averages. If there is wide breadth in the move in several ETFs (and especially if the moves are broad across industry sectors and supported by high volume), it is very telling, and you should trust the trend / directional move in the averages.

Bottom Line: Out of the many thousands of ETFs, you should select a set of 40 or less, like the list above, to focus on. These represent the typical industry sectors that you want to periodically get exposure to. You can then ignore the rest.

"Your inner financial genius requires both technical knowledge as well as courage. If your fear is too strong, the genius is suppressed. Take risks, be bold."
- Robert Kiyosaki

Chapter 3

Fundamental Stock Analysis

LEARNING OBJECTIVES

- Use fundamental analysis to help you determine what to buy or sell

- How to complete the homework for fundamental analysis

- Additional fundamental analysis rules

"Know what you own, and know why you own it."
- Peter Lynch

When you buy a stock, you are really buying a piece of a business. The evaluation of that business – its products, services, earnings, cash flow, debt, etc. is essential. You need to understand how it makes money. All of these items can be grouped under the heading of 'fundamental' stock analysis.

Many self-proclaimed trading gurus say that fundamental analysis is no longer relevant. These supposed experts think fundamental analysis is old-fashioned and that anyone practicing it as out of touch with modern times and modern markets. Critics say that in today's world of high-speed trading, the retail investor cannot compete with the algorithms and artificial intelligence by doing fundamental analysis. Their erroneous conclusion is that all a retail investor needs to know is reflected in the charts and can be divined by looking at technical indicators and 'price action.'

I disagree. Despite what you may read from the technical (charts and indicators only) traders online, fundamental stock analysis is not dead. Remember, I routinely beat these technical only traders in net annual gains and I do so handily. My experience shows me that this charting only / technical only view is not the way to outperform the market indexes over time. Charts and technical indicators definitely help with the timing of trade entries and exits, but they are not all you need to try to beat the market indexes.

I freely admit that since I started trading in the late 1980s, the value of fundamental analysis has diminished while the value of technical analysis has increased. As mentioned, this is especially true when it comes to spotting trends and selecting trade entry and exit points. However, fundamental stock analysis is still very powerful and relevant.

The only investors who can skip the fundamental homework on specific stocks in my view are those who exclusively trade in indexed funds or ETFs (comprised of baskets of over 100+ stocks). When you diversify across hundreds of companies, then sector analysis and macro-economic analysis is more important than the fundamentals of any specific company in the ETF 'basket.'

Use fundamental analysis to help you determine WHAT to buy or sell

I used to tell people in the early 1990s that fundamental analysis accounts for 80% of what moves stocks, and that 20% of the price movement can be explained by technical trading and the overall market. Today, however, I would estimate (based on hundreds of studies) that around 40% of the movement in a stock price is explained by the fundamentals of the company itself, approximately 30% is explained by the buying & selling of ETFs & indexed funds, and 30% is explained by quantitative or technical trading programs (algorithms) and high speed traders. These percentages are just rough estimates, based on my study and experience, not an exact statistical result. The point, however, is still relevant. Fundamental analysis is still a very worthwhile endeavor.

To be clear, I am not advocating that you do fundamental analysis and then execute a buy and hold strategy while ignoring the technical factors. In fact, I believe just the opposite. A savvy investor should look at three factors:

- Fundamental analysis to help select with conviction WHAT to buy.
- Technical charts and analysis to select lower risk entry points, or WHEN to buy.
- Activity and macro-economic trends in the overall market indexes and sectors to put the most momentum on your side.

You need to examine all three factors. Doing so can add up to an extra 1% - 10% to your overall annual returns.

The most common reason why people skip doing fundamental analysis is because they claim that they don't have the time. This is likely true if you are still working at a full-time job and have a family. It is also true that performing the homework required to do fundamental analysis is the most time-consuming part of your trading regimen. If this describes your situation, my advice is to either reduce the number of stocks in your basket of stocks to a manageable number, say eight to ten, or trade the sector ETF in place of the stock. With eight to ten stocks, you can keep up with the 30 minutes or so of homework on each stock per week.

I generally have around 50-55 stocks in my basket of stocks at any one time. This is a large amount. Remember, I am a full-time professional trader and money manager and all of my businesses revolve around training, coaching and managing money in the markets, which I am passionate about it. If you have a career, family, and other interests competing for your time, it is perfectly fine to reduce your basket of stocks to your 8 to 10 highest conviction companies.

Regardless of the number, you should always keep up on the homework on your basket of stocks. This is true even on the stocks in your basket that you currently do not hold a position in. You should still keep these names on your "shopping list" ready and ranked, in case the market offers you bargains on them in the near future.

If you are unable to spend around eight hours a week even on this smaller number of names, then you should not trade individual stocks and just opt for a low-cost index fund or market index ETFs instead.

How to complete the homework for fundamental analysis

So, what fundamentals of a company should you focus on? The key fundamental factors that I advocate each trader to check on include the following:

- The most recent quarterly earnings as well as earnings over the past year.
- The current price to earnings (P/E) ratio.
- The earnings growth rate.
- Sales growth rate.
- Profit margins.
- Return on Equity for the past two years (ROE).
- The current debt level and how it compares to the historical long-term levels.
- Dividends and recent dividend growth.
- Recent headlines on Investors.com, Briefing.com & Yahoo Finance.

First rule: You must put in the research time on your short list of favorite stocks, or you should not trade that week or month.

I fully agree with stock pundit and Mad Money host Jim Cramer's rule – that you must do at least 30 minutes to one hour of homework per week on each individual stock you own. That is fully in sync with my experience. I do about 30 hours a week of researching stocks and markets and trading on average. I spend between 22 and 25 of those hours keeping up to speed on my basket of stocks & current trades and a few additional hours on global macro news and insights. You can use much less time by reducing the number of stocks in your basket and still do very well.

The most important fundamental analysis focuses on getting a feel for the future earnings potential of each company. Stock prices follow earnings. You do this by looking at things such as forecasts for new products and future sales estimates. By paying attention to earnings you will follow the #1 driver of a stock's future price potential.

All of the following fundamentals are easily found on many websites such as Yahoo Finance:

- The most recent quarterly earnings
- The most recent annual earnings
- Pre-announcements of future earnings revisions up or down
- Analysts revisions to earnings projections

A great source to check earnings pre-announcements and revisions quickly is on Briefing.com under the Calendar tab, then checking "Earnings Guidance."   After I get a feel for earnings and where I think earnings are headed, my specific fundamental analysis steps are as follows:

Step #1: **Industry Sector Analysis.**
Check which industry sectors are in the top 10 and bottom 10 each day you plan to trade. Compare these to your basket of stocks and see which areas within your basket sync with these industry sector results. You can check the daily industry sector rankings in Investor's Business Daily. Another free way to verify sector analysis is you can also check the sector ETF rankings at www.ETFscreen.com and going to the "RSf Trends" tab to check the "Relative Strength Factors Trends."

Step #2: **Read the 10K and the 10Q reports from your companies** *(available on www.SEC.Gov/Edgar.shtml).*
The 10K is an annual report by the company. It can take a long time to read but it is only necessary to do this once per year. You should focus on the sections related to the management discussion about growth prospects, current results, and future risks for the company.

The 10Qs are quarterly reports. When reading them, you should focus on the same topics as the 10K reports related to the management's discussion about growth prospects, current results, and future risks. You should also examine the financial statements closely and look for the following:

- ***Debt:*** You should avoid investing in companies with too much debt. This is especially true if that debt is coming due in the next 18 months (short term). You should look closely at the debt ratio, defined as the ratio of total debt to total assets, and presented as a percentage. The debt ratio shows the percentage of debt a company has in relationship to the shareholder's equity. You need to confirm that the debt ratio is low, because excessive debt can cripple a business. You should shy away from any company with a debt ratio over 35% unless it is a new, highflying company in high growth mode.

- *Total Current Liabilities:* If this number is greater than the cash flow expectations for the next 12months, then avoid bullish trades on this company.

- *Revenues:* You should look for companies where revenues increasing at a large percentage- by double digits at least.

- *Book value:* The book value of the company is the dollar amount left over after subtracting all liabilities (including preferred stock) from the assets. This results in the book value of the company. To determine the book value per share, divide this number by the number of shares outstanding. This is also referred to as the firm's "breakup value." Almost all solid companies trade at a premium to book value. Occasionally a good company will trade at a discount to book value, but this is rarer. My rule is to avoid buying if the share price is over two and a half times book value. You should look for stocks trading at one to two times book value.

- *Return on Equity:* You should look at how much after-tax profit the company is making in the current year and compare it to the prior two years.

Step #3: Read a minimum of three analyst reports for each stock in your basket every quarter.
Securities analysts are professional researchers and reviewers that follow companies and express opinions as well as target prices on them. They are effectively doing the same homework that you are

doing, but they have additional time and resources that individual investors don't have. These include things such as direct access to a company's management, tours of the company's facilities, and other advantages that will allow them to have a deeper insight into the company.
Because of this, it is valuable to read several analysts reports each quarter. Most online brokerages supply a wide variety of these reports for free. While there were concerns about conflicts of interest in the past, research analysts are much less influenced by the investment banking business their firms do with companies than they were in the past.

Step #4: Read current new news articles on the company.
While individual news articles can be biased and inaccurate, the overall trend of news stories on the companies in your basket is something you need to stay aware of.

A good column to read is "Stocks on the Move" in Investor's Business Daily. You should also check their "Most Actives" section for breaking news and I check the Yahoo Finance news feed under each company in my basket. If you do not know where to start on finding a stock or ETF to trade, start by checking these sites. There are many other good ones. If you know that you want to trade a stock in your basket today, check for breaking news first. See if any of the stocks in your basket are mentioned in these lists. If not, see if there is a new potential stock to add to your basket with a compelling story.

It is important to check if the stock has recently hit a 52-week high, because that is a very bullish sign. You may wonder why anyone would gravitate towards active, moving stocks. They may appear to be volatile and risky. However, you will see in Chapter Six why these stocks are among my favorite trading strategies, including selling options on them to take advantage of this volatility by generating premium.

For example, at the end of 2014, one of my favorite stocks was Gilead Sciences (ticker: GILD). It had wonderful fundamentals and traded at just nine times earnings. It also had exciting new products, such as a new pill that cures Hepatitis C. Then a news bomb went off – Express Scripts Holding Co., the USA's largest pharmacy benefits management company, granted exclusivity to a competing drug from another company named AbbVie.

Express Scripts did this despite the fact that most scientific results indicated that the Gilead cure was more effective than AbbVie's. When news like this hits, it overrides your fundamental and technical analysis in the short term. You need to redo your analysis and recalculate your target price to see if you still want to hold the position.

Step #5: Read the quarterly conference call transcripts or listen to the conference call itself.
Many investors don't take the time to listen to the quarterly analyst conference call for each company. I find it invaluable to hear management's thoughts on the quarterly performance, and more importantly their outlook for the next few quarters and where they see growth and opportunities.

Step #6: Check for earnings pre-announcements.
Companies sometimes revise their earnings forecasts during the middle of a quarter, between their scheduled quarterly reporting. Earnings pre-announcements are a very powerful forecasting tool. Companies only issue revised earnings guidance when they expect either very good news or very bad news, both of which can move the stock price significantly. Pay attention to whether any of the stocks in your basket have any earnings pre-announcements, and be sure to adjust your position accordingly.

Step #7: Check the last earnings date and the price action for the last four quarters in the run-up to earnings dates.
I like to see how the price and volume of each of the stocks in my 'basket' have moved as they approach the date for their quarterly earnings announcements. I do this for the last four quarters, and often find patterns. If I notice that one of the stocks in my basket has run up 5% on average in the last two weeks before earnings and then falls 1% after earnings are reported, that is a pattern that can be traded.

Step 8: Look for history of increasing dividends.
Not all of the stocks in your basket will pay dividends, especially in the technology and biotech sectors. For those that do, however, you should review the past dividend history. I favor those companies

with a long and stable history of increasing dividends. When the
share price drops on a stock that pays a nice dividend, the dividend
yield can increase nicely on a percentage basis. A company that has
a history of increasing dividends is a strong investment candidate.

I like to add to the dividend payers in my basket of stocks when they
have temporary pullbacks on no major news. This allows me to
establish a position at a higher percentage dividend yield due to the
lower share price, which will often go right back up. For example,
safe and stable dividend yielders such as Apple (ticker AAPL) and
Disney (ticker DIS) are good examples. I add to these long-term
core positions whenever they sell off with the market.

Don't chase the super high yielding divided stocks or REITS. Be
careful if the dividend yield percentage gets too high compared to
other large stable stocks. This can actually be a red flag that the
dividend may not be sustainable and may get cut. Don't buy stocks
just for a large dividend, like the REITS and stocks paying 13%,
14%, 15%+ etc. Instead, you should try to understand the basis on
which the dividend is being paid. You should also trust dividends as
a better way of returning capital to shareholders than share buybacks
by the company to inflate their stock prices.

***Step 9: Calculate the price to earnings multiple, the growth rate
and the estimated price target.*** The price to earnings multiple (also
known as the P/E multiple) and the future target price based on your
analysis are key to giving you conviction in the near-term price
growth of your trades. The P/E multiple is also the best way to
compare two stocks to each other and determine which offers the
better value. In other words, the price to earnings multiple helps you
objectively determine the relative value of the stock – no matter
what the share price is trading at.

The second most important metric to calculate after the P/E multiple
is the ***PEG ratio***. The PEG ratio is the Price to Earnings ratio,
divided by the Growth rate. PEG ratios of less than one mean that
the shares are relatively inexpensive compared to the earnings
growth rate. This is a bullish indicator. If the PEG ratio is above
two, however, this tends to mean the shares are expensive relative to
the earnings growth rate. In these cases, I am more bearish on the
prospects of near-term increases in the share price.

PEG = **P/E Ratio** divided by **G** (the earnings per share Growth Rate)

Once you have calculated the multiple and the PEG ratio and completed the rest of your fundamental analysis in this chapter, you can estimate your anticipated price target for the company. The homework allows you to form a view on both current value and future growth. I like to estimate how far the price could go up or down from today's price in the near term (next six months). You should decide whether you like the risk to reward ratio offered from your analysis.

Additional fundamental analysis rules:

A few other guardrails to keep in mind:

RULE: Don't analyze stocks that are priced under $5: You should avoid investing and trading in stocks that trade for under $5, except if you really know the company. For the most part, these are too risky. There are many online gurus who claim to have made millions of dollars by day trading peaks and troughs in cheap penny stocks. For every one of those, I will show you 500 traders who lost money doing the same thing. Unless you really study this area as a specialty and know what you are doing, avoid these stocks.

RULE: Understand the nature of the earnings: Evaluate whether the earnings from the last quarter or two are organic (from sales of products and services) or "manufactured." Manufactured earnings are those that come from one-time events such as selling off patents or a divestiture of a business. On a related note, you should analyze upside surprises in earnings. You should always check to see if they are organic, or if they are manufactured. Also:
- Take a blend of trailing earnings per share and projected earnings per share.
- Compare the P/E ratio and EPS over time to see if earnings are increasing or decreasing.

There you have it. That completes the list of the fundamental homework to do on each stock within your basket. Some of this research is done up front before adding a stock to your basket, and some of the homework is ongoing every week after you have added a stock to your basket to stay current. It is critical to get to know the stocks you trade. The process outlined in this chapter is how I have streamlined doing so. While it is still a lot of work on each company, remember you can follow eight to ten diversified companies in the BOOST portion of your portfolio and do just fine. I put each of my stocks in a spreadsheet and add the answers to each of the research results above into a column in the spreadsheet. This makes comparisons over time and between stocks easier. For example, for each stock in my basket I track the items listed in the following spreadsheet:

	Co. #1:	Co #2:
PRICE (as of <DATE>)		
EPS (Earnings Per Share as measured by the forward P/E Ratio)		
PEG Ratio (note a PEG < 1 = Cheap; PEG > 2 = Expensive)		
Debt to Equity Ratio (the lower the better), don't buy if the ratio is over 50%		
Dividend Yield (the higher the better)		
Book Value Per Share (Don't Buy if over 3 times book value, 1-2 is best)		
Trend (via 200 day & 100 day moving avg.)		

EBITDA (Earnings before interest, tax, depreciation and amortization)		
Date of next Earnings		
My Target Price (estimate based on my homework)		

"I have said that in my whole life, I have known no wise person over a broad subject matter area who didn't read all the time – none, zero. Now I know all kinds of shrewd people who by staying within a narrow area can do very well without reading. But investment is a broad area. So, if you think you are going to be good at it and not read all the time, you have a different idea than I do..... You'd be amazed at how much Warren Buffett reads. You'd be amazed at how much I read."

- Charlie Munger at the Berkshire Hathaway 2003 annual meeting

Chapter 4

Technical Analysis

LEARNING OBJECTIVES

- **How to use technical analysis**

- **The key technical tools**

- **My favorite technical indicators and rules that work**

- **Combining fundamental analysis and technical analysis together**

- **Selecting when to deploy a trading strategy**

"Every ship on the bottom of the ocean is filled with charts."
- Preston James – investor and educator

From the inception of the stock market until the early 1990s, fundamental analysis of individual stocks dominated the thinking of most professionals.

There have always been technicians reading and drawing chart patterns (many by hand before about 1985), but until the 1990s those that used technical analysis alone for making investment decisions were thought of as someone doing a rain dance to make it rain.

Back in those days every time a chart technician would show a chart pattern and make a prediction on the near-term move of a security price, it was quite easy to show examples from other historical charts showing where that supposedly 'predictive' chart pattern got it exactly wrong. It was difficult to use past historical data to predict future price moves with any degree of consistency. Critics of technical analysis would say, it is always charting price and volume history looking backwards, not the future. "You can't steer a car forward by looking out the back window" fundamentalists would say to the technicians.

With advances in computers and the increased sophistication of data analysis, artificial intelligence and mathematical models, however, this has changed. Technical indicators have become more predictive and increasingly more important in the past 20 years. This is due to a number of factors, including a massive increase in computing power, increasingly sophisticated data analytics tools and models, advanced automated trading algorithms and high frequency traders.

'Technical analysis at speed,' as we have today, drives a much higher percentage of trades. It also becomes something of a self-fulfilling prophecy. If more traders and programed algorithms are acting on specific technical patterns and indicators, those indicators work better and become far more predictive. This is true even if it is just the fact that the herd of traders acted on an otherwise meaningless pattern. By trading on it, they make the technical signals more accurate when you look back at how prices acted after the technical signal occurred. By reacting and trading as if technical patterns are true, they in fact become increasingly true. So, while I remain a fundamentalist at heart, today I teach that you have to understand and respect trends and patterns revealed by technical analysis due to the massive trade sizes from institutions trading on technical analysis.

How To Use Technical Analysis

My advice to the retail / small investor is to use fundamental analysis help you understand *WHAT* stocks to buy or sell. Use technical analysis to help determine *WHEN* to buy or sell.

I am no longer dismissive of technical analysis as a means to forecast future stock price movements. I have realized the value of some technical indicators. Simply put, they work better today because so many other traders use them and trade by them. So how should the retail investor use technical indicators? Below are my rules and favorite ways to use technical analysis as well as my favorite indicators.

Many traders believe that the most important technical indicators to look at when thinking about making a trade are the current *price action* and the trading *volume*. These are powerful signals because they show graphically how the crowd is behaving in real time.

Key Technical Tools

How do wade through the over one hundred technical indicators available today and make any sense of it? Over my years of trading, I have found that trading the prevailing trend is best. This is also known as being a trend trader vs. being a contrarian or scalper who bets against the underlying confirmed trend. Following the trend, combined with using the 10 technical indicators outlined below is the way to be most effective in leverage technical analysis. While no technical indicators work every time and all have their strengths and weaknesses, my experience has shown the following technical indicators work best.

My Favorite Technical Indicators and Rules That Work

Below is the list of the top 10 technical analysis indicators that I recommend for retail investors, and insights into how and when to use them. While I am conscious that 10 indicators are a large number to check and follow before trading, these have been narrowed down from more than 100 popular technical indicators in the marketplace today.

Each indicator performs a slightly different function in your analysis. You don't have to use them all on every trade but you should check a majority of them before each trade.

A note of caution before proceeding; I provide a summary of each of these technical indicators that I use and how I use them. Keep in mind, however, that many people go very deep into the analysis, construction and interpretation of each of the technical indicators. Each one summarized here could easily be a chapter by itself if covered thoroughly. This is a high-level summary description and how I use them. Detailed analysis of the history, construction and interpretation of each indicator is beyond the scope of this book. However, you don't need to be an expert on all of the nuances of each one to use it effectively. For each indicator, free resources exist online. You can begin your research at www.stockcharts.com.

The top 10 technical indicators are organized below into three groups:

- *Technical Indicator Group #1: Determine the trend and buying or selling pressure on a stock or ETF*
- *Technical Indicator Group #2: Confirm the Current Trend & Measure the Strength of the Trend*
- *Technical Indicator Group #3: Determine Low risk Entry Points & Exit Price Targets*

TECHNICAL INDICATORS GROUP #1 – To help you determine the trend and the buying or selling pressure on a stock or ETF:

1. **Moving averages (10 Day, 50 Day, 100 Day Exponential Moving Averages)** – Use exponential moving averages which put more weight on the recent data points (vs. simple moving averages) for getting an initial read on the price trend on the security. All charting software provides these overlay capabilities. Begin here to determine the overall trend on the stock or ETF you are considering. I suggest you check these on either Yahoo Finance or Stockcharts.com.

2. **Volume & Price Action:** Check the previous three to four weeks of price and volume action. You should look for how today's trading volume compares to the average day's trading volume. This helps you determine the reaction of the market to the latest news items. I use this price action to look for recent support and resistance levels. I write down these levels before going on to the next indicators. These can be checked on either Yahoo Finance or Stockcharts.com.

3. **The Ichimoku Cloud** (a.k.a. the Ichimoku Kinko Hyo) indicator. This is my favorite single technical indicator. If

you go to Japan and much of Asia, the Ichimoku cloud is on every trader's screen. I am still shocked at how infrequently it is used in the USA. When you first see one of these charts, it can look very complicated. However, you can learn to read one in short order after a short training.

Ichimoku stands for:
- *Ichimoku* = one look, glance
- *Kinko* = balanced
- *Hyo* = chart, graph

This indicator gives the current price trend direction. It also gives the support and resistance levels, entry and exit signals, as well as the strength of these signals. The goal of using the Ichimoku cloud is to capture the majority of the prevailing trends in the stock at the same time in one chart. It is the only "all in one" indicator that I have found (although I still use the other technical indicators presented in this list). There are four keys to reading the Ichimoku cloud:

A. *Red line – the "Tenken-sen."* This measures the highest high and the lowest low divided by two for the past nine periods. This formula is the moving average for the last nine periods.
B. *Blue Line – the "Kijun-sen."* This measures the highest high and the lowest low divided by two but for a total of 26 periods instead of nine.
C. *Green Line –* This shows the price action for the past 26 periods.
D. *The "Cloud"* - This is the most important part of the Ichimoku cloud. It shows the midpoint of the red and blue lines (calculated by adding the high and the low, and dividing by two) for the past 52 periods, and then uses that information to forecast the future 26 periods from today. If today's share price is above the cloud, this is bullish and the cloud will act as a key support level. If today's share price is below the cloud, then the cloud will act as resistance and this is a bearish signal. The theory is that it is hard for a stock price to fight through the cloud in either direction, so when it does, it represents a strong indication of a true trend

change. A share price that remains within the cloud is considered to be an ambiguous signal. You can check the Ichimoku indicator on www.stockcharts.com.

E. Crossovers – Look also for red and blue line crossovers. When the red line crosses the blue line from below, this is considered to be a very bullish signal, especially if it occurs above the cloud. When the red line crosses blue line from above, this is considered to be a very bearish signal.

4. *The ADX indicator* – After using the moving averages to determine the current trend, I check the ADX indicator to measure the strength of that trend. It works in both directions. I look for an ADX black line reading of at least 25 and I want to see it climbing. As part of the ADX indicator I also confirm that the green line (DMI+) is on top of the red line (DMI -). This indicates an uptrend.

TECHNICAL INDICATORS GROUP #2- To help you CONFIRM the current trend & to measure the strength of that trend:

5. **The MACD (Moving Average Convergence / Divergence)** – to confirm the trend and measure the strength (in addition to the Ichimoku cloud). The MACD was developed in the 1970s by Gerald Appel. It is considered one of most effective (yet simple to use) technical indicators. It simultaneously shows the trend lines of two different time frame moving averages. This becomes an oscillator showing the short moving average in relation to the longer time frame moving average, by subtracting the longer moving average from the shorter. You can read the MACD by looking at how it fluctuates above and below the zero line. I look for how the two moving averages converge and diverge. When they cross over each other it represents a change in direction and/or the momentum of the trend.

6. **OBV (On Balance Volume)** - The OBV line indicator is used to confirm the trend spotted in the moving averages and Ichimoku cloud. The OBV indicator is constructed to measure buying and selling pressure on an ongoing cumulative basis (i.e. a running total). It does this by adding

volume to the indicator on upward (buying pressure) days and subtracting volume on downward (selling pressure) days. Look for an OBV line that is slightly upward sloping if you are bullish. If you are bullish but the OBV line is sloping downward, you should refrain from trading that day as it is a bearish sign that selling pressure is dominating.

7. **The Equity Put/Call Ratio** – The Put/Call Ratio is a technical indicator that shows put volume relative to call volume. The Put/Call Ratio rises above one when the current put volume exceeds the current call volume and the ratio is below one when the current call volume exceeds the current put volume. This indicator is used by traders and investors to calibrate current market sentiment. A Put/Call Ratio at high levels is believed to be a bearish signal, and a bullish signal when at relatively low levels.

TECHNICAL INDICATORS GROUP #3 – Determine Low risk Entry Points & Exit Price Targets:

8. **Bollinger Bands** – Developed by John Bollinger, the Bollinger Bands® are a popular technical indicator showing volatility through bands placed above and below the current moving average of a stock. The width of the volatility bands changes as volatility is based on the standard deviation from these averages. The standard deviations change as volatility changes on the underlying security. The Bollinger Bands widen when volatility increases and narrow when volatility decreases. For trading signals, I like to enter trades when the security is in an upward sustained trend over several months, but with an overall market pullback, the security is trading in the bottom half of the Bollinger Band range.

9. **Keltner Channels** – this indicator determines lower risk trade entry points, on pullbacks within the broader bullish trend. Selecting lower risk entry points is very important and often overlooked. Keltner Channels are also a volatility-based indicator, as are the Bollinger Bands above. This indicator, however, does not base its range on the standard deviations from the moving average. The Keltner channels use the ATR

(known as the Average True Range) to set channel distance. The channels are typically drawn at two Average True Range values above and below the 20-day EMA (exponential moving average). Keltner Channels are used to help you understand directional trends and overbought and oversold levels in non-trending markets.

The Squeeze:
A recent development that is incredibly helpful is called the "Squeeze." The Squeeze is a technical indicator that shows the Bollinger Bands (which expand and contract with volatility) in relation to the Keltner Channels (which are static in width).

Markets don't move straight up or down; there are often more quiet periods where pressure consolidates and then rapidly moves higher or lower. When the Bollinger Band lines move inside (or squeeze inside) the Keltner Channel lines, they are said to trigger a squeeze. This tells you that there is a quiet, consolidating market building up pressure.

Don't trade when you see a squeeze forming – as initially it just shows time periods where price pressure is flat and building up pressure and ready to release a big move. Wait until you see the Bollinger Bands pop back outside the Keltner channels. Generally, the result is a large price movement in that stock either upwards or downwards. A squeeze occurs when the built-up pressure of consolidation finally releases through large amounts of buyers or sellers taking action on a consolidating stock. The move generally is fairly rapid and significant.

You should wait for the squeeze to form and then put on a short-term trade in that direction that the squeeze fires. Note that the squeeze does not just pertain to one timeframe. A squeeze can set up on a daily chart, a weekly chart, or a five-minute chart. I tend to only trade squeezes once they form and fire on the weekly chart, where the direction is typically good for eight to ten weeks, or the daily chart, where the direction is typically good for eight to ten days. Anything shorter is too speculative.

10. **Fibonacci ratios and price extensions** – when I first learned of this technical indicator, I thought it was nonsense. I have since changed my tune. I witnessed firsthand how it predicted future stock price movements with unbelievable accuracy and consistency.

    Fibonacci ratios are derived from something known as the Fibonacci sequence. This is a numerical sequence, named after the Italian mathematician who discovered it. Leonardo Fibonacci died in 1250 AD, well before the advent of the stock market, so you can see where my skepticism came from.

    While it may seem hard to believe, there is a natural ratio that occurs repeatedly in nature to describe the proportions of almost everything. It applies from the most microscopic atoms, to things like the patterns of seashells, to the largest most advanced patterns such as the movement of planets. This proportional ratio seems to help everything in nature maintain balance. Eventually, scholars applied this sequence to the stock market and it was found that stock price movements also seem to follow the Fibonacci ratio. It soon became known as the "golden ratio."

    Fibonacci ratios are numerical ratios indicating likely price extensions and retracements. As stocks trade, supply and demand imbalances occur and a predictable pattern of often emerges. When I trade short term- anything from swing trades to a few weeks- I use the Fibonacci ratios combined with retracement price overlays to help me set exit target prices. Studies show that Fibonacci ratios and retracements have a high predictive power in forecasting short-term price movements holding within the larger trend. Fibonacci retracements also can help indicate potential reversals and their price levels. These ratios hold to the mathematical Fibonacci sequence and can be overlaid with many chart packages. The most popular Fibonacci Retracements are 61.8% and 38.2%.

Combining fundamental analysis and technical analysis together

Once you have completed your fundamental analysis on the stocks in your basket and concluded that you would like to put on a new position, you now need to check timing of your trade entry using technical analysis. The steps for putting the fundamental analysis and the technical analysis together are as follows:

Step 1:	Develop your **daily macro (top-down) economic view** of the world events affecting stocks today. *If your conclusion produces a GO / GREEN LIGHT then proceed to step 2.*	See Chapter 1 for details.
Step 2:	Complete the **fundamental analysis** on each of the equities in your selected 'basket of stocks.' *If your conclusion produces a GO / GREEN LIGHT on the stock you want to trade today, then proceed to step 3.*	See Chapter 3 for details.
Step 3:	**Determine the current price trend and buying or selling pressure**. Are there more buyers than sellers pushing the price pressure upwards, or is the opposite true? *If your conclusion produces a GO / GREEN LIGHT on trend, then proceed to step 4.*	This Chapter (4) for details.
Step 4:	**Confirm the current price trend and measure its strength.** *If your confirmation*	This Chapter (4) for details.

	conclusion produces a GO/ GREEN LIGHT on the trade you are considering, then proceed on to step 5.	
Step 5:	**Select a trading strategy** based on your conviction from the six trading strategies taught within this book. Select a low risk trade entry and target price exit points.	See Chapter 4 for trade entry points and exits & Chapter 6 for trading strategy specific trading rules.
Step 6:	**Place trade** including the downside protection (options) position.	See Chapter 5 for general trading rules & Chapter 6 for my recommended strategies and trading rules.

A Few Additional Tips on Combining the Analysis:

Please keep in mind a few additional 'fine-tuning' rules and where to use each of the ten technical indicators presented previously:

Additional tips for determine the current price trend and buying or selling pressure
The key for shorter-term trades is to determine with reasonable assurance the prevailing current price trend direction. Then trade in the same direction as that trend. In addition, after determining whether today's buying pressure is greater than selling pressure:

- It is best to place near term bullish trades when buying pressure is stronger.
- It is best to place near term bearish trades when selling pressure exceeds buying pressure.

To determine these things, I check the following technical indicators:
- *The Moving Averages.*
  Specifically, I first look at the 10-day, then the 50-day, and finally the 100-day exponential moving averages.

Exponential moving averages give you a view skewed towards recent data results versus the simple moving averages.

- *Rule: look for 'stacked' exponential moving averages.* Each shorter timeframe moving average line should be stacked one on top of each other. In other words, it means the current stock price is above all of these four moving averages (in an uptrend) or below all of them in a downtrend. In addition, stacked moving averages means that each of the shorter term moving average lines today is above the longer term moving average line hence bullish buying pressure is on. For example:

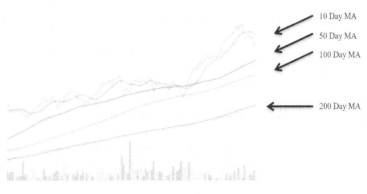

Source: Yahoo Finance

Rule: Look for moving average line crossovers from below to above:

Bullish crossovers occur when the 10-day moving average crosses above the 50-day moving average. They can occur when the 50-day moving average crosses from below to above the 100 day. The opposite is also true. Bearish crossovers are when the shorter time frame moving average line crosses down through the longer-term moving average line from above to below. Follow the trend. The whole idea of looking at moving averages is to detect when buying pressure exceeds selling pressure.

Rule: Check if the daily volume of today's and yesterday's trading is substantially higher than the average daily trading volume: Both of these figures are presented below the interactive charts on Yahoo Finance. Make note of the trend of the stock price you are looking at

and whether it is moving in or away from that trend on high or normal volume. If it is holding the longer-term trend on normal volume, you can safely move onto the next step. If, however, the stock price is breaking the 100-day or 200-day trend (up or down) on high volume – this is a powerful signal and you need to confirm the trend change. Go to IBD and check Stocks on the Move and go to Briefing.com and look up the stock symbol to see if there is any current news that is driving the stock price.

Rules for confirming the current price trend & measure the strength of the current price trend.
Once you have a good sense of the 10, 50, and 100 day trends and have determined whether there is more buying pressure or selling pressure, I then use two of the other trend confirmation technical indicators to confirm the trend to see if its strength is driven by more than mere buying and selling pressure.

Specifically, I check the following two indicators:
- **On-Balance Volume (OBV)** – Using the OBV line on the daily chart versus a weekly chart will give you another excellent confirmation picture of selling and buying pressure. Use the OBV line to confirm the trend. The theory behind OBV is based on the distinction between institutional money and less sophisticated retail traders. You read the OBV by checking if the current line is sloping upward or downward, or remains flat. An upward sloping OBV line indicates buying pressure is dominant. Higher buying pressure will help sustain the current up-trend.
- **Commodity Channel Index (or CCI)** – Though I do not consider it one of my top 10 technical indicators, sometimes I also check the commodity channel index, also known as the CCI indicator, if I have conflicting readings from the ones above. The CCI warns of overbought and oversold conditions. It ranges from -100 to +100. A high positive number indicates when prices are far above their averages. A low negative reading indicates that the price of the underlying security is far below the average. If the CCI is reading at an extreme high or low, this breaks the tie.

Selecting when to deploy a trading strategy

At this point you have formed a view on the fundamentals, the technical analysis (including trend, the buying pressure, the strength of the trend), and you have a level of conviction in making a trade. Based on your level of conviction in the future price movement, you next need to select which of the six trading strategies fits best and select a low risk trade entry point (see Chapter Six for this).

For selecting a low risk entry price, however, I like to use the Keltner channels technical indicator on a daily chart for determining a low risk entry price on a given stock. As discussed, Keltner channels are lines on the chart showing a 20-day exponential moving average with upper and lower bands at two times the average daily range. A low risk entry point on a bullish trade is when the underlying stock or ETF price drops below the mid-point between the upper and lower Keltner channel but the underlying stock is still in an overall bullish trend. Any price towards the lower Keltner channel, which represents a pull-back within a longer-term bullish trend, but where the stock still is above a green Ichimoku cloud and it still has an upward sloping OBV line is a good low risk entry point.

"Luck is what happens when preparation meets opportunity."
- Seneca (Roman Philosopher)

Chapter 5

Developing Your Personal Trading Process & General Trading Rules – Regardless of Trading Strategy

LEARNING OBJECTIVES

- Understand the importance of diversifying your trading strategies, then concentrate trades within each strategy

- Options basics

- When to place which types of trading strategy

- Setting profit targets & time frames by strategy

- Other trading rules

"Wide diversification is only required when investors do not know what they are doing." - **Warren Buffett**

Before you jump into the specifics the six trading strategies in the following chapter, it is important to understand some options basics and a few general trading rules that should govern all types of trading strategies, regardless of which ones you ultimately select. These rules will help improve all of your trades, regardless of your market outlook.

It is also critical to plan how different individual trading strategies can work together in different combinations. After you understand trading strategy diversification (covered in this chapter), the trading strategies themselves (covered in CH. 6) and trade sequencing also known as trade progression (covered in CH. 7), you can delve into and refine your trading plan and fine tune your specific rules for what is most effective and beneficial.

Let's first cover trading strategy diversification. By "trading STRATEGY diversification," I do not mean diversification of your portfolio across different stocks or asset classes. That is the traditional definition of asset diversification. In this context, diversification refers to allocating your portfolio across different trading *strategies*. In other words, in addition to diversifying your money across different asset classes, such as stocks, bonds, cash, real estate, gold, etc., you should also diversify the BOOST portion of your portfolio across different trading strategies.
You select which strategy to choose based on your view for the company over the next few months and years.

Understand the importance of diversifying your trading strategies but then concentrate your trades within each strategy

It is important to diversify the trading strategies you select. Once you have an idea of which strategies you will use, I favor *concentrating* your money within the trading strategies. These means once you have selected the dollar amounts to trade in the BOOST portion of your portfolio, you then select which trading strategies to employ for which dollar amounts. Then concentrate in one or two companies for each trading strategy selected.

For example, let's assume you analyze markets and your basket of potential securities. You determine that you want to do three of the six trading strategies taught in this book with your growth money (the BOOST portion of your portfolio). That is a fine number and you can do very well.

Remember, you have already fully diversified the BASE portion of your portfolio. Don't then over-diversify the BOOST portion as well by selecting five trades within each one of those three trading strategies. If you do this, all of a sudden you are in 15 simultaneous active trades (three trading strategies with five trades each) within the growth portion of your portfolio alone! For all but the most active professional, this is too many and will be too difficult to track, review and adjust if needed, especially when you are new to active trading.

I advise that once you have selected a few trading strategies, concentrate your position size within one or at most two stocks to trade within each strategy. Do this and your BOOST portfolio and put the rest of the BOOST portion of the portfolio in good individual stock positions (your favorites from your fundamental and technical analysis you will have already completed).
This way, your paired stock & options trades will consist of just a few trade positions to monitor and potentially make adjustments. As Warren Buffett's quote indicates, wide diversification in the BOOST portion of the portfolio is only required if and when you don't know what you are doing.

You will have achieved portfolio-level diversification already from your initial choices in building and executing your overall financial plan and breaking the portfolio into the BASE and BOOST sections. The BASE will also be fully diversified. Within the growth portion of your portfolio used for trading, you have the ability to be more concentrated.

What is the right mix of diversified trading strategies? The answer to that will depend upon your age, goals and risk tolerance. I will give you some guidelines here to do this on your own; you can also work with your Registered Investment Adviser (RIA) to help select not only the right asset allocation mix for your entire portfolio, but also the related trading strategy diversification mix within the BOOST portion of the portfolio.

To help you select, you should utilize a cone pyramid diagram of my favorite trading strategies ranked from least risky to highest risk (illustrated on the following page). This will help you select a good initial mix of trading strategies.

Generally speaking, the lower risk strategies require more capital to be effective and offer the lowest potential investment returns but are highly likely to occur. These are more conservative and should be used increasingly as you move towards retirement. The riskier strategies require the least amount of capital, but can produce the highest potential rewards, albeit with less of a chance of occurring.

My favorite trading strategies by risk & reward:

LOW RISK (**BASE PORTFOLIO** / PROTECT)

- **High Yield Money Market Funds** (cash equivalent)
- **Fixed Income** – CDs, Treasuries, Corporate Bonds
- **Buy Diversified ETFs** on Broad Market Indexes & Sectors
- **Collar Trades** (buy stock + buy medium term (3 Mo.) protective puts on the same stock + sell short-term (1 Mo.) covered calls on the same stock)

MEDIUM RISK (**Primarily BOOST only**) Strategies:

- **Covered Calls** (in the money & large unprotected covered calls)
- **Vertical credit spreads** out of the money 1 standard deviation or greater (Bull Put Spreads or Bear Call Spreads)
- **Sell Naked Puts (cash backed)**
- **Broken Wing (or Skip Strike) Butterflies** with a net credit

HIGHER RISK (**BOOST only**) Strategies:

- In the money **Call Debit Spreads (Bull Call Spreads)**
- **Call Ratio Spreads** (with a credit)
- Buy **deep in the money long calls or puts** with approximately 9-18 months to expiration; adding a stop limit order after purchase (at a 25% decline to protect the position)
- **Selling Weekly At the Money Vertical Credit Spreads**
- **Directional Butterflies**

HIGHEST RISK (**BOOST only**) Strategies:

- **Sell Naked Puts** (not cash backed)
- **Buy Calls** (out of the money / speculation)

Don't worry that we have not covered the explanations and the nuances of each of the trading strategies listed in the above diagram. Each is covered in detail in the next chapter. The key takeaway here is that you need to define the percentages of your trading portfolio to allocate to each of the above categories. The BASE vs. BOOST percentages you would have already completed (from Chapter One);

now we break down and decide on the percentages for each category of strategies for the BOOST only portion of the portfolio (how much in MEDIUM Risk strategies and how much in HIGHER risk strategies).

Remember, your trading portfolio is a subset of your entire portfolio of assets as discussed in Chapter One. That means that the riskier trading portion of your portfolio is the BOOST portion of the portfolio only. The BASE of the portfolio will be invested in fully diversified, safer asset classes.

The percentages in the examples below are within the BOOST portion of the trading portfolio total only.

For example, 30-year-old trader with an Aggressive Growth risk tolerance might have the following allocation:
- 25% low risk strategies;
- 15% medium risk strategies;
- 40% higher risk / aggressive growth strategies and
- 20% speculative strategies

A 45-year-old married father of three with a Growth risk tolerance, on the other hand may select:
- 50% Core / low risk strategies;
- 35% Medium-risk strategies and
- 15% Growth (with 0% Speculative).

A 62-year-old business owner (with kids grown) with a Moderate Growth risk tolerance, may choose to go with:
- 60% Core / low risk strategies;
- 30% Medium-risk;
- 10% Growth (with 0% Speculative).

The point is that the actual allocation will vary by individual based on age, asset base, risk tolerance, etc. Choose the right percentage mix for your situation.

Remember also to keep some of your funds in cash (or a high yielding money market sweep position) to cover fees and as dry powder to put to work when market pullbacks occur.

<u>Trading Rule</u>: A good rule of thumb is to always hold back approximately 10% of your aggressive trading capital (the BOOST portion) in cash, to be able to add more to positions that are working well, or to seize new opportunities as they arise. This will also give you flexibility when you adjust losing trades. I often have levels of 25% high yielding money market sweep (cash) in the BOOST portion of the portfolio. Cash is a wonderful hedge that is often overlooked.

Trade Sequencing (also known as Trade Progression):

Trade Progression will be covered in detail in Chapter Seven, but it is important to keep in mind here as you select your trade strategies and how to diversify across the various trade strategies.
By trade "progressions" I mean the order in which you place trades. This means, you will place an initial trade, then when and how to place the second and third trade after the result of the prior trade is known.   Trade progression answers the question, "what do I do first." Then what do I do next if 'A' outcome occurs.   Or what do I do if 'B' outcome occurs?

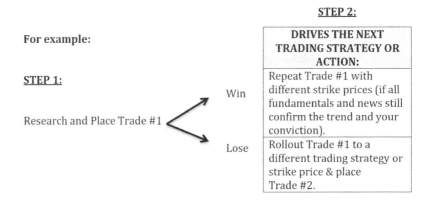

The combinations of trade progressions between trading strategies are endless. I have refined the choices to the trade progressions that consistently work best. Please refer to Chapter Seven for detailed instruction on trade progressions.

Options Basics

The rest of this book will focus on the best strategies and technics to grow the BOOST portion of your portfolio. In other words, it focuses on the more active and tactical strategies and adjustments. Each of these 6 strategies uses options (either paired with owning the related stock or ETF or trading the option outright by itself). As each strategy uses options, here is very quick primer on options and terminology for those who are not already up to speed. If you are already versed in buying and selling calls and puts, you can skip ahead to the next section entitled "When to Place Which Type of Strategy."

In options trading, there are two categories of options. The two categories are CALL options and PUT options. This is the same whether the underlying security is an individual stock or an ETF.
- *CALL Options* – Give the buyer the right but not the obligation to BUY a certain STOCK (or ETF) at a certain PRICE on a before a certain expiration DATE.
- *PUT Options* – Give the buyer the right but not the obligation to SELL a certain STOCK (or ETF) at a certain PRICE on a before a certain expiration DATE.

Each Call or PUT option Contract is made up of the following key components:
- *Option type:* CALL or PUT
- *Strike Price:* the price of the underlying security (stock or ETF) you want to have the right to buy or sell at.
- *Expiration Date:* Each Call option gives the buyer the right but not the obligation to buy the security at a specific strike price up until a specific date. This date is called the expiration date. It is defined as the last date the option buyer can exercise their right to buy or sell the underlying security or sell the option.
- *Option Premium:* For each option there is a buyer and there is a seller. The price the option contract is bought or sold at is called the option premium. The premium is set by the markets and is different for each strike price and each expiration date. Option pricing is a complicated calculation that continually changes (just like a stock price goes up and

down and changes all day long). The option premium is affected by many factors including:
- o the changes in the underlying stock or security price,
- o the amount of time remaining until expiration,
- o the implied volatility, etc.

The key to remember is if you are buying the call or put, you pay the option premium. If you are selling the call or put, you collect the option premium from the buyer.

Option BUYERS have rights but not an obligation. Options SELLERS take on an OBLIGATION to perform in return for collecting money (or for taking in the option premium). Inexperienced options traders might think it is less risky to be the option buyer because you are not obligated to do anything and can potentially profit if the underlying security goes your way. Experienced options traders know, however, that with proper strike price selection and risk management, it is actually much more consistent to win being the option seller and collecting the option premium. For each category of options, Calls and Puts, you can buy them or sell them. This is key and where most people get twisted in their thinking.

Option Category:	Potential Action:	Meaning:
CALL option(s):	Buy a CALL (or Calls)	By paying the option premium, you have the right but not the obligation to BUY a certain STOCK (or ETF) at a certain PRICE on a before a certain expiration DATE.
	Sell a CALL (or Calls)	For collecting the option premium payment up front, you have the obligation to have the stock called away from you (or bought from you) at a certain PRICE on or before a certain expiration DATE.

PUT option(s):	Buy a PUT (or Puts)	You have the right but not the obligation to SELL a certain STOCK (or ETF) at a certain PRICE on a before a certain expiration DATE.
	Sell a PUT (or Puts)	For collecting a payment up front (taking in an option premium), you have the obligation to have the stock (or ETF) put to you (or sold to you) at a certain PRICE on or before a certain expiration DATE.

Why is this tricky to keep straight in your mind? Because depending on whether you are the buyer or seller of either the call or put option your outlook on the underlying security is the opposite and everything flips logically.

For example: If you are BULLISH on the underlying stock (or ETF): the two choices from the table above that are bullish are: *Buying a Call* or *Selling a Put*. Did you catch that? Selling a put option is a bullish trade.

Buying a call option is straightforward. You lock in the ability to buy something you think is going higher in price now and you benefit as it continues to go higher. But... selling puts is also a bullish strategy on the stock. By selling a put option, you are saying to the buyer, I agree to have the stock put to me (or sold to me) at the strike price, on or before the expiration date if you pay me the option premium now. Most people struggle with this idea. Remember, buying a put option gives you the right to sell something that you think will fall in price. But we are not buying the put option in this example, we are selling puts. This means you want to get paid the put option premium up front and are willing to have the stock (or ETF) put to you if it falls to or below a certain price. As you will see, this is a great way to get paid over and over without buying the stock until it comes down to our discounted price. It is a great way to both get paid while you wait for a pullback and then to buy stocks you love at a discount.

If you are BEARISH on the underlying stock (or ETF): the two choices from the table that are bearish are: *Buying a Put option* or *Selling a Call option*. Did you catch that? Selling a call option is a bearish trade.

Buying a put is straightforward. You lock in the ability to sell something you think is going lower in price now and you benefit as it continues to go lower. This is because you have the right but not the obligation to put (or to sell) the security to someone else, the put buyer at a predetermined price. If the underlying is falling, this will be a higher price and hence more and more valuable as the underlying falls lower and lower.

Selling calls is also a bearish strategy on the stock. Most people struggle with this idea. Remember, though buying a call option gives you the right to buy something that you think will rise in price. But we are not buying the call option, in this example we are selling the call option(s). This means you want to get paid the call option premium up front and are willing to have the stock (or ETF) called away from you (or bought from you) if it rises above a certain price.

When to place which type of trading strategy

Selecting a good trading strategy should be based on a combination of several factors:
- Your view of the overall market at hand (the overall market, trend and news),
- Your conclusions from the fundamental analysis on the securities in your 'basket' of stocks that you are looking to potentially trade,
- Your conclusions from the technical analysis on the security you are looking to potentially trade to check timing and entry points,
- Current prices of the stock and related options you are considering (more on bad and good options prices and how to check the 'Greeks' in Chapters Six and Seven).

As you can see, it is a complicated process. Mastering more active trading is like any worthwhile skill; it is hard at first but gets easier and easier with repetition. I believe it helps greatly to have a decision table (or decision matrix) handy to help you select which type of trade to put on. The table in two pages shows a good trade strategy decision matrix. It is a tool to help you match your conviction level on future price direction on a security, to several correct trading strategies.

Before selecting the trading strategy, however, there is one more key piece of information to factor in in addition to price direction – the *implied future volatility*. Volatility is simply defined as the amount of movement (up or down) in the price of an asset (such as a stock or option) over a certain time period. The time period you can track volatility can be in the past (called historical volatility) or in the future (the implied future volatility). The higher the trading range has been in the past, the higher the historical volatility. If the asset has traded in a tight trading range, the historical volatility will have been low.

Implied future volatility is where we focus in putting on new trades, regardless of which strategy you select. It is extremely important for putting on new trades and investments. It means the anticipated or expected future movement in the price of a security (as implied by the price of its options) over a certain time period in the future. It shows you how volatile the market may be in the future.

Why is this implied future volatility important? It is not very important for the BASE portion of your portfolio, as you will plan to hold those positions for many years with very little trading. It is very important for more active options trading in the BOOST portion of your portfolio. This is because it greatly affects the option premium (or price of the options). As you will see, it can greatly affect whether you want to be the buyer of those options or the seller of those options. Options that have high levels of implied volatility will result in high-priced option premiums. You will generally want to be the seller of high priced (high implied volatility) options. It is just like owning any other asset, real estate, a vintage guitar, a stock, etc. When the prices are high and puffed up and inflated you want to be the seller of those assets, not the buyer.

Implied volatility (as indicated by the Greek named 'Vega') is very important, option prices on the same underlying stock at the same current price can vary dramatically based on the implied volatility factor used in pricing the derivatives by the market makers. In other words, an option's sensitivity to changes in implied volatility can be determined by Vega.

In determining the pricing of options and other derivative instruments, there are a few key inputs (time decay to expiration, implied volatility, etc.). Each one is labeled and tracked in options trading by one of five Greek letters (Delta, Theta, Vega, Gamma and Rho). There is a more detailed discussion on each of "the Greeks" in Chapter Seven. What is important to understand here in selecting each trading strategy, is that you should check on implied volatility before trading to select which trading strategy to use on different securities.

The table on the following page brings it all together and can help you answer the question of when to trade which strategy based on the implied volatility.

Many free charting platforms online can show an option's average implied volatility over time. I have researched and tracked the implied volatility readings on a security monthly back over the past 12 months. To use this chart, take the highest and lowest readings of historical volatility for a given stock over the past 12 months, and then cut this range of values of historical volatility you found into ten slices, or deciles. The lowest decile should equal the least implied volatility, the highest decile the highest readings for implied volatility. Next take today's implied volatility reading and see which decile today's reading falls in relation to the past readings for implied volatility (the range of which is represented by the deciles). By plugging in the results against the past, you can easily see which trading strategies are appropriate to potentially use for trading the security.

Implied Volatility – Trading Strategy Decision Matrix

Potential Trading Strategy Decision Matrix												
Strategy:	Potential Profit:	1	2	3	4	5	6	7	8	9	10
Buy (long) Call or Put Options	Unlimited	x	x	x							
Sell Vertical (Credit) Spreads	Limited						x	x	x	x	x
Sell Iron Condors & Butterfly Verticals Spread	Limited						x	x	x	x	
Call Ratio Spreads	Limited								x	x	x
Sell Cash Backed Naked Puts	Limited									x	x
Buy Underlying Stock/Sell Call/Buy Put (Collar)	Limited				x	x	x	x			
Sell Covered Calls	Limited								x	x	x

For more detail on the 'Greeks' (like VEGA) and trade timing, see Chapter Seven

Setting Profit Targets and Time Frames by Trade

In Chapter One, we explored the importance of matching your trading and investment goals with the timeframes for your anticipated spending needs throughout your life. It was stressed that you should spend some time thinking at the portfolio level about your current amounts of savings vs. when you anticipate needing the money. You then use the answers to these questions as inputs to create a financial plan that can achieve your objectives, with clear trading strategies, rules, and action steps.

In this chapter, we take this same analysis down to the individual trade level. The key idea at the individual trade level is that you need to set exit targets (target prices) for each trade. You should do so regardless of which trading strategy you select and regardless of whether your outlook is bullish or bearish.

Setting an exit target means selecting a key price level, date or profit percentage level that will trigger you to sell (or begin a scaled exit) from a position.

An exit or sell strategy target should have two key elements: A Time Stop and a Price (profit / loss) Stop.

Time stops: Options (calls and puts) are a decaying asset based on the time remaining to the expiration date. You can think of them like a melting ice cube. When you sell options this time decay works in your favor and you make money from the time 'melting' away. When you buy options, however, this time decay works against you and you lose money each day the trade is still open.

Before you enter a *BUYING* options trade, you need to set a time-limit (a date on the calendar) trigger that you will use as a stop to exit the trade. When I buy a long call or put option, for example, I seek to exit before the final 45 days prior to expiration. Like an ice cube that begins to melt slowly and then more rapidly as it shrinks in size, you will see that time decay accelerates as well. The most pronounced time decay occurs in the final 45 days of the life of an option. If my target prices have not been hit by then, I use a predetermined time stop to get out of the position, take a short-term loss and then adjust the trade timing (see Chapter Eight for how to do trade adjustments on loosing trades). Most trading platforms allow you to preset a sell order based on a price but not typically on a date / time factors alone, so you must make a mental note of this or input the dates to check your positions in your personal calendar.

If you entered a *SELLING* options trade, then you can wait all the way to expiration as each day of time decay on the options price works in your favor. Alternatively, some people (myself included) get a little more aggressive when the selling option trade is winning. When I sell an option, I look to close out the position when I can collect at least 75% of the time decay in my favor, if there is still a lot of time remaining until expiration date. Although the timing is different, you need to set a mental time stop for each trade, and put them in your calendar to avoid forgetting.

For Example: (note: don't worry if you cannot follow this trading strategy example yet, after reading CH 6 you will be able to do so).

Let's say I own 500 shares of AMD (Advanced Micro Devices Inc.). The current stock price is $27. The cost to buy the 500 shares of AMD stock is $13,500, or half that price if you buy it on margin (~$6,750). One of the trading strategies you will learn in CH. 6 is selling a covered call option. Options are written in 100 share increments, so 500 shares of stock equals selling 5 call option contracts. If I sold 5 contracts of the $28 strike price call options expiring in 5 weeks, the current option premium I would receive right now is $2 a contract. What have we agreed to logically? We have agreed if the option buyer will pay us $1,000 (500 shares times $2 equals a credit of $1,000 paid to me in one day) we will agree to sell our 500 shares of AMD at $28 a share anytime between now and expiration day in 5 weeks. Let's say one week later, the AMD stock price falls from $27 a share to $26 a share. The $28 call options that I sold for $2 are now worth only $.50. Remember when you sell options (as in this covered call example), you want the option price to fall towards $0 as fast as possible. This one did. The cost of the call options I sold moved from the $2 I received on the day I sold the calls, to now I could buy them back at only $.50 cents in only 1 week. This meets my guideline to close out the option position if 75% of the maximum profit has been achieved. In this scenario, I would likely buy back the 5 contracts at $.50 cents (spending $250) and close out the position. In this example I would pocket the $1.50 profit (the difference between the $2 I received when I sold the calls and the 50 cents I had to spend to buy back the position and close it out). $1.50 times 500 shares = $750 profit earned in one week on $6,750 of cost to buy the shares on margin. This is an 11.1% return earned cash on cash in one week. Now I would wait for AMD shares to rise back up to around $27 a share and then write a new covered call out four to six weeks and take in another approximately $2. **Profit & Loss targets:** The second type of **exit target** you will want to set is a sell order if the trade reaches your anticipated price target on the upside, or your stop loss limit price on the downside.

Regardless of your stock, option or ETF trading strategy, you need to define your profit and loss target prices before entering the trade. Your target can be set in terms of a percentage gain or a specific price level. In either case, it will result in you closing the trade out (selling the position) when that level is hit. You also likely will want to 'scale out' of the position meaning you sell parts of the position as different price levels are achieved. See the following example.

BUY example: if I buy a long-put option position on GE stock based on a hunch of a near-term price decline, my exit targets might look as follows:

THE TRADE: GE stock is currently trading at $11 a share. You think it will fall in the next few months. You place an order to buy 10 contracts (controlling 1,000 shares) of the long-put options expiring in three months with a strike price of $10.50. Assume for this example that the cost is $1.50 per share. Because an options contract is comprised of 100 shares of underlying stock, 10 contracts at $1.50 per share equals a total cost of $1,500. In other words, you spend $1,500 to enter this trade.

Profit Targets (I plan to scale out of the 10-contract position at different put price targets):

1. *First exit:* target price for the put option is $2.00 per contract. The action I would take if the GE puts I bought at $1.50 rise in value to $2 would be to sell 50% (or 5 contracts). Profit $.50 cents times 500, or **$250**.

2. *Second exit:* target put price reaching $2.50; the action I would take would be to sell additional 30% or 3 contracts. Profit $1 times 300 = **$300**

3. *Final exit:* watch and opportunistically sell final 20% at say $3. Profit of $1.50 times 200 = **$300**.

TOTAL profit on this $1,500 trade = $850.

Stop Loss Price Target:

o   First exit: Sell stop for all 10 contracts at 30% cash on cash loss. Meaning sell 10 put contracts at $1.05. The cost was $1.50, closed out at $1.05 times 1,000 shares, equals a loss of $450.

Also remember to add a mental TIME STOP: At 30 days to expiration, sell all positions if they have not hit my price targets.

Other General Trading Rules

I want to close this chapter before we get to my six favorite trading strategies, with my top 20 other general trading rules (or best practices). In other words, there are a few other general trading rules that apply for every one of your trading strategies that you may employ. I have and incorporated these rules into my trading over the years. While they are not accurate 100% of the time, in general they reduce risk and improve results.

I have developed some of these rules myself, but the majority have come from my study of other top traders and from their books and courses. Most of these rules come from the works of William J. O'Neil (founder of what I consider the best daily newspaper for traders and investors – Investor's Business Daily) and Jim Cramer (host of the TV shows Mad Money and Squawk Box on CNBC, author and former hedge fund manager), though there are other ideas adopted from the works of other investing and trading legends: Sir John Templeton, Peter Lynch, Warren Buffett, Larry McMillan, Chuck Hughes, and others.

My Top 20 List of Key Additional Trading Rules to Live By:

1.) **Don't buy cheap stocks**, defined as any stock with a price under $7. Most breakout stocks emerge from bases around $30. Almost no high flyers with 10 times growth emerge from a share price under $8 per share.
2.) **Don't buy a stock simply because it has a high dividend or a low P/E ratio.** You need to do deeper research on why the dividend yield is high or what has caused the P/E ratio to be low.
3.) **Cut losses at 8%-10% or less on stocks, and 30% or less on long options.** Let your winners run and be merciless about cutting your losing trades. You can always trade again another day, as long as you preserve your capital base.
4.) **Trade with the general market trend.** The 200-day moving average is the overall long-term trend on the stock or index you are looking at. Don't be a contrarian, trade with the prevailing trend.

5.) **Watch companies that have recently announced stock buybacks, and see if they are larger than previous buybacks**. Increases in the amount of share buybacks are very good for increasing a stock's price.

6.) **Whenever possible, choose trades with a large reward to risk profile.** You should always seek to risk a little while making a lot. You should try to risk two to make one on credit spreads. On long calls and puts, aim for risking 1 to get a reward of five or more. If you do this, you can be wrong more than half the time and still grow your portfolio.

7.) **Buy growth stocks where earnings per share (EPS) have been growing for the last three years at a rate of at least 25%.**

8.) **Buy growth stocks where the consensus growth in earnings per share (EPS) for the next three years is at least 25%.**

9.) **Buy growth stocks where sales are accelerating and where the company is number one in their field.** We don't ever have to buy the third best oil services company, or the three best cyber security software firm. Buy (or put in your basket of stocks) the best company in its category.

10.) *Hedge your bullish portfolio* by buying a few long puts on the overall market (the S&P 500) index or even better on the S&P500 Index Futures, goes a long way to reducing your losses in large stock market pullbacks.

11.) *Stocks are biased to go higher*. Stocks go up 65% of the time on average and historically have a long-term upward bias. It pays over the years to be more bullish than bearish. Of course, you should be wary of market corrections, but in general, it pays to be bullish.

12.) *It is better to go big in a few names.* Making larger trade sizes in a smaller number of names is generally best for the BOOST portion of your portfolio. Concentration is often better than diversification for the active trader. In fact, the really big money is often made by traders who concentrate in no more than a dozen trades, but proper risk management is essential.

13.) *Don't be arrogant – leg into and out of trade positions (scale in and scale out)* – Don't place 100% of your trade on at once, unless it is a very short-term trade. This is especially true if you are buying long-term stocks or long calls or puts. Hold winners and cut losers quickly, but do so in a scaled fashion. Don't be greedy- take some of your position off the table after every big run-up.

14.) *Buy great, high priced stocks, not more shares of cheap, lower quality stocks.* Larger stocks in general work best.

15.) *Know what you own* – Be able to explain your stocks and why you own them out loud to someone. If you can't, you should not own them. You would be surprised how many high net worth clients of mine, cannot tell me what the company they own stock in does or how it makes money.

16.) *"Buy low and sell high…volatility, that is."* This is one of my favorite Larry McMillian quotes. It is not share price but volatility that is the key. Buy calls and puts when volatility is low and sell when implied volatility is high.

17.) *Favor trending stocks that are making new 52-week highs, with stock-splits, positive earnings pre- announcements, and younger fast-growing companies.*

18.) *Use portfolio margin* when buying stocks for extra leverage. This is explained in detail in Chapter 10.

19.) *Discipline always trumps feelings*. This rule comes from Sir John Templeton.

20.) *When in doubt, trade options with expirations of at least 45 days until expiration and then seek to exit early*. This can dramatically increase your results.

There you have it. The rules and general advice from this chapter will help you be more consistent and successful. This can mean additional millions of dollars in returns to you over 20 or 30 years. While this chapter covers many rules, they can be highly rewarding when followed correctly.

What best helps a trader handle their emotions is *discipline* and following a *trading plan* with rules. I suggest you build a trading plan and put together the rules in a process and sequence that works best for you. Discipline in trading means all of the following:

- **Create your trading plan and stick to it (trust your system)**. Execute the actions you pre-planned under each scenario. This is hard to do in the real world but critical to your success. If you do so, you will have crystal clear actions and decision points.

- **In your trading plan, make sure you can answer each of these questions:**
  - How do I decide when to enter a position?
  - What portion of my portfolio is in use to enter each position?
  - What are my sell rules for each position and trade? What are my primary and secondary exit points?
  - What is the maximum loss that I am willing to risk and accept on each trade?
- **Allocate approximately the same amount of money for each trade.** Doing equal size trades in the BOOST portion of your portfolio almost ensures that your winners will outweigh your losers.
- **Allocate time to track your positions and your target exit points.**

"Fear works like faith, only in the opposite direction"
- Brian Belinda

Chapter 6

My Favorite Trading Strategies

LEARNING OBJECTIVES

This chapter gives an overview of each of the best stock & option trading strategies for most retail investors:

- **TRADE STRATEGY #1: Collars, Covered Calls & Large Unprotected Covered Calls**

- **TRADE STRATEGY #2: Stock Replacement – Buying Deep in the Money Options**

- **TRADE STRATEGY #3: In the Money Call Debit Spreads**

- **TRADE STRATEGY #4: Selling Out of the Money Vertical Credit Spreads**

- **TRADE STRATEGY #5: Directional Butterflies & Skip Strike (Broken Wing) Butterflies**

- **TRADE STRATEGY #6: Call Ratio Spreads (with a net credit)**

"In investing, what is comfortable is rarely profitable."
- **Robert Arnott**

I recently searched Google for the phrase "top stock & option trading and investment strategies." I stopped counting at 300 different trading systems, newsletters and strategies (roughly on the first 25 pages of the results). There are hundreds more on the search results that followed. It becomes information overload and overwhelming for the average investor to begin to make sense of the systems, strategies, books, courses and choices to help them make optimal investment decisions.

This is done on purpose by Wall Street firms and many individuals who have left Wall Street firms and sell investment management services and advice. The multitude of brokers, banks, mutual funds, life insurance companies and other investment professionals have a vested interest in you needing their help. As a professional financial advisor and asset manager, I am conscious that this refers to me as well. After all, navigating hundreds of investment strategy choices across numerous investment product categories virtually necessitates that most people will reach out for some form of professional guidance.

So, how can you make sense of it on your own as a self-directed investor? This book is designed to give you the tools and skills to do so. This chapter will help you cut through the clutter and narrow the hundreds of potential investment strategy choices down to a few.

Through speaking to thousands of individual investors across the USA and the Asia Pacific region (where I lived and worked for eight years), I know that most smart investors ultimately just want to know the answer to one question:

"What are the best stock and options trading strategies that consistently work in today's markets? How can I learn them use them to invest for a better future for me and my family?"

The answer to this question is that the 'best' strategies will differ from person to person. After all, people are at different life stages and have different investment goals and different risk tolerances. That said, I have tried to answer this question with this chapter. I acknowledge that the six trading strategies taught in this chapter may not be right for every investor. I therefore defaulted to the ones that I use, and the ones that work best for the vast majority of people I have advised. So, while not a fit for everyone, the strategies in this chapter appeal to the broadest range of investors for the BOOST portion of their portfolio. I suggest you meet with a financial advisor well versed in individual stocks and options (not just the buy and hold mutual fund and ETF only financial advisors, which is most of them) to assess the suitability of the strategies taught here that appeal to you.

In creating the list of my favorite trading strategies, I made the following list of assumptions about you:

Assumption #1: You need growth from your investments more than monthly income.   I am assuming you have realized by now that buy and hold stock strategies do not work for most people, unless you already have a substantial size portfolio and can hold shares for periods as long as 20 years or more. I assume you are looking for new strategies to meaningfully grow your savings more rapidly while taking some tactical action to mitigate risk and protect the downside. If you need some income from your investments, the portion of income you need for the short term (defined as the next 18 months) should not be traded in the strategies taught in this chapter. Short-term money needs to be invested conservatively, in a high yield money market fund or US Treasury Bills. Medium to longer-term money in your portfolio can be traded and invested in the strategies covered in this chapter (with a focus on the money in the BOOST section of your portfolio).

This means your primary focus, in the near term, is to grow your assets, not to live off the income generation from your portfolio. This is true whether that money is in your IRA, ROTH IRA, or in a regular brokerage account (or in multiple of these account types, as will be the case for most people reading this book).   In other words, the primary assumption is that you are not retired yet and you do not yet need to live off of the income stream generated by your investments. If you are retired, you can still consider the strategies in this chapter but only if you have a sizeable portfolio where you do not anticipate needing the money you are trading anytime soon to live on. Your primary goal is account growth.

Assumption #2: You have a reasonable risk tolerance. I don't expect that you skydive on the weekends or gamble $5,000 hands of blackjack, but I am making the assumption that you understand that with higher rewards comes higher risk. The fact is that you can lose money trading every one of the six strategies you are about to learn. Though each trading strategy taught here has protective positions, strategically limits the risk or has defined risk before you enter the trade to prevent any disastrous losses, but cash on cash losses can still happen. If losing $5,000 - $10,000 on a portfolio size of $250,000 would keep you up at night with worry, then you are in the wrong place and these strategies are not for you. Note this ratio holds for any portfolio size. For a $5,000,000 portfolio, being down $250,00 - $500,000 should not scare you or you should dramatically scale back the percentage of your portfolio you place in these strategies or don't trade them at all.

As an aside, I have known many people who say they are risk averse and would be up all night with worry if they ever lost $5,000 in the market, yet they own a portfolio of actively managed stock mutual funds that often lose much more than $5,000 in certain years. Somehow, they feel 'safe' owning actively traded mutual funds run by 'professional' mutual fund managers as opposed to taking charge of their own money and future. I find it ironic that they trust these professional mutual fund managers even when they are losing money and charging high fees for doing so.

The bottom line is that you must be willing to take some risk if you want to achieve potentially life-changing rewards.

Assumption #3: You are under 65 years old. Most of the stock and options strategies taught here are tactical in nature and are on the growth end of the investment spectrum. While my favorite strategies are hedged and have defined risk management rules (which put in a lot of safety and controls), they are still generally unsuitable for investors over the age of 65. These strategies would not be suitable if you are relying on social security to live and pay your bills.

As an exception, if you are over age 65, I approve the use of these strategies for a small percentage of your portfolio if:
- You have a lot of money in other savings and can therefore

undertake growth strategies with higher risk. In other words, if you have a $4 million+ portfolio, you can do these strategies with a small percentage of your portfolio even if you are over age 65.

- You are trading with a small percentage of your portfolio and you have strong lifetime pensions and social security. For example, if you are over 65 years old and have reasonable savings, and all of your day-to-day expenses are fully covered by guaranteed pensions and other income sources, then you can do some active trading. You would only do so if you love the stock market and you want to build additional wealth as an enhancer to be able to travel more or give more to your church, or other endeavor. In these scenarios, then it is ok to trade as long as you keep the percentage of your portfolio low. In other words, say you are age 67 and have a total investable portfolio of $1 Million but you have a guaranteed government pension and social security paying you $100,000 a year for the rest of your life. Then, these strategies are for you for a small percentage of your portfolio as all of your basic living costs are covered for the rest of your life.

Assumption #4: You enjoy studying and monitoring the stock and options markets and can spend a reasonable amount of time researching, placing and monitoring your trades and investments. As I am sure you have gathered by now, these strategies take some time, homework and monitoring on an ongoing basis. Other than helping people and spending time with family and friends, I find the stock market to be the most fascinating pursuit on earth. If this is not you, that is ok, but you should keep your trading to a minimum or don't trade actively at all.

If you have no interest in doing the homework on individual companies, watching the markets and following the news, you should not actively trade. If you enjoy following the stock and options markets but your schedule does not allow you the flexibility to check on your investments during market hours occasionally, then you should not trade. These strategies necessitate that you put in a few hours per week and know when your trades expire to make adjustments and close out trades. I am making the assumption that if you have read this far, you are interested in the subject of stocks and trading and that you are willing and able to put in the time necessary.

If not, then please do not use these active strategies. Instead, you should work with your financial advisor to select a portfolio of low-cost ETFs and index funds and CDs and be content with that.

Assumption #5: You are beginning with an account of at least $20,000 USD. This amount can be in in a self-directed IRA or in a regular brokerage account. What if you only have $5,000 USD to get started? Technically, you could do a few of these strategies, but I would not recommend doing so.

If you trade with less than $20,000, you would have to violate my risk management rules. I teach not to put more than 8%-10% of your total portfolio into any one trade. With a capital base of more than $20,000 you can do this. If you have less, you need to save more before beginning to actively trade. In the meantime, you can paper trade the strategies to gain experience.

My Top 6 Favorite Trading and Investment Strategies

The following section presents each of my favorite trading strategies. I have also included the custom trading rules that I have developed for each strategy. Remember, you do not need to trade them all. A combination of three or four of the strategies can produce great results. When first starting out, most novice traders tend to pick their favorite one or two strategies from the list of six below and specialize in those for at least one year before adding a third or fourth strategy. That progression is just fine as all of these strategies are concentrated in only the BOOST portion of your portfolio.

Most of the trading strategies that follow share a common set of themes. These themes are:
- **The careful use of derivatives**. Specifically, *options* on stocks, ETFs, indexes and commodities.
- **The careful use of margin (leverage)** to magnify returns and set up risk management (insurance) positions on your trades.
- **Selling options vs. buying options and collecting time premium** Most people think of buying options on stocks. Most of my strategies sell options and collect the options

premium. Several of these strategies allow you to trade as if you were an insurance company, by collecting lots of small options premiums and paying out very few claims in the form of losses on options premiums collected.

- **Placing trades that in combination are both long and short (bullish and bearish) at the same time**. While all of my trading strategies select a direction and are focused to be either bullish or bearish, most have built in protection in the form of a hedge position as insurance. My portfolio usually has an emphasis towards bullish positions as most of the time the US stock markets are most often in a rising trend.

- **Buying overall insurance protection on your total portfolio.** I advocate buying 'portfolio insurance' in the form of spending 1% of the portfolio and buying puts on the S&P 500 to limit the risks of a broad market sell off.

Favorite Trading Strategy #1:

Collars, Covered Calls & Large Unprotected Covered Calls – all are variations of the same strategy:

My favorite core trading strategy when I already own the shares of stock (as opposed to just trading the options on stocks I do not own), is called a '**collar trade.**' I also love the closely related variations on collars, which is selling time premium known as a **covered call** trade. I also love a variation of covered calls where you can sell call options on expensive high-priced stocks. I call this variation, **large unprotected covered calls**.

All three of these variations are at their core the *same strategy* – the covered call – but with slight distinctions and differences in risk / reward emphasis. Don't worry if you don't know these strategies or didn't follow those strategy names and details, I will explain each of these in turn in this chapter.

While I do love the flexibility and leverage of options trading, I always advocate the long-term strategy of buying and building a portfolio of high quality, blue chip stocks that pay dividends. Collar trades (and the covered call variations) are the way to put these core stock holdings to work for you more aggressively than just buy and hold, with safety.

Collar trades are especially powerful when using the massive leverage potential of margin or in a portfolio margin account. Chapter ten covers margin and portfolio margin in more detail. For now, just understand that margin and portfolio margin can give the retail investor between double and up to seven times leverage just like a hedge fund, with limited downside risk. The leverage of portfolio margin amplifies puts the returns generated by collar trades and covered call trades.

The Foundation of the Collar trade – the covered call trade:
I advise most of my clients that whenever you own shares of stock, you should consider 'renting out' your stocks to others and collecting monthly or bi-monthly cash option premiums. For core holdings, defined as steady growers with a little volatility, you will want to consider renting out your stocks and collecting cash premiums. How do you rent out your stock? By selling covered calls.

The exception is on a highflying, aggressive growth momentum stock you own, where the stock price could move up 5% or more per month. In those cases, you do not want to 'cap' or give away the potential large upside by doing any form of covered calls.

The easiest way to understand covered calls and what I mean by renting out your stock, is with an example:

EXAMPLE: Let's say you own 100 shares of Apple stock, which you bought at $175 a share. This means you have invested $17,500 in buying the stock, or 50% of that amount if you used margin to buy the 100 shares ($8,750).

Writing an option, means to sell. Option contracts are constructed in 100 share increments. In other words, one call option represents 100 shares of the underlying stock. Two call option contracts represent 200 shares of the underlying stock, and so on. Covered means that you already own the underlying stock and is considered by professionals as a conservative option strategy (as opposed to a naked option position, where you don't already own the underlying shares – going naked on options is dramatically riskier and should be avoided in most cases). Writing a covered call then, means that you can sell the right to buy your underlying shares away from you at a set price by a certain date (the expiration date). For agreeing to sell you 100 shares at a certain strike price by a certain expiration date, you get paid by collecting the option premium.

Back to the example, after you have purchased and own 100 shares of Apple stock, you decided to 'rent out' your 100 shares and take in some money. Apple is trading at a price of $175 today. You decide to write one call contract with a strike price of $190 with an expiration date five weeks in the future. Let's say the call option premium for the $190 strike price is $2. This means you will get paid $2 times the 100 shares represented by selling one call option with a strike price of $190. You collect $200. The call premium is akin to rent payments collected in real estate.

So, what have you agreed to? You have agreed that any day between today and for the next five weeks (until the expiration date) you are willing to sell your 100 shares of Apple stock that you bought at $175 if it reaches $190 or greater. You only agree to do this if the call option buyer pays you the $200 option premium right now (options settle in one day).

Remember you bought the shares at $175, so if the stock does go above $190 in the next five weeks you will keep both the $200 option premium you collect now to agree to sell it at $190 AND you will sell it at $190. This means you will also get to keep the $15 difference between the $190 you sell the shares at and the $175 you bought the shares at times 100 (or an additional $1,500).

In five weeks, if the underlying stock shares rise above $190, you make a profit of $200 for selling the call option + $1,500 for selling the 100 shares at $190 = $1,700 profit. This is a one-month return of nearly 10% if done on a cash basis and a 19% return if the trade is done using margin. Not bad and all of your cash is back to safety and ready to do the next trade. Even if Apple does not rise above $190 in the next five weeks (which it is likely it will not), you keep the $200 option premium. After five weeks the option you sold expires worthless and you look out four to five weeks and do it again, taking in a another ~$200. If you were able to do this process twelve times a year without getting the shares called out (or called away from you), you could make an additional $2,400 a year vs. buying and holding the 100 shares of Apple. You make even more if it does get called away from you, say at $190 and you keep the extra $1,500.

You can collect this monthly 'rent' payment on your Apple stock month after month. The alternative, which most investors do, is just holding the 100 shares and making nothing extra. Remember you also still collect the quarterly dividend payment on your 100 shares as you own the 100 shares of the stock. In addition, whichever month the underlying stock may finish above your strike price ($190 a share in this example), you keep all of that extra money ($1,500 in this example) from the difference between the strike price and the share price.

Selling (or "writing") out of the money covered calls (meaning at strike prices higher than you bought the shares and higher than the current stock price), works great on core holdings. The great companies you own with strong, mature businesses that are gaining but are mature and slower growing. This strategy works for stocks or ETF holdings that have decent volatility such as AMD, Facebook, Under Armour, and Apple. On these core stock holdings, you should be selling covered calls to rent out your stock and collect premiums along the way while you hold them. If you are not selling covered calls, you are leaving free money on the table.

Don't sell covered calls on your high flyers: The exception to renting out your stocks by selling covered calls would be if you believe the shares in a stock that you own are about to move sharply higher (a high growth, momentum stock, also known as a high flyer). If the stock moves higher and you have sold away your upside (by selling covered calls a dollar or two above today's share price), then this is an incorrect strategy as you give up a potentially large upside gain. If you believe a stock is about to explode higher, you would not sell covered calls and give away the upside above the call option strike price you sell.

What is the downside risk to selling covered calls? The downside risk within the basic covered call strategy is the lack of downside protection if the stock falls. You only offset your potential downside losses in the stock price falling by the amount you collect up front for selling the covered call (the option premium you took in). After that, there is no further downside protection. That's a large risk in significant stock corrections and market pullbacks. Due to this painful risk, I personally, rarely sell a traditional straight covered call strategy. Instead, I almost always use one of the three variations on the traditional covered call strategy below.

Variation #1: **The Collar Strategy – the safest variation on covered calls and my bread and butter trade strategy.**

The collar trade uses the power of the covered call trading strategy, just outlined, but adds an extra protective floor on the downside for safety.

My favorite way to reduce the risk on downside of covered calls is to do a collar trade. A collar trade is a variation on buying stock and writing covered calls. In a collar, you still do an out of the money covered call trade exactly as described in the Apple example before. Instead of just selling (or writing) the calls out of the money as before, you also add buying a protective put option, with a strike price ~10% lower than today's stock price to protect the down side risk.

Buying these put contracts in an equal proportion to protect the number of shares of stock you own protects your downside from a stock collapse but it does cost some money as you have to buy these put option contracts.

The following figure demonstrates the collar trade process:

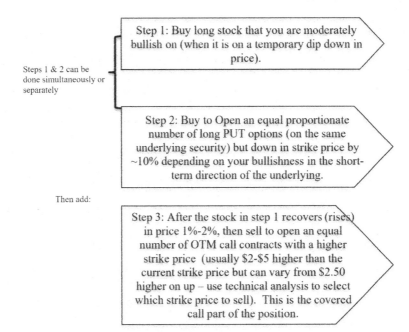

Steps 1 & 2 can be done simultaneously or separately

Step 1: Buy long stock that you are moderately bullish on (when it is on a temporary dip down in price).

Step 2: Buy to Open an equal proportionate number of long PUT options (on the same underlying security) but down in strike price by ~10% depending on your bullishness in the short-term direction of the underlying.

Then add:

Step 3: After the stock in step 1 recovers (rises) in price 1%-2%, then sell to open an equal number of OTM call contracts with a higher strike price (usually $2-$5 higher than the current strike price but can vary from $2.50 higher on up – use technical analysis to select which strike price to sell). This is the covered call part of the position.

Adding the protective puts to the covered calls allows you to capture covered call premium with safety as the puts completely cap my downside risk below the level of the strike price on the put options.

I like to buy the protective puts with an expiration date of about three or four months in the future and then sell the covered calls with an expiration date of about four or five weeks in the future. That way we hope to have the calls expire worthless (keeping the premium as profit) in about one third of the time of the protective puts. We then write a second batch of covered calls after the first ones expire worthless. And then after the second ones expire worthless, we write a third batch. This 'selling three covered calls for every one put protection' generally is a great money-making ratio. This protects you if stock you have bought and written covered calls collapses in price and you feel like you are stuck with it because you have written the covered call(s). If the underlying stock falls dramatically, the put protection you purchased allows you to put it to (or sell it to) someone else. This saves you from making really bad covered call trades when the stock crashes after you enter the covered call.

EXAMPLE: Let's say you own 400 shares of the stock of AMD (Advanced Micro Devices, Inc.), which you bought at $25 a share. You spent $10,000 to buy the 400 shares without margin or you spent 50% of this amount on margin ($5,000). You decide to Collar these shares.

Step 2 is to buy protective put options (four contracts to match the 400 shares you own). I look at the puts expiring in about three or four months in the future with a strike price down ~10% from today's share price. So, in this example, I would price the $22.50 strike price puts expiring in approximately 90 days. They currently have an option price (option premium) of 40 cents. I buy them and spend $160 (400 times .40) = $160.

Step 3 is to write (to sell) the four contract covered calls, expiring in approximately four weeks. In this example, the $27 strike price calls are going for $1.70. Selling four contracts would bring in cash of $680 (400 times the $1.70 option premium).

Now we wait and watch. If the shares do not rise and finish above $27 in the next four weeks, the call options expire worthless and I keep the $680 and then look out four weeks and write the next set of covered calls. No adjustments to the protective put contracts or the underlying stock are needed.

Let's say is the second round I take in $600 by selling the next four covered call contracts. If this one also expires worthless, I would do it a third time. Let's say we take in $650 the third round. If this too expires worthless, you made a great series of trades with this collar. At the end of all three rounds, we still own our 400 shares of AMD and our protective put expires worthless (loss of $160) but we keep the three covered call premiums we sold. The math would be $680+$600+$650= $1,930 profit, less the $160 = a total profit of $1,770. This occurred in three months on our investment of $10,000 in AMD without margin. This is nearly an 18% return in 90 days. With margin it would be even more exciting. With margin it is a three-month profit of $1,770 on an investment of $5,000, or a 35% return.

Warning: don't do collars on low-beta stocks – the underlying needs to have at least medium volatility for these to work well. Good stocks as of this writing to do collars on are Twitter (ticker: TWTR) and Exelixis, Inc. (Ticker: EXEL)

When collar trades are done with the added leverage of portfolio margin (see Chapter Ten), they are safer than in-the-money covered calls and can be very powerful. Note that adding portfolio margin to your brokerage account typically requires at least a $100K minimum account size. If you do not qualify, look at the large option unprotected covered call strategy below or collar trades.

Variation #2: Writing 'In the Money' Covered Calls
Another variation I like to do in IRA's, ROTH IRA's and other tax advantaged accounts (as it adds safety), is the *in-the-money covered call(s)* strategy variation.

Selling in the money covered calls means:
- You have purchased stock in the company and
- You sell an equivalent number of call contracts representing the same number of shares you purchased, but you deliberately sell a strike price $3 to $15 or more *below* the current stock price and collect a larger premium.

Why would you want to agree to sell the stock $3 to $15 below today's market price for the stock? Won't you get called out for sure? The answer is likely yes and that is what we want. Why? Because it still locks in a tidy gain if the stock goes up or stays the same and at the same time greatly reduces potential for a loss if the stock price falls. Selling in the money call premiums greatly reduces your downside by giving you downside protection down to the strike price sold (which is far below today's stock price) plus the larger amount of call premium collected.

I typically do this strategy at strike prices between $3 lower (for low priced stocks like Exelixis [ticker: EXEL] which is currently $20 a share) to $15 lower for medium priced stocks like Microsoft (ticker MSFT) currently at $115 a share. The strategy will also work for high priced stocks, but I tend to not do these because owning 100 shares (the minimum to write one call contract) of a $400 stock is too expensive for most traders.
The second reason selling in the money covered calls is so effective

is because the premium you collect for doing so will be large. These large premiums you collect generate cash. This large cash inflow reduces your margin requirement and allows you to do other additional trades during the time while you wait to get called on the expiration date of the calls you sold.

If the stock does happen to crash in price, you keep the entire cash premium collected, which reduces the loss on owning the stock. If the stock rises – we keep the time premium portion of the calls we sold (as the time to expiration will have gone away) and we give back the intrinsic value. Remember there is no protective put in this variation (like with the collar trade) so your loss to the downside is technically uncapped but you are protected down to the strike price you sold + the time premium. This variation provides strong downside protection and is the next best thing to a collar and you do not have to spend any money buying the put protection.

The only risk to doing in-the-money covered calls is the rare occasions when the underlying stock falls below the far in the money strike price. This means that after we have bought the stock and sold the covered call but before the calls we sold have expired the underlying stock has fallen a great deal. Specifically, the underlying stock which we own has fallen far enough that even adding our call premium protection in, we are still losing money. When the underlying stock falls huge like this, then after our current call options expire all new future call strike prices available to be sold would lock us into a loss.

To help prevent this risk, below are my key rules to follow when picking the types of stocks to do in-the-money covered calls and collar trades on and how to trade them.

RULES TO SELECT & TRADE COLLARS AND COVERED CALLS:
1. **Pick stocks with high dividends**. Limit yourself on this strategy to stocks with a forward annual dividend yield of greater than 2%. The dividends offset our margin costs to some degree and add safety.

2. **Don't write covered calls during the week of earnings announcements**. The underlying share price is too

volatile and could drop fast.

3. **Use stocks on which you are moderately bullish and you believe will gradually go higher, but not ones you think are about to explode higher**. In general, you want to select more volatile and liquid blue-chip stocks to write calls on, as the premiums will be larger. Don't select names like Clorox, Coca-Cola and Procter & Gamble, as they are not volatile enough to make real money selling the call options. Instead, select stocks such as Facebook, AMD, Palo Alto Networks and Apple. They are blue chip names but have decent volatility and nice call premiums to sell and collect.

4. **Make sure the combination of buying the stock and writing covered calls does not take up more than 10% of your total portfolio** for any one trade. I aim for 5% of the BOOST portion of my portfolio for each trade.

5. **Buy the stock on a dip near the lower band of the Keltner channel and then wait for it to rebound. Sell the calls on strength.**

6. **If you think the stock you own may stay flat or fall, sell the covered calls in-the-money** – this takes in more premium and gives you a greater cushion to the downside. If the stock goes higher you still win, but you will have to give back some of the premium collected unless you adjust or roll out the trade prior to expiration.

7. **When not using portfolio margin, select stocks in the $8-$45 range to buy and write calls on as the premiums are still nearly as good as more expensive stocks. When using margin or portfolio margin, however, use large cap stocks with high premiums and good dividends** such as Apple or Microsoft.

8. **When possible, sell monthly covered calls against stocks as monthly premiums will average nearly double the premium collected over time compared to bi-monthly or eight weeks out call premiums.** The risk

is that there is a greater chance of getting called out of the stock. Sometimes this is a good thing, as getting called out periodically forces you to take profits rather than endlessly rolling over a trade. I often close out winning monthly covered calls just before expiration and roll out and sell the next month's calls to continue to collect new premiums and compound my profits. Occasionally I just let the stock get taken from me at expiration to lock in profits. When not called out, monthly premiums give me a higher return for less risk.

9.   **Potentially use strategic "over-writing" on these in-the-money covered calls to generate the most income with safety and accelerate the compounding effect.** This means that when you have bought stock and sold calls against that stock and the calls are about to expire, go ahead and sell the next in the money covered calls a day or two before the current ones actually expire.

We do this to capture the last few days of time decay that will occur after our current calls expire which can be substantial on options with less than 45 days until expiration. Mechanically, this means selling the next set of calls naked for one to two days (so be careful). Once the current calls expire worthless, the new ones replace them and you are covered again.

If you generate large premiums before they expire and the stock gets taken away from you three times per year, you can use that cash to do additional option income trades all year long with good downside protection.

Variation #3: The *Large Unprotected Covered Calls Strategy.* A powerful variation on the covered call strategy, which I love, is writing covered calls on very expensive stocks with good growth prospects and some volatility. I call this covered call variation strategy writing *Large Unprotected Covered Calls.* The strategy is called unprotected, because there are no protective puts bought to protect the downside moves in the stock (as in the collar trade) and we are selling at the money or slightly in the money call strike prices, so we do not have as large of downside protection from the in-the-money strike prices.

Why is this still a good strategy? By proper stock and option selection and going far enough out in time, such as six to nine months, these trades are not risky. We will collect a very large cash premium up front to protect our downside. When done right, this strategy can make average annual returns of 30% to 45% each year (cash on cash) with low risk. This can be done in accounts that are too small to qualify for portfolio margin (under $100K portfolios) to gain additional leverage. *See Chapter Ten for the details on trading using Portfolio Margin.*

This strategy is mechanically the same as the in the money covered call strategy discussed previously, but with the following changes:

- **Employ the Large Unprotected Covered Call strategy on high priced stocks that you have a positive view of for the next year but that has high volatility** (a high-implied volatility number). Make sure the high volatility translates into large option premiums on the calls you will write.
- **Do Large Unprotected Covered Calls on stocks where selling the call contracts will bring in a large premium.** You should try to do this strategy on expensive, volatile stocks that allow you to generate a large amount of call premium into your account.
- **The Key Rule** – the call options you sell must have a large amount of extrinsic value (time premium) built into the premium. That large time value in the premium is likely all you get to keep if the stock performs and goes higher as expected. Remember, when you sell in-the-money calls for safety, you have to give back the intrinsic part of the option premium sold unless the stock falls dramatically. The extrinsic value, or time value, is what you will keep if the stock moves higher. This is your profit and if done right, can be substantial.
- **Doing these covered calls slightly in-the-money can also be done and takes away much of your potential risk to the downside** as it builds in a large cushion in the event that the stock falls dramatically. By writing in the money calls as a variation on this strategy, you can take in as much cash immediately as possible and adds safety. This combines

variation #2 and variation #3 in this chapter.

- **Select a stock that pays dividends** to offset the margin loan costs on buying the stock and holding it for six to nine months. You won't always find this. For example, Alphabet (Google) and Regeneron currently do not pay dividends, but you should seek companies that pay a dividend when possible (i.e. Apple, etc.).
- **Close the trade when between 75% to 90% of the call premium profit has been realized. As the underlying moves up close (and roll out and double dip if you feel aggressive).** The goal is to close and roll out before the time is up in order to accelerate compounding. Aim to collect at least 40% of the original cash in your covered call portfolio on day 1 by selling deep in-the-money covered calls. Then let the trade work over time. Take profits on each covered call when you reach 75% to 90% of the maximum potential profit. This allows you to close out many of your covered call trades out weeks before expiration and double dip, compounding your returns.

Here are a few examples of why the large unprotected covered call strategy can be so powerful:

Example #1: Regeneron Pharmaceuticals Inc. (ticker: REGN)– stock is currently trading at $400. The trade: Buy 100 shares of stock (on margin if possible):
- Cost of the stock would be 100 shares at $400 = $40,000, Cost of the stock on 50% margin = $20,000.
  Note this cost can be reduced further using portfolio margin (refer to Chapter 10 for details on portfolio margin) but this example assumes regular margin.
- Sell one contract of the $350 calls out six months with a current option premium of $100 (which is made up of intrinsic value of $50 and extrinsic value / time premium of $50).
  The results:
  Stock cost = $20,000 on margin; the total option premium collected is $10,000. The total trade entry cost is $10,000.
  (Your goal is to get called out and keep the extrinsic or time premium part of the premium, or $5,000 less commissions and margin interest)

Final Results of this trade:
Called out at $350 after six months. These means we sold the 100 shares at $350 per share and we purchased them at $400 per share. The result is a -$5,000 loss on the 100 shares of the stock. We get to keep the +$10,000 for selling the call option. So, the overall total return on the trade is +$5,000. Did you follow the math? In other words, we spent $20,000 plus commissions (on margin) to buy the stock, then sold the calls and took in +$10,000 options premium. When we got called out at $350, which means we collected 100 shares times $350, or $35,000. So, on the stock we lost $5,000 ($40,000 - $35,000) but on the option we get to keep the $10,000. Net profit is $5,000 on our $20,000 investment. This equates to a six-month cash on cash return of 25%. This is not a bad return, and you can do two such trades with the same money in a twelve-month period (a 50% annual return less margin interest and commissions, with $50 of safety on the stock falling). It ties up your capital for only a moderate amount of time and is very safe. Remember to roll out early if the stock makes a large upward move.

Large Unprotected Covered Call Example #2:
Alphabet (GOOGL) – stock at $1,000. The trade: Buy 100 shares of GOOGL on margin:

- Cost of the stock = $100,000. Cost of the stock on 50% margin = $50,000;
  Note this cost can be reduced further using portfolio margin (refer to Chapter Ten for details on Portfolio Margin) but this example assumes regular margin.
- Sell one contract of the $750 calls out six months with a premium of $350 (which is made up of intrinsic value of $250 and extrinsic value / time premium of $100)

The results:

Stock cost =	($50,000)
Total option premium collected =	+ $35,000
Equals	($15,000) total

(Your goal is to get called out and keep the extrinsic part of the premium, or $10,000 less commissions & margin).

Final Results of this trade: a total target return of $10,000 /
$15,000, equating to a six-month cash on cash return of 67%.
You can do this twice in one year - high returns with safety.

The bottom line: **Writing large, in the money covered calls takes
in the most premium and ties up the least cash vs. writing out-of-
the money covered calls.**

Favorite Trading Strategy #2:

**STOCK REPLACEMENT – Buying deep in the money Call
Options (or buying deep in the money Put Options when
bearish) with long term expiration dates.**

Buying a directional long call or put is the simplest of all option
strategies. This is where most people start their options experience.
Buying long calls is typically everyone's first trade when they begin
to discover the magic of using small amounts of money to gain
magnified returns through the leverage of options trading.

Why do so many people believe that trading options is risky? It is
because of this trade strategy (when done incorrectly). Options
trading can be risky but only if you do not know what you are doing.
Buying cheap long option positions far out of the money is very
simple and cheap, but according to the Chicago Board Options
Exchange (CBOE), 80% of these trades expire worthless. That is the
wrong way to trade long calls, I will show you the right way which
will dramatically de-risk them and puts the odds in your favor.

 The reason why 80% of option buyers lose on each long buy trade is
because they typically see the power in the leverage provided by
options and they shoot for 'home-run' trades. This equates to
gambling. By home run trades, I mean these speculators look for a
stock they think will rise and they buy cheap, out of the money
options expiring in 30 days or less. They are looking for maximum
gains and maximum leverage for minimal cost. Investors quickly
find out that these out of the money calls and puts are cheap because
they almost always lose. Since this is what novice investors most
often buy, they mostly lose and walk away from options trading.

Don't let the typical experience of novice traders convince you that buying long call or put trades are destined to lose. The key to taking the risk out of long directional options is to buy 'deep in the money' calls and puts, not the cheap out of the money strike prices. When you buy deep in the money calls or puts, when selected correctly (through the homework taught in Chapters Two, Three & Four) with proper risk and trade management controls placed (as taught in Chapters Six, Seven & Eight), these stock replacement option trades can be the highest return and least risky of all pure options trades. You still gain phenomenal leverage and upside potential by selecting deep in the money strike prices, with the advantage of substantially minimizing your downside risk. In addition, there are typically no margin costs to buy long calls and long puts.

My method to do "stock replacement" buying call options, deep in the money, with lots of time to expiration.
Let's unpack this. The stock replacement strategy simply means buying deep in-the-money calls with lots of intrinsic value built in. Intrinsic value is defined as the difference between today's share price of the underlying stock and the strike price of the deep in the money call option you are buying on that stock. The remaining value in an option premium is what is known as time value (or extrinsic value).

Let's look at an example. Let's say you like XYZ company and the current share price is: $25 a share. Through your homework and research, you believe XYZ's stock price is going to $35 a share in the next six months. The 'at the money' call options with a strike price of $25 expiring in seven months (always buy more time than you think you need) are priced at $3. This $3 cost you would pay is all time premium (all extrinsic value). Not good. Buying the at the money call options gives you the right to control XYZ's upside from today's $25 share price upward for the next seven months. If it moves higher to $35 as expected, you will make good money. But... what if it does not move higher? If it moves lower or stays the same, you will lose 100% of your $3 investment times the number of contracts you purchased. $300 for one contract; $600 for two contracts, etc.

I would not buy the at the money calls. Instead, in this same scenario, I would find the call options three to four strike prices lower. These are called 'in the money' because these strike prices are lower than the price of the stock in the open market. We want to buy those even though they are more expensive. Why? Because a large part of the option premium I am buying is real value (intrinsic value) vs. all time premium that decays every day up until being gone at the expiration date.

For this example, I would likely buy the $22 calls expiring in seven months. These $22 calls contain both intrinsic value (the difference between the strike price of $22 and the current share price of $25) and time premium (or extrinsic value). The time premium cost will be much less, say $1.50 vs. the $3 in time premium for the at the money call options. Yes, these would cost more, in this case $4.50 per contract instead of $3 for the at the money calls ($3 intrinsic value +$1.50 extrinsic value or $4.50) but they are dramatically safer than the at the money calls. As you can see, you now own something with $3 of real value and are paying a lot less for the time premium. Even if XYZ finishes unchanged in 6 months, say right at $25, I own the $22 strike price calls. This means my options will still have at least the intrinsic value of $3 (the time premium will have melted away as there is no more time) but I still own something worth $3 due to intrinsic value that I paid $4.50 for vs. a 100% loss of my $3 if I bought the at the money calls.

When you do the stock replacement call buying strategy, what you are paying for is almost all real intrinsic value, plus a greatly reduced time premium.

This is the opposite of the strategy of buying out of the money call options, the 'homerun' attempts, which lose 80% of the time and have zero intrinsic value. By buying deep in the money calls or puts, the options will move virtually in lock step with the underlying security but you can still control many more shares at a cheaper price than buying the stock.

This gives you great built in leverage of options without using any margin requirement and at a much lower cash outlay than simply buying the stock. You can do this in an IRA or retirement account as well, as it does not require using margin.

Though it is called *stock replacement*, you can also use the same strategy to buy long calls on ETFs and play a whole sector or the whole market. Using ETFs works just as well but with more built in diversification than playing one individual company (no single stock risk). The popular index tracking ETFs such as the SPY for the S&P 500 index or the DIA for the Dow Jones industrial average are so liquid that they often have fifty-cent increments between strike prices. This can lead to multiples of the returns on your long calls or puts at lower cost when you buy deep in the money calls or do tight vertical credit spreads (to be explained in an upcoming strategy).

When using the stock replacement strategy on individual companies, you will find that the best common stocks have too high of a stock share price for most individual traders to buy enough shares to make meaningful gains. For example, think of the cost of buying 100 shares of:

- Alphabet (Google) at over $1,100 per share or
- Apple over $205 per share or

These stocks are simply too expensive for most small retail investors to own a significant number of shares. If you don't own a meaningful number of shares, even if the stock increases significantly you don't benefit very much. And if you do buy a meaningful number of shares – you risk a large amount of capital if the stock price goes down. Don't buy the stock shares – it is too risky. Buy instead the ability to track the gains in movement of the same stock through in the money calls (or track the shares falling through buying deep in the money puts).

Using the stock replacement strategy and buying calls instead of shares, uses far less capital and gives the small investor exponential leverage while minimizing your down side. Options allow you to control much more stock while drastically reducing the amounts invested, and reduce your risk at the same time.

Pros and Cons of buying long calls when you are bullish:

PROs	CONs
Very simple trades to enter and exit. The trading mechanics are very easy to understand and execute.	**Most directional, long calls or put trades lose.** Most call or put buyers lose due to the trader selecting strike prices to buy that are at the money or out of the money (swinging for the fences)
High leverage. Unlimited upside and limited, defined downside. Essentially stock replacement trades allow the trader to buy the stocks you like for 10% to 35% of the cost of buying the stock (when done deep in the money).	**You are buying an asset with a limited life span** – all options have an expiration date and hence experience time decay. This is especially in the last 2 months, so make sure you buy enough time when buying long calls or puts.
Less risk than buying the stock outright: buying long calls gives the trader the full speculative exposure to the upside of a stock with a capped / limited downside risk.	**No dividend income** – You are not entitled to collect the dividends when you own the calls or puts, nor do you enjoy voting rights.
Many ways to do trade adjustments to protect and lock in profits or adjust to minimize losses	

My rules for stock replacement /the long call buying strategy

Over the years, I have developed rules that will increase returns on the stock replacement strategy and reduce risk. When my fundamental analysis leads me to believe that the stock is poised for explosive growth in the near term, I look to buy long calls. I then validate a low risk entry point using my technical analysis. If both the fundamentals and the technical analysis line up, then I use the following rules:

- *RULE #1:* **Scale in – don't buy all the call options at once. Initiate a deep in the money long call position.** This means if I ultimately want to be long ten call

contracts (controlling 1,000 shares), I will initially buy
50% of this amount, or five contracts to open the position.
If the underlying falls a little in price, then the calls get
cheaper and I will buy more at a lower price.

- *RULE #2:* **Buy only in a clearly trending market**. Use
  the 100- and 200-day moving averages to determine the
  longer-term trend. I trade long calls or puts *with* the trend
  (not contrarian to the trend).

- *RULE #3*: **Buy deep in the money calls or puts (with a
  Delta of 80-90)**. Delta is one of the option 'Greeks'
  (Covered in CH. 7) and is the best weapon to win on these
  trades. This is in many ways the most important rule for
  this strategy. Any strike price with a delta above ~80 is
  suitable. Don't overpay for time premium. A good rule
  of thumb is, don't pay more than 8% of the stock price of
  the underlying in *time premium* for an option purchase
  with five to six months until expiration. The Delta is
  given next to each strike price in most option chains in
  most online brokerage software (you don't need to
  calculate anything).

- *RULE #4:* **Pay no more than 20% of the stock price for
  the option**. Deep in-the-money options can be expensive.
  That said, don't pay for a premium that cost more than
  20% of the cost of buying the stock shares (with no more
  than 8% of the stock price in time premium).

- *RULE #5:* **Select a low risk entry point.** I use either the
  lower half of the Keltner channels or check when the
  Bollinger bands squeeze inside the Keltner channels. See
  technical analysis in Chapter Four for details on "The
  Squeeze."

Trade management rules for buying deep in the money options
After I have initiated buying long calls or puts, I manage the trade by
doing all of the following:

- *RULE #6*: **Set a stop loss sell order down 30% cash on
  cash downside**. This becomes my maximum acceptable
  loss. It sets a floor. Essentially, if you lose 30%, you walk
  away; this cuts your losses. While 30% is a high
  percentage, buying long calls or puts is a low dollar trade,
  usually no more than $4,000 total to buy in on any one

trade. 30% of $4,000 is a $1,200 loss. Most trades are closer to $3,000 total to get in. A 30% loss would be $900. Not fun, however it is manageable.

- *RULE #7:* **Take profits by adjusting winners to lock in gains once the long option position has an unrealized gain of 50%.** Once my long call or put has an unrealized gain of 50% or more, I lock in gains by adjusting the trade into a market neutral strangle. What does this mean? Adjusting to a market neutral strangle just means buying at the money puts on the same underlying as my long calls, but only out a few weeks. This locks in the gain but still allows you to keep the unlimited upside open for further gains.

The trade entry mechanics of converting to a market neutral strangle are as follows:

Step 1: you start with an initial long call purchase (or in the trading vernacular, Buy to Open long calls). If you are bearish and playing long puts, all of these rules hold true- just in reverse.

Step 2: Place your downside stop loss trade on these options at a 30% loss of the capital invested. This open stop protects your capital while you are waiting for the underlying to rise. Note that we will remove this "insurance" stop in the next step.

Step 3: Once your long call trade has an on-paper gain of 50%, cancel the stop loss trade from Step 2 and immediately buy to open an equal number of put contracts to match your existing long calls. Do this at-the-money or one strike price out of the money. This will turn your long call trade into a market neutral strangle and protects your profit while allowing the upside to continue. It also locks in the return on this winning trade. This is how to protect profits.

This is one of my favorite trades because once Step 3 is in place, every scenario in the future on this trade is substantially profitable. This solves the age-old question on winning trades – do I close out and take my profit, or let the winning trade run in hopes of earning more upside? This trade adjustment does both. It wins whether the underlying stock goes up, stays the same, or goes down. The profit potential to the upside remains unlimited and the total risk, or maximum loss, to you is the amount paid to enter the two legs of the trade (i.e. the cost of the original long calls plus the cost of the long puts).

It is true that you will give up some of the upside with the cost of adding the long puts but if done right, it is not a substantial reduction in your overall profit.

- *RULE #8:* **Buy as much time as is cost effective when entering the Stock Replacement strategy – no less than four months to expiration.** Unless you are playing a specific near-term catalyst event such as an earnings announcement or new product launch, you should buy four to nine months of time left until expiration of the deep in-the-money long calls. Anytime my homework leads me to believe that a stock will make a dramatic move higher in the next six months, and my target price is substantially higher than today's price, I buy the long calls with as much time as is cost effective without violating the other rules in the trade entry section above.

- *RULE #9:* **Use time stops in addition to your 30% downside stop orders.** Long options lose value over time due to theta, or time decay. As a rule, you should exit a trade when 75% of the time since you entered the trade is gone if not sooner. Typically, this time stop happens automatically as we place an actual sell-stop order at a 30% cash loss of our original purchase. When enough time has passed, the time decay triggers this stop loss price and you are out. You should track the time decay anyway; it is a good practice and a good way to keep cautious.

- *RULE #10:* **Roll over long calls or puts when they near expiration.** If your fundamental conviction and technical indicators still indicate that the underlying will move in the direction you thought, roll over the calls near expiration. This locks in the gains and opens up more time for additional profits.

Rollovers allow you to compound your gains and lower risks by adding a new trade with more time. You should do these rollovers as a spread order in your online brokerage software to lower the cost and receive better pricing on the bid-ask spread. When you roll winning stock replacement positions out to the future, you compound any gains. Occasionally on these rollovers, you will also adjust the strike price based on how far the underlying has moved.

At the expiration date, 4 potential actions can be taken:
1.) Let the long calls or puts that you purchased expire worthless.
2.) Sell the options prior to expiration
3.) Roll out the purchase to a later date to add time for the trade to go your way
4.) Exercise the calls and buy shares at the strike price you purchased.

Key Note: the only time in the market cycle that I do not recommend buying long calls and puts is when the market is extremely turbulent or even crashing. In turbulent times, the implied volatility spikes rapidly and makes buying long calls or puts extremely expensive, which greatly reduces your chances of making a large win. In such turbulent environments, you want to be a seller of options, not a buyer. Please refer to my other favorite trading strategies that follow for details.

Bottom line – my experience has been that buying deep in the money long calls or puts has produced my largest cash-on-cash percentage gains and is the best way to make big money from a relatively small account.

Trade Example – stock replacement strategy and then conversion to a market neutral strangle

In 2018, Apple stock was selling for $156.50 a share.
>   *Step 1:* Buy 5 Apple call option contracts with an in the money strike price of $145 (delta = 82) that have 6 months until expiration for a price of $13.52. (500 shares times $13.52 = $6,760 cost):

>   *Step 2:* After this long call order is filled, immediately enter a Good Until Cancelled (GTC) order to sell the 5 contracts (also

known as a sell–stop limit order) at ~30% loss. This is your protection "exit trade" after entry. If implemented, it would mean a 30% cash-on-cash loss on the $13.52 price paid. This means you would set the sell-stop order at $9.45. It does not need to be exactly a 30% loss, just approximate.

Step 3: Wait for the trade to rise until you have an unrealized gain of 50%. On the cash spent ($6,760) this would be when the calls are worth approximately $10,150. This can happen quickly even if Apple only gains a few dollars per share. Say Apple stock is now $169 per share. A small move in the stock creates a magnified option move. At that point, look at the next month out at-the-money put contracts and buy to open five contracts of the at the money puts at around $3.10 per contract.

Apple PUTS

Expiration = May 2017	Strike Price = $170	Price Paid = $3.10 times 500 shares or ($1,550)

This locks in a gain of 30% after buying the puts while keeping the trade open for more upside. You have in effect converted a long call position into a market neutral strangle.

Step 4: If this trade approaches the final two days to expiration close it out and take your profits. Or if you still feel that the underlying Apple stock is on a buy signal and going higher, you can roll out the long call leg only of the trade out another few months. Roll out means sell to close the current calls and then buy to open new calls out four to six months in the future. Your gains will pay for most or all of this new purchase. Rolling the trade out if you are still bullish allows the gains to compound. The profit from the first trade greatly lowers the breakeven price as well as the risk. You can effectively then start playing with the "house money" by using your winnings to place a large part of the new trade.

In general, I prefer buying the protective puts and turning the trade into a guaranteed winner but you do not have to. The downside to selling OTM calls instead of buying the puts and doing a market neutral strangle, is that your downside (the risk of a stock decline wiping out your gains) is not taken away.

Buying Long Calls (or Puts) on Industry Sectors using ETFs
Another favored way to profit from long calls (or puts) in any type of market conditions is by betting on entire sectors that are performing well, instead of trying to select the individual stocks that might win. This will often limit explosive upside gains, but also limits downside losses as the ETF gives you some diversification across many stocks in the same sector.

The goals of sector trading are:
1.   To identify and trade the strongest market sectors (or the weakest if doing bearish long put option trades).
2.   Participate in these sector moves by using highly correlated sector ETF's or, more likely, the options on these ETFs. You can even use the more highly leveraged two times or three times leveraged sector ETFs if you have a very strong conviction in a directional move.
3.   Reduces risk and volatility by trading ETFs vs. individual stocks.

This example of the stock replacement strategy buys call options on the ETFs representing the strongest industry sectors with positive momentum. The easiest way to screen the approximately 200 industry sectors for the last five day or 21 day industry sector strengths and ranking is by going to either IBD (Investor's Business Daily) or go to www.ETFScreen.com and selecting the "RSf Trends" menu (which stands for Relative Strength Factor trends) on the home page. The highest ranked sectors then come up. The default screen is the past five days, but you can change to the past 21 days, which I do to get a longer strength indicator reading. Select those ETFs with a relative strength reading of at least 92, or under eight if you are playing the bearish / weakest sectors.

As there are many ETFs by numerous different firms, you will notice that the strong sectors will have several different ETFs that sound similar. This makes sense. When, for example, Biotech as a sector is performing well, all of the various companies with a

Biotech ETF will likely be grouped near each other in the relative strength rankings. I like to choose one from each industry sector (so if four sectors are strong with many ETFs readings above 92, I will select one ETF in the list from each of these 4 industries).

As with all long call or long put trades, scale in (leg-into) the trade by putting on 1/3 of your position at a time. Find a low risk entry point by waiting for a small pullback within the overall trend. Lower risk entry points tend to reduce the chances that you will get stopped out with your 25% downside protection open trade. This 25% downside is the walk away point. You should still use the 40% -50% upside rule for when to put on the protection spread leg to lock in your gains. On ETFs I usually lower this 50% gain rule to 40% gain as ETFs do not generally have explosive upsides, as can happen in individual stocks.

Favorite Trading Strategy #3:

In the Money Call Debit Spreads (also known as vertical debit spreads or bullish call spreads).

Call Debit Spreads are consistently winning strategy. Let's define each term in the trade strategy:
- **Bullish:** means the trade bets on the underlying stock (or ETF) rising in value.
- **Call:** means we will use call options for this strategy
- **Debit**: Means there will be a net cost to the trade. In other words, we will spend money to enter the trade (as opposed to credit vertical spreads where we will take in money to enter the trade – see favorite trading strategy #4 for more on credit spreads).
- **Spread**: A spread trade means there are two call options, or legs, to the trade (or two trades in one) to create a range between the lower strike price and the upper strike price. Specifically, if means the simultaneous buying and selling of two options on the same underlying security. One leg is the trade where money is at risk (where we are trying to make money on the trade) and the second leg is the hedge,

to reduce cost or to buy a form of insurance (to protect the downside risk in case we are wrong). In the call debit spread the second leg is to reduce the cost of buying the at-risk leg.
- **In the Money:** Means we select call options strike prices that are lower than today's market price for the stock. This adds safety if the stock price pulls back during your trade.

Mechanically, a *call debit spread* means that you:
- Buy to open, one or more call option contracts on an underlying stock (or ETF) that you believe will go up in the near term. You should look for calls with a delta of at least .70 for this leg (more on the option greek named 'Delta' in Chapter Seven).
- Simultaneously sell to open an equivalent number of short call contracts further out of the money (usually $5 but can be tighter or wider depending on the stock price and your degree of bullishness on the projected movement). The purpose of this short call is to reduce the cash outlay to buy the long calls.
- The strike price of the short calls is higher than the long calls. This creates a net debit upon entering the trade. I usually do $5 strike price difference for the two legs.

Over years of trading I have moved from shunning this strategy to using it all the time. Why have I warmed up so much to what on the surface looks like a mere directional long call trade (Favorite Trading Strategy #2) but with a capped / limited upside? It is for all of the following reasons:
- **Lower Trade Cost & Better Leverage** – call debit spreads are a way to execute a 'synthetic' covered call strategy (see my favorite strategy #1) but at a much lower cost to enter the trade. The debit call spread substitutes the expensive stock purchase part of the covered call trade with buying long term, much lower cost, in-the-money call option(s) instead of buying the stock. You then sell the short calls in the same way for both the covered call and the call debit spread. This dramatically increases the potential returns on a cash-on-cash basis. It can reduce your required up-front cash outlay by as much as 70%-80% while maintaining the

equivalent upside potential. This dramatically increases the potential returns over a traditional covered call trade on a percentage basis.

- **Limited risk** – the maximum amount at risk on a debit spread is the amount spent to enter the trade. This completely eliminates the downside beyond this cost point. When the trade is done in the money, the risk can be drastically reduced even further.
- **More consistent profits / winning percentage than my vertical (credit) spread strategy (see my favorite trading strategy #4)**. From 2014 through 2019, I have been averaging 80% wins on debit spreads versus an average of 55% wins per year on credit spreads. One only has to be right less than 40% of the time to be consistently profitable on debit call spreads when done in-the-money.
- **These trades require no margin and you can do these in a self-directed IRA** and other retirement accounts.
- **In some cases, one can completely pay for the long call position with the amount collected from the short call leg of the trade.**
- **You don't need to analyze all of the "Greeks" (covered in Chapter Seven) on these trades as much as with other trades**, which makes the set-ups easier for less experienced traders.
- **Reduced likelihood of a "blow-up" on these trades, even if the underlying stock declines**. This lower risk is due to a lower break-even price than just buying a long call option and due to the limited maximum risk, which is limited to the amount spent to enter the trade.
- **A wide profit zone**. The trader makes money on call debit spreads if the underlying stock goes up, stays the same and even if it falls slightly.
- **One can "leg into" debit spreads by first buying the long calls and then only adding the short call leg later when it is the right time**.

As with all trading strategies, there are some ways to lose money and risk / reward tradeoffs. The downside risks to doing call debit spreads are:

- **No dividends collected,** as you do not own the stock. In this respect, the covered call where you actually own the stock is superior.

- **You usually need to hold the call debit spread all the way until expiration** to collect your profit. This is not necessarily a downside, but the point is that this is not a strategy to use when you want to quickly move in and out of a position to capture a small, short term moves in the underlying stock. You need to keep the trade open until such time as the value of the short call leg erodes. When you do this, you realize the gain for your next long call leg. If you do not intend to hold the position all the way to expiration, you will have to buy the short leg back at a loss if the underlying stock moves higher, as it is expected to do. You also will still have to spend money on commissions for both entry and exit of the trade.

- **You should go two to four months out in time to expiration date, to increase your chances of a profitable trade.** You should not do debit spreads on weekly or bi-weekly call options. Going out in time two to four months greatly increases the premiums that you can collect, while reducing the probability of losing trades. I usually go out three months and after I have collected ~ 80% of the profit potential, I close out the debit spread.

Spreads – choosing strike prices by time to expiration:

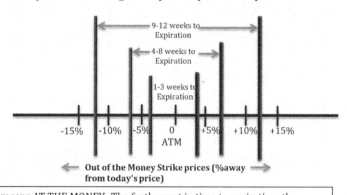

ATM means AT THE MONEY. The further out in time to expiration, the further out of the money strike prices you can sell and collect good premium from when placing spreads. Most of the time you can close further out in time spreads early with a large majority of the profit.

The bottom line: with call debit spreads, you can effectively share the risk and reward with someone else (the person who buys the short leg of your call spread) and still make great consistent returns. There are two types of call debit spreads that I focus on:

Type #1: **Vertical Debit Spreads** (also known commonly in the industry as Bull Call spreads). These have the same expiration date on both legs of the call options (both legs of the spread) and are the ones I do most often.

Type #2: **Diagonal Debit Spreads** (also commonly known as bull call _calendar_ spreads) – these have different expiration dates for each leg of the spread. Typically, I buy the long calls with about 8-12 weeks until expiration and then sell weekly calls (at a higher strike price) against the long calls each week or two until the expiration week of these long calls that I purchased. I find this trade harder to manage and keep track of, so I typically do Type #1 above.

Rules for my version of the call debit spread trading strategy:

Rule #1: Use mid-priced stocks or ETFs. Both options on stocks and ETFs work great for bull call debit spreads. Shares trading at a price higher than $125 work well, but not as well as mid-priced stocks or ETFs.

Rule #2: Do call debit spreads, In the Money. I generally do bull call debit spreads with a strike price that is at least one standard deviation in the money for extra safety and protection. You do not need to calculate standard deviation; you can estimate it. To do this, just look for the strike price for the lower of the two call strike prices, that has a 68% chance of winning (given on the option chain in your brokerage software). This distinction de-risks the trade tremendously as opposed to doing strike prices at-the-money. The key for in-the-money call debit spreads is to **select stocks with some volatility**. You need the volatility to ensure the call premiums are larger for collecting time premium in the leg of the trade you are selling. You are seeking to lock in and collect the time value portion of the option premium as your profit.

Rule #3: When the debit spread is winning and very close to, or at, expiration and you feel confident that it will not reverse, you can close the protection leg of the trade (the short leg) and let the long call position run. On expiration day, you can sell the winning call option and lock in the profit.

Rule #4: If the short calls leg of the trade is in the money a day or two before expiration, close out the short leg of the trade to avoid assignment meaning you would be obligated to deliver the shares which you don't own at the short call price.

The bottom line: trading call debit spreads, especially when done in-the-money, lets you enter a directional trade on a stock you hope will rise in price, while allowing someone else to repay you for some of the costs by collecting premium on the short leg of the trade. The tradeoff is that you also share some of the reward if right if the stock rises above the price of the short calls we sold in exchange for sharing the risk. The profit potential is capped. If the underlying stock price finishes at or above the higher (short call) strike at expiration, you would exercise the long call component and would be assigned on the short call. As a result, the stock is simultaneously bought at the lower (long call strike) price and sold at the higher (short call strike) price. The maximum profit equals the difference between the two strike prices, less the initial debit paid to establish the spread. I typically do $5 spreads – meaning the difference between the long call strike price and the short call strike price is $5.

Example: You have done your research and homework and you feel Twitter (ticker: TWTR) stock will rise but not explode higher over the next three months. The underlying twitter stock is currently priced at $39 a share. You decide to place a bull call spread (debit spread) to capture the movement without owning the stock.

Mechanics: You pull up the option chain on TWTR. In the option chain, you find that the $33 in the money strike price call option, expiring in three and a half months, has a 32% likelihood of finishing OTM (out of the money). This means the $33 strike price has a 68% chance of finishing ITM (in the money) – this is what we want. A 68% chance of finishing ITM means there is a 68% chance that the market stock price for TWTR will finish above $33 a share in 100 days. We buy this strike price as it is approximately one standard deviation in the money from today's market price of the stock. Then sell the $5 higher strike price to create the call debit spread and to help pay for the call we purchased. In this case we would sell the $38 strike price with the same expiration date. The trade entry would be:

- *Step one* – Buy to Open, 10 contracts of the $33 strike price call options expiring in three and a half months. The price is $7.35 per contract. Our cost would be $7.35 multiplied by 1,000 shares, or a cost of **$7,350**.

- *Step two* – Sell to Open, 10 contracts of the $38 strike price call options expiring on the same date, three and a half months into the future. This is also known as the short call leg. The price is $4.45 per contract We take in $4.45 times 1,000 shares for selling this, or a credit of **$4,450**.

- Total spent to enter this Call Debit Spread is +$4,450 minus $7,350. **A net debit of $2,900.**

- This trade wins if TWTR stock finishes above $33 + $2.90 debit spent to enter the trade. So, if TWTR finishes above $35.90 this trade will be profitable. This is a good bet as the stock is currently at $39 and has lots of good news and earnings. The max profit potential is the difference between the two strike prices ($38-$33) times the 1,000 shares = $5,000 less the amount paid to enter the trade (the debit of $2,900). The max profit is $2,100. The max loss potential is the amount spent to enter the trade $2,900. The break-even price is $33 + $2.90 or $35.90.

Favorite Trading Strategy #4:

Vertical Credit Spreads (also known as Bullish Put Spreads & Bearish Call Spreads).

Which industry has historically generated more money than any other in the world? The insurance industry. Why do insurance companies make so much money? They take on the obligation to insure risks that they have calculated with relative certainty will not occur frequently. They collect many premiums on these infrequent risks and pay out few claims. This is the same principle behind my favorite trading strategy #4, credit-spread strategies.

With vertical credit spreads, you become like the insurance company. You collect many premiums on stock scenarios that your probability calculations prove will not occur often, and you keep those premiums once the obligation expires. Sometimes you have to pay out a loss (like an insurer pays a claim) but you try to have many more winners than losers. I like the risk management and flexibility of vertical credit spread as a strategy and I like that you get paid on day one to make the trade.

The drawback to vertical credit spreads is that it is really hard to predict with any certainty if a stock will be higher or lower in price in the next one to four weeks into the future. No one can do this with consistency. You will find with vertical credit spread trades, you will win some and you will lose some (when you lose you will need to rollout the trade to gain more time to be right– more on this later in this chapter).

As I tend to have a bullish bias in stocks, **bullish put credit spreads** are a core strategy that I use when I am bullish on a company. Though I do them rarely, a bearish call credit spread works the same on stocks you want to bet fall in price in the next few weeks. Yes, you can do these out in the future longer than four weeks to expiration but as you want to maximize the time decay you collect, the last month is the steepest time decay and tends to work best.

On vertical credit spread trades, the maximum profit potential you can make is limited to the initial net credit taken in on the trade when you place it. You essentially get to collect the max profit up front and then see if you get to keep it or have to give it back as the trade works towards the expiration date.

The downside loss is capped at the difference between the two strike prices you select for the spread, less the net credit received when you place the trade, which you get to keep no matter what. Essentially you are selling time premium on these trades to produce income while capping your downside. Just like the insurance company, you become a time merchant (selling and collecting the time premium of the option) and these can supplement your income dramatically.

I tend to sell the strike price that is one to three strike prices out of the money to try to de-risk the trade in my favor but still make good money. This means take the current stock price and *sell* the put option that is one to three strike prices lower in price (on a bull put spread) or one to three strike prices higher that the stock price on a bearish call spread); then *hedge by buying* the put strike price $5 below the strike price you sold. This adds the protection leg on a bullish put spread. Alternatively, you would buy the calls $5 higher than you short call strike price on a bearish call spread.

An Example will illustrate the Bull Put Credit Spread Trade

BULL PUT SPREAD:
You have done your homework and you feel Microsoft will go up over the next four weeks. Instead of spending money and buying the MSFT stock, nor buying a call option on MSFT, you decide to take in money (a credit) instead but benefit if the MSFT share price rises. You can do this by selling a bullish put spread. It is exciting to take in money instead of spending it to enter a trade.

- MSFT stock is currently trading at $125 per share.
- The price for the $122 strike price put options (three strike prices down from today's stock price of $125, to de-risk the trade), expiring in four weeks is $2.25.   You sell this one.
- The price for the $117 strike price put option ($5 lower) are priced at $.90 cents. This is our hedge or insurance leg – you buy this one.
- This sets up a credit of +$2.25 - $.90 or a net profit of $1.35 per share. What this means is you can make $1.35 times the number of shares in each option contract. So a one contract bull put spread would pay you $1.35, multiplied by 100 shares, or $135. A two-contract bull put spread would pay you $1.35 multiplied by 200 shares, or $270. A five-contract credit spread would credit you $675. A ten-contract spread would credit you $1,350 less commissions. These credits are the maximum profit potential on the trade.
- What is the max risk? It is the $5 difference between the strike prices (the difference between the short put strike price and the long puts bought for protection), times the number of contracts less the amount taken in for the credit.
  - So, the max loss potential on a one contract spread is the $5 spread between the strike prices (of $122 - $117) multiplied by 100 shares minus the $135

credit taken in. This means a max potential loss of **$365**.

- o   The max loss potential for a two-contract spread would be $1,000-$270 or **$730**.
- o   For a five-contract spread, the max loss potential would be $2,500-$675, or **$1,825**.
- o   For a ten-contract spread it would be $5,000 - $1,350 or **$3,650**.

To place the vertical credit spread, you would open up your brokerage platform and open an options chain to examine the prices offered. Then go under the TRADE menu and select Option, then Spread.

Vertical credit spread – Bull Put Spread Trade Mechanics:

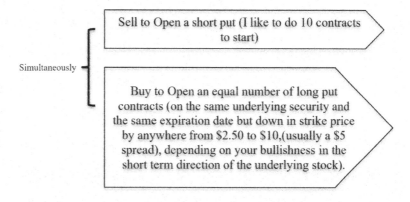

Simultaneously

Sell to Open a short put (I like to do 10 contracts to start)

Buy to Open an equal number of long put contracts (on the same underlying security and the same expiration date but down in strike price by anywhere from $2.50 to $10,(usually a $5 spread), depending on your bullishness in the short term direction of the underlying stock).

The benefits of doing credit spreads are as follows:

PROs	CONs
Credit spreads provide a nice cushion for directional error in the underlying – when done with slightly out of the money ("OTM") strike prices. You can stop trying to predict where the market will go and instead focus on predicting	**Difficult to know how to balance how far Out of the Money ("OTM") to place each trade**. To be conservative – you collect less up-front premium by doing vertical credit spreads further OTM. If you go too far OTM,

where it won't go. Our only concern is if the stock or ETF goes against and past our OTM strike prices so substantially that they cause the trade to lose.	however, you will win a high percentage of the time, but one loss can erase 10+ wins due to the low premium collected on the wins vs. the high loss potential if you lose. The key is to balance the risk / reward.
Collect nice income / premium up front as soon as the trade is placed. Getting paid to place the trade is nice and since there is typically four weeks or less to expiration date, rapid time decay.	**Spreads can be difficult to trade on more highly volatile stocks** high volatility stocks pay you more in up front option premiums but they are more unpredictable. They often can cross several strike prices in a month time period – blowing through your short leg and your protection leg and causing a max loss.
Limited loss / capped loss with the long protection leg of the credit spread.	**You are not entitled to collect the dividends** when you do credit spreads.
Lots of ways to adjust and lock in profits these trades	**The high percentage likelihood to win when you enter the trade can change quickly after you are in the trade.** The 75% likelihood credit spread trade when you enter it, can become a 40% likelihood trade in a couple of hours. This sometimes makes entering adjustments or closing out trades difficult to do in a timely manner.
Credit spreads can essentially be used at any time in any market conditions and with any optional security (stocks, ETFs, etc.).	

On a volatile stock, I like to set my protection leg of the initial credit spread trade more narrowly (set tighter protection than a $5 spread). I usually look at $2.50 spreads on volatile stocks. On less volatile stocks, or names that I have a strong conviction will make a directional move, I like to set a wider spread and keep more of the initial net credit premium.

As you are selling time premium, don't be tempted to check every tick of the underlying stock or ETF right after you place the trade. Place the trade and walk away. Give it some time to work. The Thursday and Friday into the options expiration date are typically the focus, unless the underlying has made an unanticipated move well before expiration. There is more on how to handle these moves in the risk management and adjustments section in Chapter Eight.

My rules for trading vertical Credit spreads:

RULE #1: **Concentrate in a few trades and positions** vs. putting on a large number of short-term credit spreads. If you want to put more money to work, make bigger trades in a few positions. Use higher priced stocks as they work better.

RULE #2: *Sell approximately one standard deviation (or slightly more) out of the money strike price for each credit spreads.* In other words, sell the strike price that is at or past one standard deviation or has a 68% likelihood of finishing out of the money. It does not need to be exact but use 68% as a minimum, or guideline. Then buy the appropriate protection leg based on your conviction in the move of the underlying (when in doubt, do a $5 spread width). Check the chart and also ensure that you are selling a strike price just under the resistance points (the 10-day, 30 day or 50 day moving average) based on the past price action.

RULE #3: **Do credit spreads on large, well-known liquid stocks or ETFs** – those with strong fundamentals and good technical set-ups supporting the direction that your trade needs to go in order to win.

RULE #4: **In strong bullish markets with a confirmed uptrend be more aggressive with the strike prices you select, sell the risky leg of the spread leg closer to ATM. In uncertain markets, be**

more conservative and sell the legs at further out of the money strike prices. Target 2%-5%+ monthly cash-on-cash returns. Ensure the strike prices selected yield a minimum net credit of $1 or larger on each credit spread. Otherwise, commissions and slippage will eat into your gains too much. I aim for a minimum of $1 net credit on any number of contracts less than 20. If I am trading over 20 contracts, then the minimum net credit I target is 75 cents.

RULE #5: **Do longer time frame credit spreads (specifically out one to three months to expiration) until you have a lot of experience.** This is for three reasons:

    1. It allows you time to be able to place trade adjustments (discussed in Chapter Eight), which increase greatly your chance of ending with a profit.

    2. It allows you to sell further OTM strike prices at good premiums (generally 15% - 20% out of the money from today's stock price) vs. short term expiration dates which have a higher percentage of winning.

    3. Strike prices further away from at the money lose their time premium sooner than at the money strike prices. Since time premium is what we are collecting, this means you can collect 50% - 70% of your time premium profit long before expiration and close it out early- usually in a month or less.

Rule #6: **Avoid trading in the direction of very large open interest.** Every option chain and every strike price will show the open interest for each strike price. You don't want to go against the large institutional investors.

The conservative approach to start with is to sell three months out credit spreads further out of the money. You should aim for 12%-15% OTM from today's underlying security price. Once the trade is executed, these further OTM strike prices should lose time value, or theta, much faster than the front month contract. This means that the trade can generally be closed out at 60%+ of the net credit in four to six weeks of placing the trade. You have up to 3 months to be right if it doesn't move your way in the first four to six weeks.

Variation #1 - Writing Weekly Vertical Credit Spreads:
Many small investors try to speed this process up by writing vertical credit spreads that expire each Friday (also known as writing weekly

credit spreads). These are a more aggressive approach as they have faster expiration dates with strike prices that are much closer to being at-the-money. It is much more exciting in action! A problem with this strategy, however, is that there is very little time to adjust losing trades. Otherwise I endorse it. If you are going to do weeklies, here are a few tips:

- **Make sure you open the spread position by selling the premium and collecting the net credit on the Thursday or right at the open Friday during the week before expiration day (leaving the weekend plus five business days until expiration).** The reason is to get the benefit of the time decay from the weekend before expiration working in your favor. By trading the Thursday before the weekend, you avoid being hurt by the market makers expanded spread over the weekend, which gives you slightly more favorable premiums.

- **Do tight spreads with less risk** – I like to do $1-$2.50 wide credit spreads when I do weeklies on active stocks like Apple, etc. On one month to three-month long credit spreads, I will widen the spread to $2.50-$5. Remember, tighter spreads equal less risk to you. If you have to rollout a losing spread it gives you the flexibility to slightly widen the spread on the rollout position at better strike prices. You should seek to risk $1 to make $1 (one to one risk to reward ratios). You can often get $.80 net premium on a $2.00 spread or $1.35 net credit on a $3.00 spread. Try to get as close to a 1:1 risk to reward ratio as possible.

- **Sell one strike price OTM and buy the protection leg $2.00 - $5.00 further OTM strike price.** The width of your spread and hence risk will depend on the price of the underlying security, its strike price choices, and the strength of your conviction in an upward move over the remaining week.

- **Don't sell weeklies within seven days of an earnings announcement.** There are too many unpredictable price moves in the immediate run up to earnings. Avoid this week. If you need to rollout an existing spread into an earnings week that you did not plan on, you should roll it out two weeks to expire the week after earnings and tighten up your spread or move it further out of the money and keep the same width.

- **Only sell weekly vertical credit spreads on underlying stocks that have weekly options.** This may sound obvious but remember, not all stocks that have options, have weekly options. Some only have monthly options. Going into the third Friday of each month (which is the expiration date for Monthlies), every stock and ETF becomes a weekly. I have made the mistake of forgetting this, selling the weekly credit spread, having it go against me and needing to roll out the trade to buy more time and then realizing the next set of strike prices to roll to is one month to expiration, not one week. Your weekly strategy will turn into a much slower monthly rescue trade. You can check the current list of stocks with weeklies on the CBOE website under the Products tab.

- **Only trade weekly credit spreads in trending markets.** Stable long-term up trends or downtrends work best. Avoid choppy action. Otherwise, you should trade out longer in time to expiration (no weeklies) and look to close out early with 50% - 85% of maximum profit. Refer to Chapter Four on technical analysis for how to confirm the strength of a trend.

- **Try to enter a bullish credit spread on a pullback within the longer-term trend** using the Keltner Channels or squeeze technical indicators to achieve a lower risk entry point.

- **If the underlying stock or ETF that you did the spread on goes against you while the trade is open, just close it and roll it out.**

Variation 2: Iron Condors -writing both a Bull-put Spread and a Bear Call Spread together:

One very attractive variation of the credit spreads strategy is the Iron Condor. When a trader does not want to try to take a directional bet when placing a credit spread but rather does both of the directional credit spreads at the same time on the same underlying stock, this is called an iron condor. It is the combination of a bull put spread and a bear call spread at the same time with the same expiration date on the same underlying security. It is in essence a 'double credit spread.' I like to do iron condors with both sides around one standard deviation out of the money.

My rules for Iron Condors:
Rule #1: **Place Iron Condors further out in time** as longer-term options allow for a larger range of strike prices that work well that are far OTM and have high likelihoods of success. You should select a time period between six weeks and two months. Select plus and minus 15% above and below today's stock price for the strike prices (or just select 2 standard deviations in both direction which are easily found on all good charting software and websites). Two standard deviations is equivalent to 95% confidence (or 95% certainty) that the underlying instrument will stay safely in the channel and your positions that you sold will expire worthless and you will keep the premium collected. Tactically, this means you sell the strike price both above and below the current at-the-money strike price that is near two standard deviations and then buy the strike price $5-$10 further out of the money as protection.

Rule#2: **When placing an Iron Condor, my expectation is that the stock / ETF price will stay within a fairly tight range in the channel that I have created between the bull put spread strike prices and the bear call spread strike prices.** This implies placing these trades on fairly stable stocks, or even better on ETFs or on market indices.

Rule #3: **If after placing the trade the underlying stock price starts to move unexpectedly and rapidly towards one side of the channel you have created with the iron condor, add a few long puts (or calls) in the direction of the developing trend.** Selling calls equals small insurance, while buying puts equals big insurance.

Rule #4: **As your accounts grow, don't be tempted to come closer and closer to the ATM price to make more money.** This will lower your statistical chances of winning. In place of transacting closer to the ATM price, you can just do higher numbers of contracts and stay out at or near two standard deviations.

Rule #5: **I also recommend that you do aggressive rolling out on these one to two standard deviation iron condor positions.** This means that after you place the trade, monitor the position until approximately 40%-50% of the time premium has eroded. You will know this is the case by just looking at the unrealized gain on the trade.

Once you have an on-paper gain of around 45%-50%, go ahead and take that profit by rolling out the position to a new iron condor on the same instrument. I do this in time to the equivalent amount of time originally put on trade I am closing and collect a second premium. This reduces your risk, resets your strike prices to match the moving market and accelerates the time of compounding your gains. This is a key secret to growing your accounts quickly.

Rule #6: **Remember to also hedge your entire portfolio against a major stock market correction whenever you have credit spreads on – this provides extra portfolio insurance.** I usually take 20% of the proceeds from all of the credit spreads and iron condors I have placed and buy that amount of puts on the S&P 500 out six to eight weeks as portfolio insurance.

KEY BONUS STRATEGY: Writing Cash backed Puts (with Protection)
When you want to buy a stock that you don't own at a reduced price and get paid to do so. Don't sell cash backed puts alone, instead it is safer do a very wide bull put spread.

I almost included a 7th favorite trading strategy in this book. This is the strategy of selling naked puts backed by cash (also known as writing cash backed puts) in your account when you want to buy great stocks at a lower price. It is a simple and powerful strategy. The logic is, if you like a company and you want to buy the stock in the company, but you feel it is too pricey at the current share price, what can you do? The answer is, you can sell puts at a price you would be willing to pay for the stock and collect premium while you wait for it to pull back to your price and then you buy it. Remember selling long puts means you are willing to have the stock put to you (or sold to you) at the strike price on or before the expiration date. If the shares never fall down to your target purchase price, you keep the option put premium and once it expires, do it again and collect another put premium. This is a great strategy, you get paid over and over while waiting for a stock you want to buy to fall to the price you want to buy it (so remember , you must keep the cash to buy it on hold in your account, in case it does fall and gets put to you).

I refrained from including this as a favorite strategy due to two reasons.

1) This is in effect the very risky strategy of selling naked puts. You are backing the naked puts with cash (cash on-hold in your brokerage account) in case you must perform and buy the shares. Factually, however, it is still selling naked puts. Selling naked puts, while safe most of the time, does technically have limited gain and *unlimited* **risk**. This means that they can wipe you out in rare extreme circumstances. Generally, this occurs when large unforeseen events occur such as a scandal, a takeover, an accounting fraud, etc. These are of course rare, but they do happen. I once had to console a trader who had sold 100 naked put contracts with a strike price of $40 on a stock trading in the open market at $45 / share. The company came out with accounting irregularities and a massive investigation by the regulators was announced. Overnight the stock fell from $45 to $11 a share. This trader collected $12,000 in premiums on day one for selling 100 contracts of the naked puts that at the time were $5 out of the money (he sold the $40 puts when the stock was trading at $45). Overnight, this trader now was obligated to buy 10,000 shares of the stock at $40 (around $400,000). While this event is extremely rare and the trader had way too big of a position on, the consequences of unlimited downside trades are too severe. I don't teach this strategy without the variation discussed below. This trader lost the equivalent of

a house overnight. The easy $12,000 up front gain that he collected (he had collected that $12,000 premium ten times / ten months in a row without assignment) are not worth this kind of a blow up. The trader was all but wiped out. The lesson is don't ever sell options (calls or puts) naked.

2) The easy solution for the risk of selling naked puts is a wide bull put credit spread (just as we learned my favorite trading strategy #4). What I mean by this, is that there is a very cheap and easy way to collect all of the advantages of selling cash backed naked puts without the risk of a blow up described above. Just buy the equivalent amount of puts with a strike price down $5 from the ones you sold. In effect you are doing a put credit spread instead of selling naked puts. If the trader in the selling naked puts example had bought very cheap puts with a $35 strike price further out of the money, the loss when the stock fell to $11 a share would have been greatly mitigated as he could have 'put' the shares to someone else at $35 (instead of buying and owning 10,000 shares worth $11 and dropping).

How can you use this to your advantage? If your goal is to buy stocks you like wholesale and collect short term put premiums, do an out of the money bull put spread. It is a great strategy. Structure the trade as a bull put spread, not by just selling cash backed naked puts. By doing this, you can continue to collect these short term, out of the money put premiums over and over until you are assigned the shares to buy. By adding just one more step, you dramatically reduce your risk compared to selling naked puts. On a $45 stock, you can buy the $35 strike price long put expiring in 30 days for five or ten cents per put contract. That is very cheap insurance and prevents the catastrophic loss I described above. In effect, you have just placed a wide bull-put credit spread. If the underlying stock price falls below your short put strike price, you should still be prepared with cash backing in your account to buy the shares, even if it requires using margin. Remember, you only do this on stocks that you want to buy anyway but at a cheaper price.

Favorite Trading Strategy #5:

Directional Out of the Money ("OTM") Butterflies and Skip Strike "Broken Wing" Butterflies

What is my favorite strategy for using tiny amounts of cash at risk, with a high risk to reward ratio? The answer is the two variations on the butterfly trade discussed below.

I love the risk to reward of utilizing butterfly strategies. The down side is that they don't win as frequently as some of the other strategies taught in this book, but when they do, they can be huge winners with very little cash at risk. The other large benefit is that the downside risk is fully capped. The low price you pay to enter the butterfly trade is the maximum possible risk.

A butterfly is a key way to play a stock when I expect the underlying to move to a specific price at option expiration date. My two preferred butterfly strategies are variations on the basic butterfly strategy. The following two types of butterfly variation trades are the best for small investors to trade:

1.   **An Out of the Money Directionally Skewed Butterfly**
2.   **A Directional Skip-strike, or "Broken-wing" Butterfly**

Lets' go over each of these two butterfly strategy variations in turn. First, however, I will cover a quick recap of what a traditional butterfly strategy means. This will set a baseline of understanding before getting to the two variations I prefer.

A *traditional butterfly* is a non-directional (neutral) trading strategy where you expect the underlying stock to stay in a tight trading range between today and the expiration date. It is to be used when you believe that you can predict with a reasonable amount of certainty the price at which the underlying will finish at on the expiration date of the options. The closer to your predicted finishing price, the more money you make with a butterfly.

A butterfly is the combination of a bull call spread and a bear call spread that share the same strike price on the short leg of each spread. You construct a traditional butterfly by using an "All in

One" ticket in most online brokerage software. Some brokers will let you select a "butterfly" ticket to enter the trade. A butterfly is a three-legged trade (which means it contains three simultaneous positions) on the same underlying you do all of the following:

- **Sell two at the money call contracts** at the target price you believe the stock will finish at on expiration day.
- **Buy one ITM call contract** with a strike price one to two strike prices below the strike price you sold and
- **Buy one OTM call contract** with a strike price one to two strike prices above the strike price you sold. Make sure it is the same proportional distance away from the strike price as the two sold call contracts.

You can place the butterfly with larger numbers of contracts than the 1:2:1 example above. I usually do 10:20:10 or 20:40:20 size trades. Just make sure to hold to the same 1:2:1 *ratio* between the buys and sales. Let's look at an example with a diagram.

EXAMPLE – Traditional Butterfly: Today Facebook (ticker symbol: FB) trades at $180.72. You believe that in 30 days it will close at $182.50 a share. You decide to play it with a butterfly trade. You would place all of the following:

- **Sell two call contracts** at the target strike price you believe the stock will finish at expiration date, which is $182.50. The cost per contract is $1.30 but as you are selling this leg of the position, you will collect this amount as a credit multiplied by the two contracts (200 shares). *Credit = $260.*
- **Buy one call contract** with a strike price one to two strike prices down at $177.5. The cost per contract is $3.85 cents per contract – this is a cost to you, multiplied by one contract (100 shares)). *Cost = $385.*
- **Buy one call contract** with a strike price one strike price up at $187.50. The cost per contract is $.21 cents – this is a cost multiplied by one contract (100 shares). *Cost = $21*

TOTAL NET DEBIT (COST) TO ENTER THIS BUTTTERFLY = $146 plus commissions.

The diagram below is how this traditional butterfly would look:

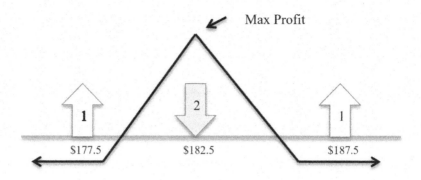

Now let's look at the two butterfly variation strategies that I prefer over the traditional butterfly:

My strategy variation #1 - A Directional (Out of the Money) Butterfly.
This strategy takes the traditional butterfly trade and makes it even lower risk and higher reward. This can reduce your risk in the trade by minimizing your initial spend when entering the trade by anywhere from 75% to 100%. Use this strategy when you believe the underlying stock will make a nice upward move of around $5 to $9 over the next month. Do the same trade entry mechanics as the traditional butterfly but instead of doing the trade near the money or at the money, put it on out several strike prices in the upward direction that matches your forecasted $5 to $9 upward move expectation. Using the previous Facebook trade example, the directional butterfly would look as follows:

EXAMPLE (Directional, Out of the Money Butterfly): Today Facebook (ticker symbol: FB) trades at $180.72. You believe that in 45 days it will close up $6.25 at just under $187. You decide to play it with a low risk directional butterfly trade. You would place the following orders:

- **Sell two call contracts** at the target strike price you believe the stock will finish at expiration date. In this case $187; the cost per contract out 45 days is $.60. As you are selling you will collect this amount as a credit multiplied by the two contracts (200 shares). *Credit = $120.*

- **Buy one call contract** with a strike price slightly down at approximately $183. The cost per contract is $1.18 cents per contract. This is a cost to you, multiplied by 1 contract (100 shares)). *Cost = $118.*

- **Buy one call contract** with a strike price above at an equal distance to the one you bought below. In this example, the strike price is $191. The cost per contract is $.05 cents. This is a cost multiplied by one contract (100 shares). *Cost = $5*

Total net debit (cost) to enter this directional, out of the money butterfly = $3 plus commissions.

You can see the better risk to reward of this trade compared to the traditional butterfly. You spent just $3 (plus commissions) to enter this directional butterfly trade as opposed to spending $146 plus commissions to enter the traditional butterfly. With this trade the underlying would have to make a larger move for you to make money, but if it does your risk to reward ratio is much higher here.

Your maximum downside is the $3 plus the commissions you spent to enter the trade. This specific cost is so low that you can afford to do more contracts to make this trade worthwhile. Usually this is done in a ratio of: ten contract, twenty contract, ten contract butterfly. You buy ten contracts of the two 'wings' of the butterfly and sell 20 contracts of the 'body' of the butterfly. Your maximum risk on the trade would then go up only to $30 plus commissions.

Your maximum reward on this trade (at the 10:20:10 ratio) would be if the underlying stock finished exactly at your target price of $187 on expiration day. If this occurs you could make a maximum profit of $4,000 less commissions. This is an amazing risk to reward ratio for risking $30 plus commissions.

The formula for calculating the maximum possible profit on a butterfly trade is as follows: ***Max Profit*** = *strike price of the short call minus the strike price of the ITM (lower strike price) long call less the net premium paid to enter the trade less commissions.*

**My strategy variation #2 - A *broken wing (or 'skip strike')
butterfly***
This strategy is also a directionally skewed butterfly as in the
example above, but with one significant difference. On the out of
the money long call purchase, you skip a strike price and go further
out in distance from todays at the money stock price compared to the
downside / in the money long call. I often do broken-wing
butterflies for an initial *net credit*. I will go over a couple of
examples to illustrate this below. These trades have Greek levels
that are more favorable to the trader compared to vertical credit
spreads such as bull put spreads or bear call spreads, and have lots of
wiggle room on the underlying security price movement before they
lose.
For example: You have researched and selected a stock that you
think will go higher in the near term based on fundamental and
technical analysis. That stock (let's just call it XYZ company) is
currently selling for $52 a share. Your research tells you it should
rise to $58 in the next four to five weeks. Set up the directional skip
strike butterfly as follows:

**NOTE: enter all of the below as a single 'all in one' ticket order
on your online broker (or as a butterfly order in other brokerage
software systems):**
- Sell two times the calls at or near your target price of $58
  (for $1.00 credit per contract in this example).
  Credit = $200.
- Buy one call contracts at a strike price $5 below our target.
  In this example at a strike price of $53 (for $1.70 per
  contract in this example). *Cost = $170.*
- The SKIP STRIKE leg – Buy one times the calls at a strike
  price $10 above our target, or a strike price of $68 (for 5
  cents per contract in this example). *Cost = $5*

  **TOTAL NET DEBIT (COST) to enter this directional,
  out of the money skip strike butterfly = a *net credit* of
  $25 per contract (less commissions).**

As with all butterflies, you can do as many contracts as you want as
long as they all have the same expiration date and you maintain the

1:2:1 ratio above. In this example, by doing this broken wing butterfly trade directionally and skipping one strike price on the upside, you can sometimes establish these for a net credit. However, a very small net debit is fine and more common. This amount is the most we can lose. Because of this, you have cut your risk by reducing your amount at risk while maintaining the profit potential. I do these often with stock indexes so there is no chance of early assignment and less chance of a shock move upward as compared to individual stocks.

This strategy wins if the stock closes around or below the targeted strike price I picked by expiration date. A regular butterfly would lose if the stock falls too much, so this version of the trade has unlimited downside protection. The tradeoff is that a larger loss occurs on a broken wing if the stock rallies dramatically above our skip strike long call on the upside.

*EXAMPLE: **Bullish Broken Wing Butterfly***: (assumes trade was established for a net credit):
- The goal = The underlying stock finishes as close to 'B' as possible.
  Max profit = B – A
- Max loss = Difference between the strike prices of C and D minus the net credit received.

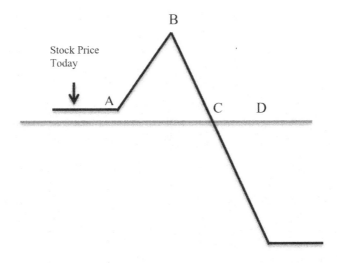

Bearish Broken Wing Butterflies:
You can do broken wing butterflies skewed whether you are
bullish using call options or bearish using put options. The
example above is skewed upwards using calls, as it is a bullish
trade. I do this type most often. If you do a skip strike /
broken wing butterfly trade skewed bearish, you are betting on
a targeted downward move in the underlying stock or ETF.
The mechanics of the bearish trade are the same, except that
you use puts instead of calls and the leg of the trade where you
embed the 'skip strike,' is on the downside long put leg (or
wing) of the butterfly.

Favorite Trading Strategy #6:   Call (or Put) Ratio Spreads, with a net credit

This strategy recommendation is for the more advanced retail self-
directed trader. It is called a call ratio spread. It is placed for an
initial net credit (takes money in at the open).

This is the most advanced, also the riskiest, of all of the six trading
strategies taught in this book. Don't start with this one if you are a
novice trader. Once you get some experience and are doing a nice
job of building up your accounts, you can add this strategy to your
toolkit.

This strategy is a great way to win whether the stock goes down,
stays the same or goes up slightly. A stock that goes up slightly but
not too much is the best winning scenario in this strategy. In fact,
the only way to lose money on a call ratio spread with an initial net
credit is if the stock makes a dramatic, unexpected move higher
while you have the trade on.   Stocks in theory can rise to infinity so
be careful if there is a chance of a dramatic unexpected move higher
(as with all of my strategies there is a potential hedge against this).

I typically do this strategy with call options to capture large gains on
a slight upward move in the underlying stock. Some investors prefer
doing put ratio spreads due to the slightly better risk/reward tradeoff;
the stock can only fall to $0 whereas with call ratio spreads the risk
to the upside stock price is unlimited.

I prefer to do Call Ratio Spreads for a net credit only when I feel the market is reaching the top of a cycle. If the market is already making all-time highs, the chances of a major move higher is lessened. In addition, when the market is making all-time highs, there is a good chance it will drift higher slowly – which is the best result for this trade – or retreat and retest moving averages, which still wins with this strategy.

When done correctly, with an initial net credit, one can make money even when the market moves in the opposite direction that you guessed it would.

RULE: Select a stock or ETF that you believe will move slightly higher over the next month, but has a little chance of moving sharply higher. Do not do this strategy on a high volatility stock like cannabis stocks, Netflix or Tesla, as these can hurt you in this trade.

Trade Mechanics:

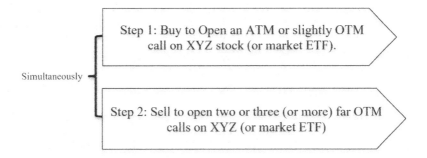

Simultaneously

Step 1: Buy to Open an ATM or slightly OTM call on XYZ stock (or market ETF).

Step 2: Sell to open two or three (or more) far OTM calls on XYZ (or market ETF)

Any underlying security price at expiration that is under the strike price of the higher leg will result in a profitable trade. If the underlying goes up slightly but not above the high trade break-even price and this trade wins big.

The benefits of a call ratio spread placed with an initial net credit include:

- **A wide profit zone** – the stock can move down an unlimited

amount, stay flat, or even move up a little and you will still have a winning trade. This eliminates the need for the trader to have to predict exactly how the stock will perform.
- **The trade starts with the underlying price in the profit zone.** Try for a 2:1 ratio; a 3:1 is still acceptable.
- **Less margin is required** if the trade goes against you.
- **If the trade goes up slightly as predicted, there will be significant profits in the sweet spot of the profit zone**.

The **drawbacks** to the Call Ratio Spread are:
1. **They are a little more cumbersome to put in place** as they require three options and scouting for premiums that work to produce the initial net credit.
2. **Higher commissions** due to a three-legged trade.
3. **If the stock does explode higher, there is technically unlimited loss potential as the stock price goes higher and higher**. Note that this risk can be protected by buying a call far out of the money as a form of catastrophe insurance.

EXAMPLE: Call Ratio Spread with a Net Credit: a 3:1 Call Ratio Spread with a net credit

The Stock price of XYZ company today = $52 a share.

The trade:
LEG #1: Buy to Open, ten contracts of the $55 strike price, expiration in three months, option price is $4 per contract. **The total spend would be** ($4* 1,000 shares) **$4,000.**
LEG #2: Simultaneously, sell to open, 30 contracts of the $70 strike price call options with the same expiration date. Collect $1.50 for these. Multiplied by the 30 contracts or 3,000 shares means **we collect $4,500**.
NET CREDIT – This trade produces an overall **net credit of $500**.

Potential outcomes (omitting commissions):
1.)   If the STOCK FALLS = If the stock goes down by expiration date, both sets of contracts we bought and sold expire worthless and we keep the **$500 as a profit**.

2.)   IF STOCK STAYS THE SAME = both option positions also expire worthless and we keep the **$500 as our profit.**

3.)   IF STOCK GOES UP SLIGHTLY = the $70 strike price calls we sold expire worthless and we keep the amount we collected on them. The $55 strike price calls go to approximately $5.25 per contract for **a gain of $5,250 as our profit. Add this to our original net credit of $500 and we have won big. A $5,750 net profit.**

4.)   IF THE STOCK GOES UP SIGNIFICANTLY = In this scenario we have lost big. If the stock goes to say $85, the $70 calls we sold have to be bought back to close and they are now worth $15 each for a cost of $45,000, in other words a loss of -$45,000 (remember we sold 30 contracts of these). We do get to keep our original credit of $500 and our $55 long calls (of which we only own ten contracts) have increased in value nicely and are now worth +$30,000. **The overall result is a $14,500 loss on the trade.**

5.)   To minimize this large loss potential, do these ratio trades only at the top of a market cycle. Also, as a trade adjustment, buy ten additional far OTM calls with an $85 strike price if the stock price goes from $52, with substantial time to expiration.

The opposite of the Call Ratio Spread with a net credit is the Put Ratio Spread with a net credit. This is also a promising trade but everything works in the opposite direction. I generally only favor doing put ratio spreads with a net credit as a trade hedge on another position or more often as a hedge on the entire market. I usually have 80% bullish trade positions on at any one time across my entire portfolio. This is because I like to be an optimist and find things I think will go higher. I then hedge all of these bullish positions by buying puts on the overall S&P 500 (using the SPY) or with these put ratio spreads.

My rules for trading call (& put) ratio spreads are:
RULE #1: Use wide spreads between the strike prices you buy and sell. This minimizes the risk of the underlying security moving through your short leg and causing losses.

RULE #2: **Due to the unlimited risk of this strategy, add a stop loss order to trade if the underlying reaches a certain threshold level representing the maximum loss you are willing to take.** When you set these trades up correctly, you can go years without losing or getting stopped out. You can do these on commodities as well and get nice premiums far out of the money. In fact, call ratio spreads with a net credit are my favorite commodities strategy.

RULE #3: **When doing PUT ratio spreads, do them on stock indexes using optionable ETFs rather than individual stocks.** Put ratio spreads work great as they often provide a reverse implied volatility skew that never seems to disappear. Sell far OTM puts on the index and buy not so far OTM puts on the same. You can often sell the far OTM puts so far out that it would be almost risk free from a probability standpoint, and even more so when using futures on the stock indexes. For example, at some points you can sell out 90 days to expiration a strike price that equates to the Dow Jones Index falling 4,000 points. Can the Dow Jones Average fall 4,000 points in the next 90 days? Technically, yes, but it is extremely unlikely. Sometimes the farther you go out of the money, the more you have to increase your ratio to get the net credit. For example, to go that far OTM for the Dow, you might do a 3:25 ratio spread.

In summary – remember the wide profit zone where all scenarios win below a certain high price is the main benefit for doing call ratio spreads. The best-case scenario on call ratio spreads occurs when the underlying rises slightly but does not reach the short leg.

There you have it- my top six trading strategies for individual investors. These strategies work consistently and offer the best risk to reward ratio for the non-professional trader. As mentioned in Chapter Five, I believe that the best returns are achieved by investors who diversify across these six strategies, as well as across industries. Don't start with more than two strategies. Then work up to all six over time. The mix will change based on your age, risk tolerance, and capital base.

As of 2019, I have the growth portions of my portfolio diversified across the following strategy mix:

Percentage of Portfolio:	Strategy Diversification:
50%	Collars, In the money Covered Calls & Large Unprotected Covered Calls – using Portfolio Margin
20%	Long Calls and Puts – deep in the money (stock replacement) directional trades
10%	Call Debit Spreads (in the money)
5%	Credit Spreads (Bull put spreads or Bear Call spreads or both at the same time, known as Iron Condors)
5%	Directional Butterflies & Skip Strike (Broken Wing) Butterflies
9%	Call Ratio Spreads with a Net Credit (as the market is currently making all-time highs)

NOTE: I also hedge the entire bullish portfolio by buying out of the money put options on the whole market (puts on the S&P 500 index and / or NASDAQ index) with ~1% of your cash.

"Concerning all acts of initiative and creation, there is one elementary truth – that the moment one definitely commits oneself, then providence moves, too."

- Johann Wolfgang Von Goethe

Chapter 7

Trade Selection and the "Greeks"

LEARNING OBJECTIVES

- **Use probabilities for stock & option trade selection**

- **The key option 'Greeks' to check prices**

- **Determine your target exits before entering trades**

- **Trade progression vs. going all in**

- **Pre-trade checklists & order placement enhancers**

"Everything should be made as simple as possible, but not simpler."
- Albert Einstein

We have now learned the six best trading strategies for the non-professional trader to stack the odds in your favor. You have the keys to both the trade mechanics and to the bespoke rules that I have developed over the years to de-risk each of the trading strategies.

This chapter will help you decide when to select each trading strategy at the individual trade level. In addition, this chapter will help you remember all of the key steps from the chapters so far by providing you with a summary of my pre-trade checklists. You should print or copy these and run through each before executing each trade until you are comfortable. Think of these pre-trade checklists to be just like a pilot's pre-flight checklist before takeoff.

After selecting each trade strategy and your outlook for the underlying security, you will then need to quickly choose from among the hundreds of various strike price and expiration date choices available to select the individual trade. While these choices may seem confusing, or even intimidating, this chapter will teach you rules to cut through the clutter. My rules for selecting which strike prices and expiration dates work best, largely center on using statistical probabilities and the option 'Greeks' as shortcuts. Through these tools you can more easily decide which strike prices expiration dates to trade.

Lastly, before putting each trade on, you need to determine your target exit points. Target exits, are specific price points that will trigger your next buy or sell action. The typical actions will be to exit trades or to make trade adjustments. This chapter will help you quickly determine and set your exit target prices (both gains and stop loss prices) before you enter each trade.

Exit targets are part art and part science. There is always a balance between killing off bad trades quickly and letting your winners run while taking some profits along the way. The best way to select target exits is to become familiar with statistical probabilities on strike prices and related options prices.

Use probabilities for trade selection. How to use statistical probabilities and the "Greeks" to select trade strike prices and expiration dates

Once your research has revealed what you believe to be a good trade opportunity, you are faced with several decisions. You will need to choose which expiration date to choose and which strike prices to trade. The most important three rules in selecting which option strike price and expiration date to choose for your trade (from among the hundreds of choices available) is to do so based on:
1. *The current levels of the "Greeks."*
2. *The statistical probabilities of trade success* at trade entry and as the trade progresses
3. *When the next earnings date is coming.* Avoid placing

any short-term trades (less than three months in duration) that cross over the earnings announcement date of the company. Long-term trades are ok to cross over earnings announcement dates.

Let's address each of these three in turn (trade selection using these three rules is the focus of the rest of this chapter):

RULE #1: The first most important rule in selecting which option strike price and expiration date to choose on each trade is to base your selection on using the Greeks.

The key "Greeks" to check and how to use them for trade management

Throughout this book I have alluded to the importance of the option "Greeks." You don't need to know everything that there is to know about the Greeks, but a few essentials are critical to the trading and selection of options.

The reason the Greeks are important is because most of the strategies in the last chapter use the power and leverage of option contracts. Without doing a deep dive on the history of how options are priced, when you understand the basics of options pricing and how the prices change it can help you make improved decisions about which option expiration dates and strike prices to play. You can use a few simple rules about the Greeks as guidelines to trade more effectively.

There are five Greeks in all. The most important of the Greeks for the retail trader are only three of them: delta, theta and vega. You can essentially skip the Greeks called gamma and rho unless you are a professional trader.

> The key Greeks for options trading and why:
> - Delta – Buy high deltas, sell low deltas
> - Vega – Volatility, the key Greek for options
> - Theta – Be like the insurance company – sell time premium

Understanding Delta

The option's delta measures the degree of correlation between the movement of the option price and the price of the underlying stock. In other words, if the underlying stock or ETF moves one dollar, how many cents will the option price move? Delta tells us this. The relationship is strong when the option has a high delta (for each $1 move in the stock, there will be high related move in the price of the option, say 80 cents or 90 cents). The relationship is weak when the option has a low delta and the price of the option won't move very much if the underlying moves up or down by $1 (say 20 cents or 30 cents). In options with high delta, you will sometimes hear the term 'tick for tick' meaning the option price and the underlying are moving in direct proportion. If the stock moves up $1.00, the option price also moves $1.00.

The delta can range from +1.0 (a direct positive relationship between the option price and the stock price) to -1.0 (a direct inverse relationship). Call options will range from +1 to 0. A delta of 0 represents no correlation in the movement in the call option price when the underlying stock moves.

The delta of a put option will range from 0 to -1. A delta of -1 would indicate a direct tick-for-tick relationship with the underlying stock or ETF, while a delta of 0 would indicate no movement in the option price with a move in the underlying. Generally speaking, an option that is at the money will have a delta of approximately 0.5. *How to Use Delta:* So, what do you need to know to use Delta to help you select which options to trade? Remember this rule:

RULE on Delta: ***Buy high Delta options and***
                   Sell low Delta options.

This rule is a variation and the opposite of the old saying of "buy low, sell high" related to stock prices. Keep in mind that option prices are divided into two components. The first piece is the "intrinsic value" or the portion of the option price that is in-the-money and the second piece is the time value (or 'extrinsic' value).

The time value is the portion of the option price left over after subtracting out the intrinsic value. If the option strike price is above the price of the underlying stock, ETF, Index, then there is no intrinsic or real value – the entire price of the option is time value. This is important because when the option gets closer and closer to expiration, the time value can have a negative effect on the delta. This explains why sometimes you will see the price of your option go down even when the price of the underlying stock is rising. A high delta can help keep the option price up near expiration – when you buy options this helps you but when you sell options this hurts you.

Rule #1: **Buy long calls (or puts) with a delta of .80 or higher. Sell options with a low delta of .50 or lower.**
This applies to the stock replacement strategy and all covered calls, collars, debit spreads and credit spread strategies. The exceptions to this rule are:

- The long protective put that we buy to protect the downside on the collar trade (Strategy #2) will have a negative delta (usually -.2 to -.4). This is the insurance leg of the collar trade so this rule does not apply.
- The long call in the call ratio spread (strategy #6) will be at the money or near the money, this delta will be closer to .45 or .50.

Understanding Vega:
Implied volatility and changes to implied volatility are very difficult concepts for non-professional traders to understand. It is critical to master this, as this is the key 'Greek' for selecting most options trades. Vega can make a material difference to your overall trading results. Professional traders focus the vast majority of their attention on volatility.

Volatility is the statistical measure of how erratic a stock or ETF or commodity price has been in the past (historical volatility) and is likely to be in the future (implied volatility). Implied volatility is the key, as it shows the up to the minute mood of the market. The implied volatility gets priced into the option premiums and can make the option premium larger (fat and juicy for selling) or smaller (good for buying). The market makers can change the implied volatility based on the perceived risk of future price movement between now and expiration. Vega increases leading up to major events due to increased uncertainty (earnings announcements, government rulings,

FED interest rate decisions, new product events, etc.). After the event occurs, there is often an implied volatility crush as the unknown event outcome shifts to known outcome.

As a retail trader and investor, we can use implied volatility to our advantage in several ways. It is important in selecting your trade strategy and also selecting the specific strikes of your options. It can easily be looked up in your online options trading platform. For example, credit spreads and other strategies that collect time premium are even more powerful in situations where there is high-implied volatility. Volatility readings and the changes in these readings over time on your basket of stocks, allow you to pinpoint when volatility is cheap and when it is expensive. There are volatility charts for this reason to help you track volatility and its changes. Knowing this allows you to buy and sell options at the most opportune times per the historical average. You can also tell if the option price today is cheap or expensive historically.

> *RULE on Vega:*   *Buy low implied volatility*
> *(options will be less expensive)*
> *Sell high implied volatility*
> *(options will be more expensive)*

A great website to track volatility is www.ivolatility.com. This website plots both the historical and the implied volatility with a 30-day look-back. The historical volatility line and the implied volatility line generally move in tandem, but they do diverge from each other at times. The key is to compare present volatility with the past average to see patterns and opportunities.

You saw the chart below briefly in Chapter Five. This chart helps you decide which trade strategy type to consider placing depending on the current volatility vs. the historical volatility.

Remember that buying long options are positive vega trades. They are hurt by decreases in implied volatility. Selling or shorting options are negative vega trades, meaning they are hurt by increases in implied volatility. Collar and spread trades neutralize vega.

To use this chart, take the highest and lowest readings of implied volatility for a given stock over the past 12-18 months. Then cut these range of implied volatility you found into deciles. The lowest decile should equal the least implied volatility. Finally, plug the results into the following strategy table to help decide which trading strategy to use:

Implied Volatility / Relative Volatility – Trading Strategy Chart

Potential Trading Strategy Decision Matrix												
Strategy:	Potential Profit:	1	2	3	4	5	6	7	8	9	10
Buy (long) Call or Put Options	Unlimited	x	x	x							
Sell Vertical (Credit) Spreads	Limited						x	x	x	x	x
Sell Iron Condors & Butterfly Verticals Spread	Limited							x	x	x	x
Call Ratio Spreads	Limited								x	x	x
Sell Cash Backed Naked Puts	Limited									x	x
Buy Underlying Stock/Sell Call/Buy Put (Collar)	Limited				x	x	x	x			
Sell Covered Calls	Limited								x	x	x

You can also use implied volatility to determine if the option strike price you are considering buying or selling is a good deal. Below are my rules to simplify it:

RULES on Vega:
Buy low implied volatility (under 25% is best, and never buy over 35%). If the implied volatility is over 35, you are paying a large premium for that strike price based on expected volatility.
Sell high implied volatility (minimum of 35% and over 50% is best). If the implied volatility is under 35, you are not getting adequately compensated by collecting enough premium for selling that strike price for your short leg

The VIX Indicator. The gauge of volatility for the S&P500 (US stock market) as a whole is the CBOE Volatility Index (also known as the VIX Indicator). It technically measures the expected volatility in the S&P500 index options in the near term. It has been described as the "Fear gauge" of Wall Street because the VIX typically rises when stocks fall and vice versa. Any VIX reading below 18 is considered low compared to historical averages. A VIX reading over 25, however, is considered high and is an indicator that stocks are correcting and more volatility is expected. In highly volatile markets, as indicated by a high VIX reading, you should sell options with large premiums. In markets with low volatility, you should buy options which will now be priced lower.

Understanding Theta:
Theta refers to the time decay of the option. As you know, options all have a time limit and then they expire. The rate of this price decline in the time value portion of the option price is measured by theta. Theta quantifies the risk of time passing and measures the rate of price decay as time winds towards expiration. Time decay helps you when you sell options and collect the premiums, and it hurts you when you buy options.

> ***Rule on theta: Put time decay on your side by being a seller of options most of the time. The only true exception is the stock replacement strategy (favorite strategy #2).***

As mentioned previously, I love selling covered calls and selling puts and calls as part of spreads. When selling vertical credit spreads such as bull put spreads, iron condors, and bearish call spreads, I recommend selecting strike prices that are one standard deviation out-of-the-money. This is a good rule of thumb to put the odds in your favor. Comparing the probability of winning against the premium being offered, is a good way to balance the risk and reward when selling vertical credit spreads. When you sell options, time decay works in your favor on all strike prices. It works especially well with at-the-money strikes or strikes that are one strike price out of the money.

When you are long calls or puts, theta hurts your position, but it hurts it most in the last two months leading into expiration. The key to keeping time decay from hurting our position too much is to buy enough time in the future to keep the time decay small. This is why you should do the stock replacement / long call strategy with a minimum of four months to expiration. The longer the better, eight or nine months to expiration, is best.

Time decay works to your advantage in covered calls and collar trades as well. When you sell calls against a long stock position, time decay works in your favor.

RULE #2: The second most important rule in selecting which option strike price and expiration date is when the company's next earnings date is scheduled:
Trading over an earnings date is dangerous for short-term trades and especially for options trades. This is because as a small move in the stock produces a magnified move in the options. In choosing which strike prices and expiration dates to trade from the many choices available, it is key to know when the next earnings date for the stock is occurring.

This is important because each of the four quarterly earnings reporting dates can often be the most volatile four days of the year. Major price fluctuations are common right after earnings are announced. Many times, I have been in profitable spread trades that I decided to hold or place over earnings announcements and had a 60% winner turn into a loser five minutes after earnings are announced.

The rule that I now follow is: **For all short-term trades (call ratio spreads, butterflies, debit spreads or credit spreads), avoid trading during earnings.** Make sure that all trades you choose have an expiration date before the week of the earnings announcement.

- The exceptions to this rule are if you have done spreads on an ETF or an index as these are broadly diversified. The earnings announcement of one company will not impact the entire index.
- The other exception is the long call (stock replacement) strategy. This strategy has a four-month to nine-month potential lifespan. By definition, this trade will likely be held over at least one if not two earnings announcements.

RULE #3: Select Option Strike Prices base on the statistical probability of success

The last filter to determine which expiration date and strike price to choose for each trade, is the statistical probability of success. This means the likelihood that the option you are looking at will finish successfully on or before its expiration day. All modern online brokerage software provides full and detailed option price chains. These options chains can provide the statistical probabilities for finishing OTM on all option strike prices, at all expiration dates, for all optionable companies. They are continuously updated as the prices of the underlying security change.

An example of the table of statistical probabilities that will appear in the options chain screen would look like this:

APPLE (ticker: AAPL) JULY 2019 $185 Put	
Current Stock Price: $190.07	
Strike Price Put Option: $185	**Probability of Touching:** 50.22%
Days to Expiration: 90	**Probability of Finishing Below:** 25.64%
Implied Volatility: .214 or 21.4%	**Probability of Finishing Above:** 74.36%

In most online brokerage software, probabilities such as this can be brought up instantly on every strike price for every stock, ETF, or index that has options.

The table shows you all of the following under the "Probabilities" tab:
- Today the underlying stock is Apple (ticker symbol: AAPL)

and it is trading at a share price of $190.07.

- The put option you are looking at has a strike price of $185 and expires in 90 days.
- The statistical probabilities are 74.36% that Apple's stock price will finish above $185 on expiration day.

You can see that if you play this option with a bullish trading strategy, 74.36% of the time you will be correct if you build the trade to win if Apple finishes above $185 based on current prices. The tradeoff you are evaluating when looking at the probability percentages is that in exchange for a higher percentage likelihood of winning, you earn a lower amount of money on the trade. If your likelihood of winning is very high, you are collecting a much lower amount of money. This means the higher the likelihood of winning, the more money you are risking. The conclusion and the 'art' of trading is that you must strike a balance between the likelihood of winning and the risk.

I have known traders who follow the exclusive strategy of selling vertical credit spreads two standard deviations out of the money, representing a 95% chance that they will win on every trade. While this high winning percentage is great, they only collect very small net credit amounts on each trade because they are so far out of the money. It is very easy to determine the strike prices to sell to have a 95% chance of winning using the probability table in the option chain above. The problem with this strategy is that you end up risking roughly $1,000 for every $100 you make in profit – you are risking ten dollars for the chance to make just one dollar. That's not a good risk to reward ratio. It is true that you will win the $100 in profit on each trade,95% of the time. The problem is that one time you don't, you lose $1,000 and wipe out the profit from ten winning trades. It's not worth it in the long run unless you are very good at trade adjustments (see Chapter Eight for trade adjustments by strategy).

The probability table also shows the implied volatility. We discussed this earlier in the chapter when we discussed VEGA and the VIX volatility index. It is worth repeating here, that to put the statistical probabilities on your side when selling options, make sure the option premium is juicy enough to warrant taking the risk on the trade. Conversely, when you are buying an option, check the implied volatility to make sure you are not overpaying for the option premium. Every trader has only a limited capital budget, and it is important to allocate your capital to the trades that generate the most premium on a risk-adjusted basis. We will look further into measuring the changes to implied volatility in the next section under the Greeks.

My Trade Rules – for the best statistical probability of success:

To stack the statistical odds in your favor when trading, follow these rules:

- **For collar and covered call trades, first select the stock you believe will rise moderately. Second, select a call contract to sell that has a large amount of time premium.** The time premium is what you will keep as profit for selling the call options (if the underlying rises in price as expected). Therefore, implied volatility levels above .30 (or 30%) or .35 are best. This is more important than the statistical probability of the stock price finishing above the option strike price. For maximum profit in these trades, you want the stock to be called away from you. Make sure the statistical probability that the underlying stock price will finish above today's stock price is more than 50%.

- **For deep in the money long call (stock replacement) trades, select call contracts with an 80% + likelihood of the underlying security price finishing above the option strike price you buy.** You should buy options with a delta above 80.

- **For call debit spreads, just like covered calls and collars above, the delta is the most important selection criteria. Select an in the money long call with a delta of at least .70 and a short call with a Delta of .40-.50.** These will give you the best statistical probability of winning.

- **For vertical credit spread trades (bull put spreads, bear call spreads and iron condors), use approximately one**

standard deviation out of the money strike prices for trades with a high probability of success. You do not need to calculate the standard deviation. Pull up the options chain and look at the out of the money put contracts, select the strike price closest to where the option chain shows that there is a 68% or 70% chance that the underlying stock price will finish above that strike price at expiration. Close enough. For call contracts, select the out of the money strike price showing a 68% chance of the underlying stock price, finishing below at expiration. You can get the standard deviations for free on www.stockcharts.com. This rule will give you approximately a 70% chance of winning on each trade. You should go out in time between three to eight weeks to expiration to make sure that the premiums work this far away from the current price. If the option premiums for the trade you are considering are too small at that timeframe, then go out further in time until they do, or until you determine that doing the trade doesn't make sense.

- **Directional butterflies and skip-strike butterflies will have lower probabilities of winning but they pay off significantly when they do. Try to target the short leg of the butterfly at a strike price with a statistical probability of as close to 40% as possible.** The minimum percentage chance of success that you should look for in a directional or skip strike butterfly is 33%. This means that there is a one-third chance that the underlying stock price will finish above the strike price of the options you are selling. Any further out and the likelihood becomes low that the underlying will move that far by expiration. With butterflies, you should not be as concerned with the likelihood of the underlying stock finishing above the short strike price as you are trying to pinpoint the exact finishing price at expiration. You want the underlying to move towards your target strike price even if it does so well before expiration, so that you can lock in large portions of the total potential profit early.

- **For call ratio spreads with a net credit, target a 9% to13% likelihood of finishing in the money.** The key aspect of this strategy is the risk leg of the trade. This is the out of the money calls that are sold vs. the calls we buy that are at or near the money. Try to sell far out of the money calls with a low probability of finishing in the money, yet ones that still produce enough in premiums to produce a net credit on the whole trade. Typically, in a 2:1 ratio call spread where you seek to produce a net credit at trade entry, you would sell far out of the money calls with between a 10% and a 15% likelihood of finishing in the money. On a 3:1 ratio spread, you would sell out of the money calls with between a 9% and a 13% likelihood of finishing in the money. The chance of finishing in the money is a low probability event, but if it does occur, you will have a large loss on the trade. Aim for 9% to 13%.

Determine your target exits before entering trades
Knowing when to sell your positions before you enter the trade is critical. I have heard is described as 'know your exit before you go through the entrance.' I like that description.

Exiting trades at the optimum time is critical for your long-term success (especially in the BOOST portion of your portfolio) and is one of the most perplexing decisions for most investors. Your profit is determined when you get out of a trade, not when you enter it.

The guide to knowing when to get out of a trade are as follows:
- Determine your target exit prices before you place the trade. Do this on the upside, so that you know when to take profits, and also do so on the downside (the stop-loss) so that you know when to cut a losing trade.
- Scale in and out of trades. You should only exit a trade all at once if it has less than four weeks to expiration.

Writing down your exit points (both winning and losing) beforehand is a key discipline that you need to practice. This means determining both the stop-loss price target on the downside and the target profit price on the upside.

Use these guidelines for determining your target trade exits:

- **Enter the trade correctly using high probability trade strategies and at favorable prices that put the statistical percentages in your favor.**

- **Exit the position if the reasons why you entered the trade have changed.** If the circumstances around the company and the bullish story about the new products, services, management or whatever reason you liked it have changed, get out. Examples are wide and varied, such as a negative corporate development or an unfavorable news item, etc. A good rule of thumb to follow is: If you would not buy the company and put on a bullish trade today, then adjust the trade or sell it now.

- **Set target profits using a sliding scale that factors in your target profit and time to expiration.** The table on the next page illustrates when to get out and what scale-out points are acceptable. Remember these are guidelines – not hard and fast rules. This is where the art and science of options trading come together.

		Time to Expiration (abbreviated as "exp")					
	Cash on Cash Profit (or) % of Max Profit Achieved so far:	60% of time to exp. (or more)	50% of time to exp.	40% of time to exp.	30% of time to exp.	20% of time to exp.	10% of time to exp. (or less)
PROFIT	40%	X (see Example #2 on the next page. Exit 1)					
	50%	X	X (see Example #1 below. Exit 1)				
	60%	X	X	X			(Example #3, Exit 2)
	70%	X	X	X (see Example #2 on the next page. Exit 2)	X		
	80%	X	X	X	X (See Example #3, Exit 1)	X (Example #1, Exit 2)	
	90%	X	X	X	X	X	X (Example #2. Exit 3)

You can use this chart as a guideline to scale out of profitable trades. Interpret the graph is by being aware that:

- Option prices move quickly and exponentially compared to the moves of the underlying stock. Overnight, option position can go from losing 10%, to an 80% gain. Rapid price changes and the fact that you scale out of winners across several exit prices leads you to utilize multiple exit points in relation to time.
- The "X's" means that these are all acceptable exit points for different trades under different scenarios.

Example #1: You have sold options in a vertical credit spread trade strategy. Both legs of the trade will expire in five weeks. The short leg of the spread represents your risk on the trade. As the time premium erodes in your favor, two and a half weeks into the trade you notice you have an unrealized gain of 55% of the maximum possible profit with 50% of the time left in the trade.

- Per the chart: trigger exit #1: Sell $\frac{3}{4}^{th}$ of the position and let the other $\frac{1}{4}^{th}$ run.
- Later in the trade, with 20% of the time remaining, you notice you have achieved 80% of the maximum possible profit. Per the chart, take Exit #2 and close out the rest of the trade.

Note: If none of the "X" in the chart are triggered and the trade is not triggering a loss, keep the full position on. Allow time decay to have a chance to work in your favor.

Example #2: You have placed a deep in the money long call (stock replacement) trade expiring in six months. After only three weeks in the trade, the underlying stock makes a rapid move higher causing the call options to jump to a 40% cash-on-cash unrealized profit. You should convert the trade to a market neutral strangle by buying short term at-the-money puts and by doing so set a floor under the profit. Alternately, you could:

- Exit #1: Sell to Close half of the position at a 40% profit and let the rest run.
- Exit #2: Since exit #1 hit so quickly, if the underlying security keeps rising, sell another 30% of the position when

the cash on cash profit hits 70%.

- Exit #3: When cash on cash profit hits 90%, even if less than 10% of the time remains, sell all but one contract. Let the final contract run for the chance of a homerun.

Example #3: You have placed a directional butterfly trade expiring in six weeks. You anticipate a $6 up move on the underlying and set your short leg at that strike price. The maximum possible profit on this trade is $3,750. The underlying stock begins to move up $4 from where it was when you placed the trade. Four weeks into the trade, you have an unrealized gain of 75% of the maximum possible profit with 30% of the time left in the trade.

- Exit #1: Buy to close 75% of the position in order to lock in the majority of the profit. Let the rest run.
- Exit #2: With three days to expiration, the underlying stock starts to move away from your target price and triggers a loss. Close out the remaining 25% on the short leg only which brings your total gain on the trade from 75% of the max to 60% of the max and you have closed out of all risk. Let the long calls run as a lottery ticket for the chance of a homerun.

- **Cut losses at 8% to10% or less on long stock purchases and 25% to 30% or less on long option positions.** Set your loss exits up front using these percentages as guidelines and stick with them. If you are doing the collar trade, you will automatically set your stop when you place the protective put leg of the collar. Sticking to your loss target exit percentages is difficult but it is critical to preserve your capital base and enhance your gains.

- **Some take the emotional exit price target. Close out part of a trade when you would be happy right now with taking most of the profit and letting the rest run.** Take this example:

You are 75% invested and have 25% of your portfolio in cash awaiting new opportunities. You think the market is a little turbulent and the high amount you have at risk makes you nervous. You think it might make sense to reduce your exposure. You scan your positions and see no obvious candidates to sell. You notice that one trade has an unrealized profit of $1,000 on $5,000 at risk (for a 20% cash on cash unrealized profit). There is still twelve weeks of time remaining on the trade until expiration. You realize that you have earned $1,000 in the eight days that you have had this trade on. You are happy with that return, because you don't trust this market in the short term. You decide to close out 80% of the position for an $800 profit and let 20% run.

CONCLUSION: You should never be hesitant to take profits, reduce your exposure and lighten up your portfolio.

It is very important to track your trades on a spreadsheet. Include one column for your target profit exits points and another on your loss exit targets. Over time you will place many trades and you may lose track of them if you do not write down your profit and loss target exit prices.

A written tracking system, with target exit prices written down, also provides the discipline to trigger you to act when your emotions will be telling you otherwise. Writing down your target entry and exit points also serves as an invaluable written trade diary that can help you reflect on and improve your trading when you make mistakes and don't honor your trade exits.

Use a strategy of Trade Progression vs. Going All-In with One Strategy
Some of my clients ask me, 'why not keep this simple and only trade one strategy for the BOOST portion of the portfolio?'

In my experience, analyzing thousands of my past trades, indicates that diversification across a minimum of three trading strategies (with equal size trade amounts) achieves better results than only trading one strategy. Trading 3three to four or more of the strategies helps achieve higher overall portfolio gains. I found that it is not best to just select one trading strategy that you feel most comfortable with and only trade that one. Once you feel proficient, however, it is best to diversify across at least three of the six trading strategies covered in Chapter Six.

Over the years, I have tested this "one versus many" trading strategies many times. I ran tests to see if my results improved by using just one trading strategy. I found that my overall results improved by at least 5% annually when I diversified across at least three trading strategies and traded them simultaneously as opposed to trading only one strategy. I concluded that it is best to diversify across strategies. This led me to experiment with various trade strategy combinations as well as the progression of my trades to fine-tune my results for optimum performance.

After you have determined your percentage mix across the low risk and high-risk strategies, there still remains the issue of creating a plan for trade progression. In other words, in *what order* do you put on the trades and what do you do after the outcome of the trade is known?

Here are my favorite trade progression strategies:

TRADE PROGRESSION Example#1: When you are bullish on an individual stock and the overall industry sector and the overall market in the short term (next six months or less):
- First trade: Sell out of the money, cash backed puts (or a put credit spread as taught in CH. 6, selling the short put at the strike price you want to buy the stock). Collect this premium every four weeks or so until the shares get put to you or your outlook on the stock or market changes. You can repeat this process again and again. When the current options expire, just sell new puts at a strike price you are comfortable buying the stock for the next four-to-five-week time period.
- Second Trade: if the shares of stock get put to you, you will be forced to buy the stock (this will happen automatically and is why we do these cash backed, so you have the money to buy the stock on hold for when the shares get put to you).
- Third Trade: Collar the stock by buying protective puts with three to four months to expiration. Select a strike price that is ~10% below the current stock price. Buy enough contracts to fully cover the number of shares that were put to you. After you have purchased the protective puts, complete the

collar by selling covered calls that expire in three to five weeks. Select a strike price that out of the money (generally up $2-$5 above today's stock price).

- Fourth Trade: keep selling the covered calls with expiration dates out three to five weeks until you called out of the stock.
- Fifth Trade: if the stock rises above the strike price in the calls you sell, the stock will automatically be called away from you. If this occurs, check if any value remains in the protective puts you owned. If they have not gone to zero, then sell those puts after your stock shares are called away from (automatically sold from) you.
- Sixth trade: Repeat your research on the same stock to confirm if your original view still applies in the current market conditions. If you are still bullish, sell again the naked puts and start the cycle over.

TRADE PROGRESSION Example #2: When you are bullish on a stock over the longer term (nine months or more)

- First trade: Stock replacement – meaning that you buy deep in the money long calls (with nine to twelve months until expiration).
- Second trade: once the trade has increased in value, buy an equal number of long put contracts on the same underlying with expiration on the same day as the long calls position. Do this second trade at-the-money to set a floor and lock in the gains achieved so far while allowing the upside in the long calls to continue.
- Third Trade: If the original trade achieves gains of 100%, then sell half of the calls. Do not sell the long puts you bought for protection. Now they will double in size, which is ok if the stock reverses direction.
- Fourth Trade: If stock reverses meaningfully, sell 50% of the long puts you bought.
- Fifth Trade: if the bullish trend continues and the original calls from the first trade have gained 200%, sell another 30% and leave 20% of the original trade open.
- Sixth Trade: unwind each remaining side (the remaining 20% of calls or the 100% of puts) as the market oscillates in the final few weeks or months into expiration.

TRADE PROGRESSION Example #3: When you are Bearish on the stock:

- First trade: Sell an out of the money put credit spread (known as a bull put spread) and collect the net credit amount in your account. Aim for a 40%-50% return (cash on cash) for a good risk to reward trade with an expiration date three to four weeks in the future (the shorter the better for achieving the target return).

- Second trade: If you are wrong and the underlying stock falls slightly in price, then sell an out of the money bear call spread (turning the trade into what is known as an iron condor). You now have two trades on (or a four-legged trade, or iron condor).

- Third Trade: If the stock price then holds in the channel between the bear call spread and the bull put spread (which is what you want) let both spreads expire worthless and keep both premiums.

- Fourth trade: If you put on the iron condor and the stock falls (and you are comfortable buying the stock at the strike price you sold as part of the bull put spread) allow the stock to be put to you at expiration and then begin a new trade progression by collaring it.

You can easily create your own trade progression strategies in addition to using these. The key is to use the fundamentals and to form a directional view on the stock. Then just start with your favorite bullish or bearish strategy in the given market conditions as indicted by your worldview and other homework. Think through the trade outcome possibilities. Lastly, think through the best choices for placing a second trade based on the outcome of the first trade. Repeat this for the outcomes of the second trade and into the third and future trades.

Pre-trade Checklists & Order Placement Enhancers

Are you now all set to begin trading? Sadly, no. One last pre-trade discipline is needed. As an airplane pilot has the final steps before take-off, I have created the equivalent for trading, the pre-trade checklist. It is a final set of checks you need to make before deploying capital.

Experience has taught me that having the discipline to do these 'final checks,' even when I think I don't need to, adds 5% or more per year to my overall returns. It does so by preventing me from impulsively jumping into trades. These final checks should be done just before you make each trade. The good news is that after you have been through the checklist a few times, these final checks can be done in just a few minutes. Many of the steps are the same for all trading strategies.

Below is my set of general pre-trade checklists for all strategies and trade entries, followed by a few additional pre-trade checks specific to which one of the six trading strategies taught in this book. Many steps are simply double checks of pre-trade homework to ensure you have done your fundamental and technical analysis steps. If you have, they can be checked off in seconds. They follow a top down approach of checking the overall market, then the industry sector, and finally the stock itself.

GENERAL PRE-TRADE CHECKLISTS - ALL TRADE STRATEGIES

STEPS:	Notes & ✅ :
#1 Re-verify the direction of the overall market cycle – is it bullish, bearish or consolidating? Remember that 70% of individual stocks move in the same direction as the overall market cycle. The specific two checks you can do are *1)* Check the front page of IBD (Investor's Business Daily) to confirm the market trend such as "Market in Confirmed Uptrend," etc.). Pay attention to changes in the IBD Market cycle ratings (especially if the sentiment changes by two or more grades) – this indicates a significant reversal in the market cycle. You don't want to go against this move.	

Check the S&P 500 index, the Dow & the NASDAQ.

2)   Check the opening 30 minutes of the market and watch the four major averages (the S&P 500, Dow, Nasdaq & Russell 2000). If they are all up as well and the IBD is bullish, it's a green light to buy.

#2 Ensure you have checked today's headlines and built your top down macro worldview. Re-confirm your summary of your overall world view and current macro political risk events as well as the headlines on the stock you are about to buy or sell. Check Yahoo Finance & IBD online for headlines on your stock. Also check Briefing.com to build out the calendar of upcoming newsworthy events on each of my top 10 positions. It will show things like upcoming analyst events, FED meetings, key industry conferences, and product events. All of these can have an impact.

#3 Verify that your stock is in the top ranked (or bottom ranked if you are bearish) Industry Sectors – preferably in the top 10 and bottom 10. At least 30% to 40% of individual stocks move with their industry sector. Also check Briefing.com and check the earnings calendar, the sector ratings & news on the stock.

#4 Check the Greeks to determine which strike prices to select for your trade so you are choosing high probability trades. Select trades with at least 70% chance of winning. Check the delta and choose very low deltas when selling puts or calls.

Check very high deltas on ITM calls / puts if intending to buy as these have the best chance of winning and finishing OTM.	
#5 Final check of the stocks chart for entry points. Perform a final check of the moving averages, the Ichimoku Cloud (green cloud / stock price is well above the cloud), upward sloping OBV line for bullish trades to confirm the trend & where within the Keltner channels the stock price is trading. From your earlier Technical analysis you should know where the price of your intended buy or sell is in relation to the cloud, OBV and Keltner Channels but give each a 30 second double check as many hours may have passed since you last checked it to ensure stock is well above the cloud. Make sure all are green for entry point on the trade. Also do a final check of the exponential moving averages to ensure that the 50-day Exp. Moving average is above the 100 day (and check if there is a recent cross-over). Find the resistance line / open interest below the current price and place trade just under that.	
#6 Final check of your fundamental analysis and the IBD Stock Checkup screener. Recheck your last fundamental analysis results and update the key ratios and numbers. Ensure the story has not changed). Also ensure a 90 or above rating for buys / bullish trades (97-99 is ideal) or below 40 for bearish trades according to the IBD Stock Checkup rating system.	
#7 Final check of the current trade volume on the underlying stock vs. the daily average trading volume. See if the	

volume is abnormal for the day and if so, check the trend with the high volume. Remember the volume column means the # of contracts that have traded today. Open interest means that the current number of contracts that are open positions. It is updated at the end of each day.	

<u>**Additional Checks for Individual Strategies:**</u>

<u>*STRATEGY #1: Collars, Covered Calls, Large Unprotected Covered Calls:*</u>

* Check all of the General Pre-Trade Checklist Steps and then add these:

Action Item:	Today's Pre-trade Result:	✔
1. Check that the premiums work. On the collar trade, select protective puts with a strike price down approximately 10% below today's stock price. Evaluate and select the puts that are not too expensive relative to the calls you will sell and collect premiums on. On the call portion of the trade, ensure the in-the-money calls you want to sell **have good time premium** in the price. Ensure that the OTM collar trade calls sold have good premium relative to the cost of the longer-term puts, etc.		☐
2. Check that you are not trading over earnings week.		☐

3. Verify the stock pays a high dividend if possible. A forward annual dividend yield of < 2.0% and closer to 3%+ is best.		☐
4. Verify the combination of buying the stock and writing the covered calls against these shares together does not take up more than 5% of your total portfolio		☐
5. Are you using portfolio margin on this trade? If yes – use large expensive stocks If no – lower cost stocks in the $10-$35 range		☐

STRATEGY #2: Stock Replacement – Buy Deep in the money Long Calls

* Check all of the General Pre-Trade Checklist Steps and then add the following:

Action Item:	Today's Pre-trade Result:	✔
1. Re-check that the stock is **in your 'basket of stocks'** & that it is highly ranked.		☐
2. **Check the last Earnings' date** & last four quarters price action in the run up to earnings dates.		☐

3. **Recheck the key 200trike200al:** - The Ichimoku Cloud and ensure the current price is well above the cloud and the cloud is green and strong uptrend - The OBV line is upward sloping - The Moving Averages (ensure the 50-day EMA is above the 100 day and 200-day EMA) - & look for crossovers. - The MACD is in bullish crossover.		☐
4. Check for high probability trades using the Greeks. **Choose very high deltas (80%+ is ideal)** as these give the best chance of winning and finishing OTM (to keep the premium collected).		☐
5. **Select the expiration month (out four to nine months)** based on your fundamental analysis and when you expect a large move to happen. When in doubt – buy more time.		☐
6. **Check if the price is at or near the 52-week high** (if so, this is very bullish).		☐
7. **Set the stop loss exit trade at 25% - 30% below the cost** on a cash on cash basis. Keep this trade open "Good Until Cancelled."		☐

STRATEGY #3: Call Debit Spread (Bull Call Spreads):

* Check all of the General Pre-Trade Checklist Steps and then add these:

Action Item:	Today's Pre-trade Result:	✔
1. Check that **the Delta's** of the Call debit spread are **at least .70-.85 for the long call leg and between .40 and .50 for the short call leg**.		
2. **Check that the time to expiration is out between two and four months.** Three is perfect. This timing greatly increases the premiums collected, while reducing the chance of losing trades.		
3. **Use mid-priced stocks or ETFs.** Higher than $125 a share stocks work well but not as well as mid-priced stocks. Ideal range is $25-$100.		
4. **Evaluate bullish conviction.** Do Bull Call Spreads one standard deviation in the money for extra safety if not confident of a bullish move. If		

the trade is done ITM, ensure the call premium has good amount of time premium in the price.		

STRATEGY #4: Vertical Credit Spreads:

* Check all of the General Pre-Trade Checklist Steps and then add these.

Action Item:	Today's Pre-trade Result:	✔
1. **Check the last earnings' date & last four quarters price action in the run up to earnings dates.**		
2. **Check for high probability trades using the Greeks.** Choose very low deltas (8-15 is ideal) and high probability 68%+ winning trades as these give the best chance of winning and finishing OTM, allowing you to keep the premium collected.		
3. **Trade short leg below the current downward support line (when possible)** so there is a lot of buying pressure above the short strike sold. This defends the trade.		
4. **Ensure a minimum net credit of 75 cents per contract** (meaning the credit for the short leg		

minus what we have to pay for the long protection leg, yields at least a 75-cent net credit to us).		
5. **Check if the price is near or at the 52-week high** (if yes, this is very bullish)		☐
6. **Use a Limit Credit order upon entry** to ensure you get the target net credit you want.		☐
7. After the trade is filled, remember to **use sell stops** to determine your exit point.		☐

STRATEGY #5: Directional Butterflies and Skip strike Butterflies:

* Check all of the General Pre-Trade Checklist Steps and then add these:

Action Item:	Today's Pre-trade Result:	✔
1. Check that the broken wing **(skip strike) butterfly is established for a net credit** (or at least no more than a 20-cent net debit).		☐
2. Check that the **Directional Butterfly** is established for a **net debit of no more than 50 cents** (closer to 20 to 25 cents is better and can be found frequently).		☐

STRATEGY #6: Call Ratio Spreads with a Net Credit:

* Check all of the General Pre-Trade Checklist Steps and then add these:

Action Item:	Today's Pre-trade Result:	✔
1. **Check if you are doing this trade on an ETF. If on an individual stock, verify that the stock being used is not too volatile.** Do not do this strategy on a highly volatile stock.		☐

2.	Check that **the trade is not being done over an earnings week**. An earnings announcement with a large upward stock price move can hurt this strategy badly. Ensure the earnings announcement does not happen during the life of this trade.	
3.	Select **wide spreads between the strike prices you buy and sell.** This minimizes the risk of the underlying security moving through your short leg and causing losses.	
4.	**Add a far out-of-the money stop out leg for protection**. Due to the unlimited risk on this trading strategy if there is a large unexpected move to the upside, add a stop out call option for protection if the underlying stock reaches a certain threshold level representing the max loss you are willing to take.	

"If I had eight hours to cut down a tree, I'd spend six sharpening my axe."

- Abraham Lincoln

Chapter 8

Trade Adjustments – What to Do When Trades Go Wrong

LEARNING OBJECTIVES

- How to decide if & when to adjust a losing trade position

- Executing trade adjustments – what to do when things go wrong on a trade

- Additional rules for handling losses & trades that go against you

"Strength does not come from winning. Your struggles develop your strengths. When you go through hardships and decide not to surrender, that is strength."
- Arnold Schwarzenegger

No one likes losing money. The reality of trading and investing is that losses will happen regularly. This is normal and needs to be expected. This chapter is about what to do when losing trades occur. The set of skills, decisions and techniques necessary to manage poorly performing trades is called *trade adjustments or managing trade losses*. It is critical to long-term success for all traders to be able to manage and handle losses emotionally.

Despite everything you have learned in this book, some trades will simply go against you. Whether you place directional or non-direction trades, you will be wrong on occasion. You will lose more often than people expect when they begin managing their own money. At times, the markets can seem cruel, irrational and like they are out to get you. An old saying in trading is that there are a thousand reasons to get into a trade, but once you are in and your money is on the line, none of those reasons matters anymore. Once in, long term success is all about how you manage losing trades emotionally and sometimes with actions.

Winning trades are easy for even beginning investors to watch, monitor and exit. However, losing trades will handcuff most inexperienced traders. You *will* feel fear and frustration when you are wrong. We all do. The pain of such unexpected losses causes the majority of new traders to quit and just go back to buying and holding mutual funds and indexes.

The good news is that all is not lost when you are facing your inevitable losing trades. The fact is that the most consistent winning traders and long-term investors don't just pick the right stocks and trades at an above average rate (using high probability trades and the 'Greeks' – both taught in this chapter). In addition, consistent traders know how to manage and adjust their loosing positions. The best hedge funds and professional traders do this very well. The key for you is to have an investment strategy where a substantial number of losing trades are assumed and built into the system and it is still successful! Combine this with the know-how to adjust some losing trades into winners and your chances for overall portfolio success increases greatly.

The best traders tend to outperform their peers, year in and year out. How do they do this? Admittedly, some of these men and women are geniuses at stock selection and reading company news and trends. I have observed that much of what they are doing, however, is knowing how to manage trades that go against them. Trade management skills are rule based and can be learned. With options, many low-cost trading adjustments are possible and can be placed while your original trade is still active. Trade adjustments, placed at key moments in a trade's lifespan, can help turn losing trades into potential winners.

You can radically change the probabilities on the outcome of your trades after they are placed through adding adjustment trades.

This chapter will teach you how to do it.

I know of very few other bets in life where this is true. In most other fields, when you are wrong there are severe consequences. If you don't know how to risk manage your portfolio and adjust losing trades, this can be true for stock & option trading as well.

How to decide if and when to adjust a losing trade position

It is important to point out that the whole subject of "trade adjustments" is a controversial one. Adjusting losing trades is not universally agreed on as a good thing to do by professional money managers and traders. Many professional traders do not believe in making trade adjustments at all. Those in this 'never do trade adjustments' camp will argue that trade adjustments are just a reluctance to admit when you are wrong. Basically, a form of denial of the facts. Even worse, sometimes your losses are magnified when you spend additional money on trade adjustments and they fail to save the trade. Sometimes you even spend money adjusting a trade and then the underlying reverses and your original trade would have won anyway. Critics of trade adjustments will argue that when trade adjustments fail, now you are out the original trade loss plus the additional cost of the adjustment trades. They feel that it is better to never adjust, just accept your losses quickly and move on.

I respect this view, especially if you like simple trading strategies. Adding trade adjustments does add some complexity to an existing trade (as it typically adds a new options leg to the existing trade strategy). If you fall into this never adjust camp, it is a legitimate viewpoint. You can just accept your losing trades, cut your losses quickly and skip this chapter. However, if you want to make the most money possible, give this chapter a chance.

My own trading has improved through trade adjustments. I still lose on some trades (even those that I try to adjust), but approximately one-third of my losing trades turn into winners at trade closure through the adjustment trades taught in this chapter.

Before we get into trade adjustments, there is one caveat. Although I do not place many very short-term trades (one to three weeks to expiration), when I do, I do not typically adjust these. If a short-term trade goes against me, I will just close it out for as small a loss as possible and move on. Alternately, if my view of the underlying is intact but my timing was wrong, I will 'roll out' the losing trade to add additional time for it to work. Rolling out means to complete a buy back of the existing option position, which creates a temporary loss. Then immediately resell out longer dated strike prices on the same underlying security (normally at the same or nearly the same strike prices) which credits back the amount in the loss plus a new fresh profit.

Rolling out losing positions is one type of trade adjustment. Most trade adjustments in this chapter are designed for trades with more than four weeks left to expiration.

How do you decide if you should do a trade adjustment on a specific trade? The way to decide if a trade should be adjusted is if both of the following are true:
- The active trade still has adequate time until expiration, preferably a month or more, and
- The cost to benefit of adding an adjusting trade makes sense. If you have to spend more than 40% of the total possible profit to make the adjustment, it tends to not be worthwhile. This is a judgment call that you will need to make. Not an exact science.

Example #1: You have bought a long call position on a stock. It has two months of time remaining and the maximum you can lose on the trade is the $1,160 debit that you paid for the call options. Would adding an adjustment trade that costs $500 make sense to place (the mechanics of which you will learn in the next section)? The decision is up to you but I would tend to not make that adjustment. It costs too much compared to the potential benefit. With two months or more of time remaining, you could typically close this trade out for less than a 50% loss and rollout to potentially gain your loss back and gaining much more time for the trade to work. This assumes, of course that nothing fundamentally has changed with the company and the underlying bullish story.

Example #2: You are in a $5 wide vertical credit spread that expires in 57 days. It is losing. You originally risked a $3,000 maximum loss to potentially make a maximum gain of $2,000 over the 75-day life of the trade. As you are losing on the trade, you investigate potential trade adjustments. You find that you can add an adjustment trade which costs $330 but would increase your odds of winning from the current 31% to 75%. Would it make sense to place the adjustment? In this scenario, I would spend the $330 and make the trade adjustment.

Keep in mind that any trade adjustment that you decide to place will remove some of the risk from the trade in one particular direction but often it can add additional risk in the other direction. This factors into your thinking before you make the trade adjustment. Trade adjustments typically cost some money (though usually only a few hundred dollars). Because you are spending money, it will limit total potential gains on the original trade.

Executing Trade Adjustments – what to do when things go wrong on an individual trade

A trade adjustment typically means adding a new small trade, such as buying a few options contracts or adding a spread on the same underlying stock, that alters the probability that your original trade will move back in your favor. Typically, a trade adjustment costs money in the form of a net debit but has only the risk of what was spent on it to add to the maximum risk (maximum potential loss). The most effective defensive adjustments vary in their mechanics by trading strategy.

You should build in the trade adjustment into the downside price target at that time. You should not wait until you are feeling the panic of a losing trade to try to figure out your potential trade adjustments. It is easy to be tempted to take immediate action in reaction to a temporarily losing trade. When emotions run high is the wrong time to be making a trade adjustment. If you've planned out an adjustment in advance, that is the time to adjust – mechanically and at pre-determined trigger prices. This takes the emotion out of the decision. It is then simply a formula; if 'X' happens, I will adjust to 'Y.' Regardless of which initial trading strategy you initially used, it is important to keep one rule in mind:

RULE #1: *Keep your trade adjustments simple and don't overtrade.*

Some investors who learn how to do trade adjustments get "adjustment fever" and begin to change all of their losing trades every day or two in response to fluctuations of the market. Don't do this. Rapid fire trading adjustments will hurt you over time through multiple transaction costs, price slippage between the bid and ask prices and commissions. Don't add "death by a thousand cuts" to a trade that is already losing.

RULE #2: *Keep you've trade position sizes conservative for your account size.*

By properly sizing your trades in the first place, you should be able to sustain the loss from a few losing trades without serious damage to your overall portfolio. When trades are properly sized, you can make one or two trade adjustments without significant risk or financial impact. A good rule of thumb is also that when in doubt, don't place the trade adjustment.

My favorite trade adjustments for each of the six trading strategies taught in Chapter Six.

1. **Trade adjustments for losing covered calls & collar trades**

Covered calls (and protected covered calls in the form of a collar trade) are one of the most flexible trading strategies there is. There are endless potential trade adjustments on covered calls. This is part of the reason they are so powerful for all investors.

I will cover my favorite covered all trade adjustments here. Throughout this section I will just discuss covered calls, but you can assume that all of these adjustments also work for collars.

My Favorite covered call adjustment: Early roll out and down one strike price:

The way a covered call or collar trade loses is if the underlying stock declines in price. You have already purchased this stock and sold calls against it. The sold calls are your only downside protection in a covered call. Often if the underlying falls in price, it will fall by more than the amount you collected in selling the covered calls. While you always get to keep that premium from selling the original call(s), once the underlying falls further than that, you are in a losing situation.

- If I feel that decline in price of the underlying is just temporary, and not based on fundamentals, I will do nothing and ride it out.
- More likely, however, if I now believe the underlying stock price will stay down and flounder a bit and have trouble rising dramatically, I go shopping for an early roll-out. What do I mean by this?

Rolling out a covered call, simply means buying back in the marketplace an equivalent number / strike price / and expiration date of the existing short calls that I have previously sold that are due to expire soon. This creates a temporary loss but don't worry we will get it all back in the roll-out trade. I then immediately sell an equal number of the same calls on the same underlying security out in time. This effectively resets the covered call position but at a new expiration date (a date longer out into the future). For more advanced traders – you can do this in one trade ticket. When you do this, use a spread order that executes both trades at the same time. A spread order will tend to get better pricing fills on both the sell to close and the buy to open orders. This can save you hundreds of dollars in execution slippage per year.

Now that you know what rolling out is, let's show you how I like to do trade adjustments early on loosing covered calls.

Example of a covered call ('roll-out') trade adjustment:

ORIGINAL TRADE: On May 7th, you bought 500 shares of XYZ stock on margin. The stock price at that time was $18.75 and you felt it would rise moderately over the next four months. This cost on 50% margin (500 shares at $9.38 on margin) was $4,687.50. You also sold slightly out of the money covered-calls. Specifically, you sold five contracts of the June expiration calls with a $20 strike price and collected 95 cents (multiplied by 500 shares) equals a $475 credit.

It is now June 1st and the underlying stock has not risen in price as hoped. It has now fallen to $17 and you now believe it will stay there for a while. You are confident that the underlying stock will not rise above $20 before the third Friday in June expiration date. It is time to adjust this trade and go shopping for an early buy back and rollout.

Trade Adjustment: You look at the July strike prices on the same underlying security and find:
- The July $20.00 strike price calls are bid $.50 and ask $.60, and:
- The July $17.50 strike price calls are bid $1.50 and ask $1.60 (because on June 1, there are still seven weeks to expiration on the July calls, so there is more value in these than the June calls with three weeks to expiration).

Go for the $17.50 strike price as it is more cash rich (despite the lower strike price). This would be the 'roll-down' part of this trade adjustment and moving the trade out to July is the 'rollout' part in this trade adjustment. In this scenario, I would immediately buy back the June $20 calls (now priced at say 30 cents) and sell an equal number (five contracts) of the July $17.50 strike price calls for say $1.55.

What is the cash flow? You keep both the $475 you collected for selling the June $20 calls (less the $150 amount to buy them back) and you also have now collected another $775 for the July 17.50 strike price calls. For total premiums of $1,100 (minus commissions) on your cash on cash outlay of $4,687.50 spent on the stock.

What can happen now? Three outcomes can occur:
1. *If the underlying stock (which is now $17) rises above $17.50 by July expiration,* then you will be called out at $17.50 strike price you sold. In this scenario, we net a total profit of $1,100 in net premiums collected plus another 50 cents in profit from $17 to $17.50 (multiplied by our 500 shares or +$250). A total inflow of $1,350. We have lost the difference between the original stock purchase price at $18.75 and the sold stock price of $17.50, or a capital loss

of 500 shares multiplied buy the $1.25 loss, or a loss of $625.

    a. **Total Trade Profit (including adjustments)** = **$725** (minus commissions). Divide this by your cash outlay to by the stock of $4,687.50 and we have yielded a 15% return by the third week of July in a total of 10 weeks. That's not bad on a stock you were wrong on. You thought it would rise from $18.75 and it fell to $17 and then rebounded a little, yet you still made a nice profit.

2. *If the underlying stock falls and stays the same ($17).* In this scenario, we will not be called out at $17.50 and we will keep all of the stock and keep the premiums. There is an unrealized loss on the shares but since we do not get called out, it is not realized.

    a. **Total Trade Profit (including adjustments)** = **$1,100** (original call premiums collected, minus commissions). Divide this by your cash outlay to by the stock of $4,687.50 and you have yielded a **23% cash on cash return** by the third week of July (in a total of ten weeks). We still have all the stock and can immediately write more calls with an August expiration and take in more premium. Another great outcome.

3. *If the underlying stock continues to fall in value (say to $16),* then we will not be called out and we will keep all of the stock and keep the premiums.

    a. **Total Profit = $1,100** (original call premiums collected, minus commissions). However, we have now lost an additional $1 per share on our original 500 shares of stock for a total capital loss of $1,125. We have lost $25 plus commissions. Not bad. Remember, we also still have all the stock and can immediately write more August calls and take in more premium. This puts us back into a profit situation. It is a solid outcome for being so wrong and watching a stock we felt would rise but instead fell $2.75 a share (~15%).

Explanation of the trade adjustment. Did you see how the trade adjustment of early roll-out (and roll down) enhanced our profit and also limited potential loss on the covered calls? It accelerated our cash flow more quickly and we did not wait for June expiration to roll out a losing covered call. I am a big fan of early rollouts when trades go against us with a good deal of time remaining to expiration.

My second favorite covered call adjustment: Rolling down to a lower strike price in the same month.
Similar to the roll out adjustment above, if the underlying has fallen dramatically and quickly, I will occasionally just roll down while keeping the same current month expiration date.

<u>ORIGINAL TRADE:</u> On November 17th, you bought 300 shares (on margin) of a $28 stock that you felt would rise moderately over the next six months. This share purchase cost on 50% margin was $4,200. You also sold slightly out of the money covered calls. Specifically, you sold three contracts of the December expiration calls with a $30 strike price and collected $1.00 and multiplied by 300 shares equals a positive $300.

It is now December 7th and the underlying stock has not risen as planned. In fact, it has fallen significantly. The stock has now declined to $23.10. You are confident that the underlying stock will not rise above $25 before the expiration date of the third Friday in December.

Trade Adjustment: I would seek to roll down this trade immediately, keeping the December expiration date:
- The DEC $30.00 strike price calls are now bid $.00 and ask 7 cents and
- The DEC $25.00 strike price calls are bid $2.50 and ask $2.60.

Do the trade adjustment to roll-down to the $25 strike price. In this scenario, I would immediately buy-to-close the December $30 calls for $.07 cents (cost of $21) and simultaneously sell an equal number, or three contracts, of the December $25 strike price calls at $2.50. You are still in a covered call trade on the shares but now instead of a strike price of $30, you have a strike price to sell your shares at $25 and have also taken in a second premium. You keep both the original $300 you collected for selling the DEC $30 calls and you also have now collected another $750 for the DEC $25 strike price calls. Total premiums of $1,050 (minus commissions) were generated on your cash on cash outlay of $4,200 spent on the stock.

It is true that these two premiums together do not make up for the unrealized loss in the stock you have taken (the stock fell from $28 to $23.10 for an unrealized loss of $1,470) but it is close to covering the whole loss and if you do not get called out of the stock in approximately two weeks, you can immediately write the January calls and try to get profitable again.

This is the power of the buy back and roll-out. With collar trades you are protected on the downside with the protective put that you purchase for protection up front. On large underlying stock price pullbacks, you would not buy back and roll out the covered call portion, instead exercise or sell the protective puts that have risen in value when the stock price falls.

TRADE ADJUSTMENTS – COLLARS & COVERED CALLS:

Original strategy	Adjustments – based upon your new outlook on the underlying stock	Action / Effect
Collars & Covered Call Trades	If Still BULLISH: Do nothing	If the underlying stock has taken a dip but you think it is temporary and it will quickly recover, just sit tight and make no adjustment.
	If NEUTRAL: Sell a second call (equal number of call contracts) out in time and down a	Do the buy back and rollout trade adjustment after the underlying stock price has fallen. Aggressively sell the next month out (and down a strike price) calls, collecting a second premium.

strike.	
If now BEARISH: Roll down the trade to a lower strike price in the same month.	Roll down the strike price with the same expiration date if the underlying has made a quick dramatic move down.
Close trade if two and a half weeks or less to expiration	Locks in a loss but frees up remaining cash to do other trades.

2. Trade adjustments for losing long call (STOCK REPLACEMENT) & long put trades

We have covered how to execute a successful trade adjustment for winning long calls or put trades. It is done by converting a 40%-50% unrealized gain in a long call or put trade into a straddle.

Here we will cover the losing trade adjustments. I like to use two simple trade adjustments or repair strategies on a long call or long put position that is losing. These adjustments are as follows:

- *If you are still bullish on the underlying stock*: A great adjustment if your long calls are losing is to sell short term out of the money call contracts with less than one month to expiration. You need to do this on an equal number of contracts to the long calls you are already in. Doing this trade adjustment leaves your long calls, which are your main position, in place to try to capture future upside while consistently taking in short term cash thereby reducing your cost basis. Select a strike price that still has good premium to collect but is a bit higher than you actually think the underlying security will achieve by the expiration date (as you do not want to get called out, locking in a loss). Your goal is to do a series of these short-term call sales and collect a lot of little cash premiums to try to turn the paper loss into an overall gain.

- A second adjustment you can make to a losing long call position, *if you are still bullish on the underlying*, is to add a bull put vertical credit spread trade. This adjustment adds another high probability trade in the same direction of the long calls you are in. In effect you are doubling down but can also cut your loss if this trade wins but you are still down in the original long calls trade. As the underlying price has fallen since you entered the long calls trade, you are adding a bull put spread which also profits from a rise in the underlying at better prices than existed when you bought the calls.

- *If you are now directionally NEUTRAL on the underlying stock but you anticipate a big move in either direction* you can buy long puts with the same strike price and same expiration date as your existing long calls. This turns the long call trade into a directionally neutral long straddle. Now you can win if the underlying goes up or down as long as it moves significantly.

- *If you have now turned BEARISH on the underlying* you can change direction in the trade by turning the original directional long calls into a bear call calendar spread, which is a form of vertical credit spread that wins when the underlying declines. To execute this, add a new trade leg to your existing long calls by selling an equal number of call contracts as your long calls, with a strike price closer to the now lower ATM price of the underlying security. To reduce risk, maintain no wider than a $5 spread between the strike price of your existing long calls and the new sold calls. To increase profits, make sure the newly sold calls have a short life to expiration- perhaps as short as two weeks. You can do a series of these selling calls trades over the life of the long calls to collect premiums along the way and continue to reduce your cost basis.

TRADE ADJUSTMENT SUMMARY TABLE: LONG CALLS
(or LONG PUTS):

Original strategy	Adjustments – based upon your new outlook on the underlying stock	Action / Effect
Long Deep ITM Calls (the **Stock Replacement** Strategy) or deep in the money long Puts	If Still BULLISH: 1. Sell OTM short term calls (converting trade into a vertical call debit spread) 2. Add a Bull Put Credit Spread.	1.1 Creates a bullish call debit spread that can keep the trade benefiting from a strong bullish move but reduces the cost basis in the trade by collecting premium in the short calls. 2.1 Can help offset some loss in the long calls and can generate short term income.
	If NEUTRAL: 1. Buy an equal number of puts with the same strike price and same expiration as your existing long calls.	1.1 Turns the trade into a directionally neutral long straddle.

	If Now BEARISH: 1.) Sell OTM short term calls - $5 closer to ATM (turns the trade into a Bear Call Calendar Credit spread).	1.1. Changes direction on the trade. Can do several of these over the life of the long call trade.
	Close trade	No adjustments. Locks in loss on the long calls but removes all risk.

An example trade with adjustments

Here is an example of a long-put trade followed by a series of adjustments. This is an actual case study of a trade that I recently reversed from a losing trade into a winner by using trade adjustment strategies. This example is nearly a worst-case scenario, as it took seven adjustments to complete, but it ended up a win. This extreme case illustrates how wrong you can be and still turn a losing trade into a winner.

The Trade: My research and technical indicators indicated that MSFT (Microsoft) would fall over the next 100 days. My initial trade was to buy two long put contracts that were in the money ("ITM") at an .80 Delta, with five months until expiration. The initial cost of this trade and the adjustments were as follows:

Trade or adjustment description (# of contracts, etc.):	Price Paid or Received & Total:	Running Total (Profit or Loss):
Initial Trade: Bought two MSFT Put Contracts (ITM with a Delta of .80)	Paid $8.10 per contract times two contracts.	($1,620)

	TOTAL = ($1,620)	
Adjustment #1: The price of MSFT rose going against me, so I bought two more of the same puts at a lower price. Scaling into the trade. I now doubled the number of contracts.	Paid $6.85 per contract times two contracts. TOTAL = ($1,370)	($2,990)
Adjustment #2: Sold OTM short puts with one month to expiration against my long puts to recoup some of my cost at a strike price I did not think would be hit by expiration (this technically turned my long puts trade into a Bear put spread)	Collected $.97 per contract times four contracts. TOTAL = $388	($2,602)
Adjustment #3: The underlying stock on MSFT stabilized and after a couple of weeks much of the time premium in the short puts I had sold had come out of the contracts, so I bought the short puts back to lock in the gain and kept my four long puts open.	Bought to Close the four short puts that I had sold in adjustment #2 above for 20 cents per contract. TOTAL = ($80)	($2,682)
Adjustment #4: My original trade had been open for seven weeks at this point and MSFT stock price started to rise again. I bought two more of the same long puts that I currently have at a	Bought two new long puts at $5.30. TOTAL = ($1,060)	($3,742)

further reduced price		
Adjustment #5: Sold six contracts of OTM short puts with one month to expiration against my long puts to recoup some of my cost at a strike price I did not think would be hit by expiration. This turned my long puts trade into a Bear put spread.	Collected 67 cents per contract times six contracts (600 shares). TOTAL = $402	($3,340)
Adjustment #6: The stock again stabilized and after three more weeks much of the time premium on the six short puts had been captured, so I bought them back to close. My long six put contracts remained open.	Bought to close the six short puts that I had sold in adjustment #5 above for 27 cents per contract. TOTAL = ($162)	($3,502)
Adjustment #7: After nearly four months MSFT stock started to fall slightly and I was able to sell the six long puts I had bought to complete the trade cycle.	Sold six long put contracts for $7.05. TOTAL = $4,230	**NET PROFIT** (After all adjustments) **$728** on $3,742 invested at the peak, equals a **~19% cash on cash return** in four months (despite being wrong all the way through)

As you can see from the above table, I was wrong many times in what I thought MSFT would do over the three or four months I was in this trade. Many of my adjustments were also directionally wrong after the underlying stock started to move against me. Despite this, after all was said and done, I still managed to finish with a profit of over $700 USD. Remember, without adjustments, my original puts purchase price of $8.10 would have resulted in a loss when I sold them back at $7.05. With the adjustments, however, this selling price of $7.05 resulted in a profit because the adjustments had lowered my cost basis along the way. Mastering adjustments can be critical to success.

3.   Trade adjustments for a losing call debit spread trade.

Bullish call debit spreads do not need a lot of adjustments, except when the trade is winning. When the underlying stock rises up above the short strike price in your call debit spread, you are in a winning position. There are several decisions to make about closing out the short leg and rolling it up and out, or you can close the short leg and allow the remaining long calls to appreciate.

A bullish call debit spread loses when the underlying stock falls in price. If you remain bullish on the underlying and feel the current price pullback is temporary, then don't adjust. In this scenario, you should do nothing and hope that your original bull call debit spread comes all the way back to end in a profit.

As you have protection to this downside due to the limited risk of having a spread on, I only really do two types of trade adjustments to losing call debit spreads, otherwise known as bull call spreads.

My Favorite Trade Adjustment for a Losing Bull Call Spread:
An easy way to defend a bull call spread trade that goes against you is to turn it into a butterfly trade. This adds two more legs to the trade, making a 2-legged trade into a 4-legged trade. This does add commissions but it takes in more premium and gives the trade a solid chance to make back the on-paper loss from the losing bull call spread. Here is an example:

ORIGINAL TRADE: Facebook (Ticker: FB) is trading for $173.30. It is currently the middle of February and you believe FB is poised to make a move over the next couple of months above the near-term resistance of $175. You originally played this anticipated upside move with a bullish call debit spread, buying ten contracts of the June $172 calls and selling ten contracts of the June $177 calls. *Net Trade cost = $2 multiplied by 1,000 shares (ten contract spread) = $2,000 cost.*
It is now the end of March and the FB stock has not risen as planned. In fact, it has fallen to $169.50. You believe that the underlying stock will now only rise to around the $171 - $172 level before the third Friday in June expiration date.

Trade Adjustment: I would seek to convert this bull call debit spread into a butterfly. Mechanically, I would:
- Sell 20 call contracts at the $171 strike price for June expiration.
- I would then roll my original 10 contract $172 long calls up to ten long calls at $173 strike price (selling the 10 contracts at $172 and buy ten contracts of the 173's).
- Sell the original short $177 calls at a nice profit as selling calls is bearish and winning when the underlying stock price fell to $169.50.
- Lastly, to complete the 4th leg of the butterfly, buy 10 contracts at the $169 strike price for about $1.75 each.

By executing this conversion into a butterfly, the total risk on the downside decreases. There is now a lower profit cap on the upside of the trade. Because of this, a sharp upward move is more of a risk now. If FB stays around $170 or $171 at expiration, there will be a nice big profit. An expiration right at $171 is the largest possible profit scenario.

My Second Favorite Trade Adjustment for a Losing Bull Call Spread: Convert to a directionally neutral Straddle or Strangle

If the stock falls after my bull call debit spread is placed, and the future outlook of the stock is unclear, then I will occasionally convert the long calls portion of the spread into a straddle or strangle.

A long straddle and a long strangle are the same type of trade and behave and profit in the same way. The straddle uses the same strike price for buying long calls and puts, and the long strangle uses slightly different strike prices for buying a long call and put.

This alternative way of defending a losing bullish call debit spread turns the trade into a directionally neutral straddle (or strangle if I use a different strike price than the original long calls). Now that the underlying went against my expectations, I am no longer sure of future direction of the stock. I expect it, however, to move rapidly one way or the other. Mechanically, the simple trade adjustment is to buy an equal number of ATM or slightly OTM long put contracts on the same underlying with the same expiration date. These long puts turn the trade neutral to still slightly bullish by turning your original long calls into a calendar straddle or strangle.

You should only do this trade adjustment if you expect a lot of volatility on the underlying stock but are unsure of the direction (this can be due to a court ruling with an unknown outcome, a management shakeup, a scandal of some kind, etc.). Any unknown event with an unknown, somewhat binary outcome would lead me to choose this adjustment.
In 2015 I did this adjustment on both GoPro and on Alexion Pharmaceuticals. These are volatile stocks that I was bullish on and placed bull call debit spreads. When they each fell $15 and went against me, I felt that they would either gain $20 or lose another $20 very quickly. I converted my bullish call debit spreads into directionally neutral straddles. When they each moved dramatically, in the positive, I won big.

TRADE ADJUSTMENTS – CALL DEBIT SPREADS:

Original strategy	Adjustments – based upon your new outlook on the underlying stock	Action / Effect
Bullish Call Debit Spread (Bull Call Spreads) Trade:	BULLISH: *1.* Do nothing – no adjustment	1.1 Do nothing and wait for original bull call debit spread to win
	NEUTRAL: *1.* Convert the Bull Call spread into a Butterfly. *2.* Buy matching number of puts with matching duration and strike price (or slightly OTM strike price) into a straddle or strangle.	1.1 If I believe I can target near the pinning price at expiration, convert the Bull Call spread into a butterfly. 2.1 Turns the trade into a directionally neutral long straddle (or strangle if a slightly different strike price put is purchased). Needs a large move in the underlying to win. Otherwise do not place this adjustment.
	BEARISH: *1.* Close Trade	1.1. Locks in a small loss but frees up capital to re-deploy.

4. Trade adjustments for losing vertical credit spread trades

One of the best things about vertical credit spreads is they probably offer the most variety of trade adjustment options of any of my favorite trading strategies when a trade is going against you. There are no less than 8 potential trade adjustments and ways to defend a credit spread depending on your new outlook on the market and/or the underlying stock and sector.

Unless it is an iron condor, a vertical credit spread is a directional trade that loses when the underlying moves in the unintended direction. Vertical credit spreads win when the underlying moves the way you predicted or stays the same. It can even win when the underlying security moves very slightly against you. These are all good outcomes. Sometimes, however, the underlying security will move directly against the direction you predicted or expected. In the case of an iron condor, you expected not much movement and for the underlying security price to stay in a tight channel and it has instead moved sharply higher or lower. In these losing scenarios, I follow these rules to adjust:

Rule #1: **Follow the money.** If a trade is going against you, check the OBV technical indicator on stockcharts.com (or other good charting site). The OBV indicator shows the on-balance volume – an accurate picture of the current buying pressure vs. selling pressure. Use this to confirm if a new trend has emerged or if the trend you had researched is continuing. Adjust your outlook accordingly.

Rule #2: **Confirm the trend** in a second way by comparing today's price action and volume against the average daily volume, and by looking at the current Keltner channels. If the stock is falling on greater than average volume, this indicates the trend has turned bearish. If it is falling on light volume but is still within the Keltner Channels, then maintain your bullish outlook.

I use the above rules and the decision tree that follows to make adjustments when credit spread trades go awry. Note that the following list of trade adjustments are not designed to be done sequentially. Each trade adjustment is a different trade choice and they are not mutually exclusive. You can put on multiple trade adjustments over time for the same original trade. I usually select only one at a time. I may then select a different adjustment two or three weeks later.

TRADE ADJUSTMENTS – VERTICAL CREDIT SPREADS: DECISION TREE OF POTENTIAL ADJUSTMENTS

Step 1: ENTER THE Vertical Credit Spread (Bull Put Spread Example):		
LOSING TRADES: If Price of the underlying Security **Falls** (watch the Delta on the short leg of the spread – if it goes above .35 on calls, or -.35 on puts look to adjust).		**WINNERS:** If the Price of the underlying security **Rises** (or stays the same).
Adjustment #1 – if bearish, convert to a Ratio back spread – buy one to two long puts on the same underlying security. • Do ATM or Near the Money.	**Adjustment #2** – if neutral, sell a bear-call spread on same underlying & same expiration • Takes in a second credit premium-now trade is an Iron Condor. • **This is my favorite adjustment.**	**Adjustment #1** – Wait until expiration day – then Buy to close the short leg for 5-10 cents per contract. • No adjustments needed until expiration.
Adjustment #3 – if still bullish on the underlying, roll-out (& potentially down a strike price or two) to the following week. • This gives us more time with the same directional bet.	**Adjustment #4:** If Neutral, the Butterfly adjustment. I generally add a bear call vertical credit spread instead of a butterfly – but it is possible to convert the bull put spread trade to a butterfly	**Adjustment #2** – If stock recovers your way, then close out before expiration day when 75%-80% of the max credit achieved. • If the stock is now back on trend, you can roll-out and keep most of the premium and

	by selling another equivalent set of short puts as you have open and buying a higher price put set (equivalent number of contracts and expiration date as your original long put leg). *Most traders can ignore this adjustment.*	collect a second premium.
• **This is my second favorite adjustment.**		
Adjustment #5 – If I want to own the stock, take assignment of the shares at expiration. • Once assigned the shares – collect the dividends and begin collar it • No adjustment needed – just accept assignment at expiration (but note that this takes up a lot of margin).	**Adjustment #6–** If still bullish, sell a second bull-put spread on same underlying & same expiration date (but down below the now lower stock price) – Double your bet but at a much lower set of strikes • **This is my third favorite adjustment**	

A note on losing trade adjustment #3 in the table, it can be difficult to decide on a losing credit spread trade if you should roll-out and give yourself more time for the trade to go your way, or to do another type of adjustment. I will typically check the delta of the short leg of my position to help me decide. I have found that rolling out early and aggressively- as soon as you see the trade working against you and the delta of your short leg goes above .35 for calls or -.35 for puts- helps increase my winning percentage. This is true only If your overall outlook on the underlying stock has not changed.

For example, if I placed a bullish put spread on Apple stock expiring in six weeks when the stock is trading at say $180, I would typically have sold the short leg at a put strike price of $175 and bought the long (protection) leg at a strike price of $170. If the stock falls to around $177.65 in just a few days after I placed my original bull put vertical credit spread, I would check the delta on the $175 put strike price I sold. If it is above -.35, I would roll out a week and down to the $172.50 strike, and buy the $167.50 strike.

Additional trade adjustments (for My 5th & 6th favorite trade strategies from Chapter Six)

Trade adjustments on my last two favorite trade strategies, Directional Butterflies and Call Ratio Spreads, are different than the prior adjustments. For these, not much in the way of losing trade adjustments needs to be done. This is due to the low maximum amount at risk for each trade, the fully protected downside, and the net credit we strive for at trade entry on both strategies.
A directionally skewed call butterfly with a buy 10 / sell 20/ buy 10 contract ratio, for example, might be entered into at a total cost of around $135 USD. That is the maximum risk to you on the trade. Any trade adjustment we might think to add would likely cost more than the small amount of money at risk in the initial trade. Therefore, it is usually not worth it to adjust the trade. Just take your small losses on these directional butterflies when they occur and start a new trade.

There is an exception to this rule on both the Skip Strike directional Butterfly and the Call Ratio Spread. Both of these strategies can lose significantly if there is a sharp and unexpected gain on the underlying stock. We build in a great deal of safety when we enter both of these strategies to reduce this risk but it still exists. Typically, there must be $9 to $20 of upside movement on the underlying security before we would incur any risk of loss. As we all know, however, that can happen. That is why we add a protective long call option when we enter the Call Ratio Spread and we close out the skip strike butterfly if it goes too far past the middle, short leg strike price.

I have summarized each in their respective tables in the following chart. **Trade adjustments for losing skip strike or directional butterfly trades** – Directional butterfly – no adjustments needed.

Trade adjustments for losing broken wing (skip strike) butterfly trades

Original strategy	Adjustments – based upon your new outlook on the underlying stock	Action / Effect
Broken Wing Butterfly trades	Risk Control: *1.* If the underlying security price passes the short leg strike price, exit the trade early.	1.1 If an Unexpected large upward price movement occurs in the underlying security, this skip strike butterfly is at risk of loss. To cap such a loss, seek to exit the trade if the underlying security price passes the butterfly short leg strike price.

Trade adjustments for losing call ratio spreads with a net credit

We place call ratio spreads initially for a net credit at trade entry. This prevents any losses from being possible except under one scenario. If a sharp and unexpected rise in the underlying security price occurs taking it above the high OTM call strike price, we can at that point start to experience large losses. We control this by purchasing even further OTM call contracts as emergency protection.

TRADE ADJUSTMENTS – CALL RATIO SPREADS
(with a Net Credit):

Original strategy	Adjustments – based upon your new outlook on the underlying stock	Action / Effect
Call Ratio Spread trades	Risk Control: *1.* If the underlying security price passes the upper call leg strike price, exit the trade early.	1.1 If an unexpected large upward price movement occurs in the underlying security, this call ratio spread is at risk of loss. To cap such a loss, look to exit the trade if the underlying security price passes the upper leg strike price.

Handling losses trades that go against you is the key difference between pros and amateurs

We covered the mental side of trading in general in Chapter One. This chapter discussed what to do when you are in loosing trade positions and when and how to execute trade adjustments.

There is also a huge *psychological* aspect to trade adjustments. Losing trades are where trading gets very real. It is no longer an academic exercise; real money is on the line. To make matters worse, when you are in a losing trade, it is usually not just one. A broad market reversal can result in several losing trades all at once, placing you at risk of losing big money overall. The best traders do not get emotional when losses occur, however, when you are losing real money, this is very difficult to control.

If you know how to rescue losing trades through trade adjustments, it will help you control your negative self-talk and thoughts and give you a plan to follow to mitigate losses. You are following a rule-based, goal-oriented trading plan.

When you are in a losing trade (or a series of simultaneous loosing trades) and facing a potentially large draw down on your account, you will of course be feeling the primary emotion of fear. Trading on fear can make smart people do dumb things. At these critical moments you have to keep your cool. Rationally sizing up the decision to adjust and placing adjusting trades where they make sense has helps me to control my fear. I can execute adjustments without overreacting and exiting all positions at large losses. Knowing how to adjust losing trades and get them back in your favor will help keep you level headed and calm.

Keep in mind that by following a plan, using the Portfolio management rules (BASE & BOOST, etc.) using only the highest percentage trading strategies and rules taught in this book, you are limiting the possibility of major losses.

You will have the confidence to trade effectively knowing that:
- You are trading with an overall plan.
- In each trade, you are hedged with a protection position or how a small management maximum loss defined and built into the trade.
- In long direction calls or puts and debit-spread positions, your maximum losses are capped at the cost of our debit to enter the trades.
- In butterflies your maximum loss is the small debit to enter the trade.

Add all of these controls together and you have the ability to make large gains with additional layers of protection on your downside. That said, handling your emotions during loosing trading periods is the single hardest thing to do and causes more losses than any other factor.

The best way to avoid fear when trading is to have a financial plan. A written trading plan, with defined, crystal clear goals, and follow pre-planned rules for trade entries and exits and adjusting losing trades.

Remember, losing trades are inevitable. They are just part of the business of trading. But the market is not out to get you – use your rules and adjustments, as well as the risk management techniques taught in the next chapter.

"I've failed over and over and over again in my life and that is why I succeed."
- Michael Jordan

Chapter 9

Risk Management Rules

LEARNING OBJECTIVES

- **Understand the Importance of Risk Management and Following General Risk Management Rules**

- **Portfolio Level & Trade Level Risk Management Rules**

- **How to Position Size in Real Time to Maximize Profit and Control Risk**

"The word CRISIS, in Chinese is composed of two characters, one represents 'Danger' and the other represents 'Opportunity.'"
- John F. Kennedy, 1959

After reading this far, you know how to build a robust trading plan, read the market news and trends, select trades, determine profitable trade setups, look for good technical entry points, and use the best trading strategies. You also know how to adjust trades that go wrong.

All of these steps help reduce the risk of losses. Now it is time to put the finishing touch on your risk management plan. This chapter will help you to create a risk management plan at the portfolio level and at the individual trade level.

Understand the Importance of Risk Management and Follow General Risk Management Rules.

Risk management is the most important aspect of being a consistently profitable trader. But most traders either overcomplicate risk management or oversimplify it. There are two schools of thought when it comes to trading and investment risk management as it is taught today:

1. *The Over-Complicated School of Risk Management.* Many trading instructors believe that because risk management is such an important aspect of being a profitable trader, it must need to be complicated. The people who ascribe to this school of thought, use dozens of technical indicators, watch their Greeks mid-trade, and use complicated charts and stop-loss orders in their risk management program. All of this is exhausting, and most of it is unnecessary for success.

2. *The Over-Simplified School of Risk Management.* Other people, however, try to reduce all of risk management down to one rule. Usually, that rule is either to set a stop loss on each trade and don't watch anything else, or it is to just roll out any losing trade. Both of these are a little too simplistic to be that helpful. Unfortunately, setting a stop loss order or rolling out losers does not equal a risk management plan.

Proper risk management lies somewhere in between the overcomplicated and the over simplified schools of thought. It incorporates hedging at the trade level and overall at the portfolio level. When done right, risk management is what separates long term successful traders and investors from those that end up with losses and frustration.

The high percentage winner does not always make money.

The key to success and making money in the markets is to ensure that your losing trades do not cost you more than you are earning on your winners. This is a key point and it has nothing to do with the percentage of the time your trades win.

People think that the person whose trading strategy wins the most often must be the most profitable investor. This is simply not true. A trader that is managing losses well can win 40% of the time on trades and beat the portfolio returns of the guy winning 70%+ of his trades. How is this possible? The trader winning 70% of the time might be losing three or four times as much money on his losing trades than he is gaining on his winners. The one who wins 40% of the time might be winning ten times the money on her winners than on her average losing trade.

Risk management quite simply means keeping your losses small and letting profits run.

Risk Management – your most important job in trading & investing.

Risk management is so critical that it can accurately be described as the trader's most important job. Winning trades tend to be easy and take care of themselves for the most part. Most people are good at managing winners and not giving back all of their gains on winning trades if things start to reverse. Managing winning trades effectively by scaling out of them can be taught relatively quickly, even to the most novice investor.

Managing trades that go against you, however, is the hardest thing to do in investing. Risk management becomes *the entire* key to sustained performance. One trader I respect often says "killing off bad trades is your only job." While this statement is a bit strong, there is a lot of truth in it. In addition, proper risk management strategies let you sleep better at night, which in turn provides a sense of confidence that makes you a better trader.

As important as it is to "kill off bad trades," I am not minimizing the importance of risk management through pre-trade research, strategy selection and using pre-trade checklists. The proper prior selection of which stocks to choose, the levels of the Greeks on the strike prices you select, and the standard deviations you select by going further OTM or ITM are very important and are in some ways a form of risk management. My point is that no matter how well you do your pre-trade homework and selections, you will still be wrong some of the time. Managing your way out of losing trades is where a proper risk management plan comes in.

The rules I have developed over the years vary slightly depending on which of the six trading strategies taught in this book that you are using. However, some of the concepts are general and apply no matter what trading strategy you are employing. A number of the following risk management rules have appeared in other places in the book. I repeat the relevant rules here to bring all of the risk management techniques together in one place in this chapter. It can serve as a checklist. Let's start with my general risk management rules that apply to all trades regardless of trading strategy:

GENERAL RISK MANAGEMENT RULES

Rule #1: **Avoid & minimize losses!** This is Warren Buffett's number one rule and it is also my number one rule. While this rule may seem obvious, most people don't know *how* to implement it. Options and combination strategies are by definition more volatile than simple buy and hold stock or ETF trading. How do you implement this rule? Understanding that is the combination of the rest of the rules below.

Rule #2: **Plan your trades and any trade adjustments based on a plan and probabilities, not emotions.** The more you preplan your actions, potential adjustments and exit points, the better. Before you enter any trade, figure out your profit and risk parameters and exit points based on the mathematical probabilities given in option tables. For example:

- *You can choose how large of a trade size to put on* – on a $100,000 USD size portfolio, don't put more than 5% of your portfolio at risk on any one trade. On a $500,000 USD size portfolio, don't put more than 4% of your portfolio into any one trade ($20K). On a $1,000,000 portfolio, don't put more than 3% of your portfolio ($30K) into any one trade.
- *Set your target loss and profit amounts on every trade* – the target amounts change with the trading strategy you have selected but you must set these targets on the upside and downside before entering every trade. Sticking to your profit and loss targets is harder than it sounds, you must stick to them! I often select multiple targets to scale out

both on the upside and the downside by using the points of resistance and support from my technical analysis. I then set my downside exit target just outside of these technical support levels. My choices on upside and downside targets change the further away from expiration the position is. This means that is the position moves my way quickly, and I can close out the trade and lock in 60% of the potential gain, I will do so. If the trade doesn't move my way quickly and it takes three months to start to be profitable, I will then require something closer to an 85% gain. Time is a factor as well. The following chart shows my rules of how time to expiration and percentage gain work together for closing out, or scaling out of trades:

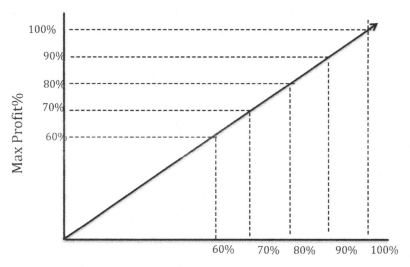

Time Amount Start to Expiration

As you can see, if I have earned 60% of the maximum possible gain (on a butterfly, covered call, credit spread or debit spread trade) on or before 60% of the time is gone – I will take my gain and close out the trade or scale it down. If it takes 80% of the time from the beginning of the trade to expiration date, I then wait for a higher percentage gain.

Rule #3: **Manage risk through proper trade sizing. Try to do equal sized trades.** This is one of the most important risk

management trading rules of all.   Position sizing is the most
important way to control how much you risk you take with any
particular trade.   Position sizing refers to how large each trade is in
terms of dollars spent or dollars at risk across the different positions
in your portfolio. You will never wake up with a shocking loss in
your overall portfolio if you position sizes your trades correctly.
Think about it – if you never risk more than 5% of your total
portfolio size on any one trade, and most trades are closer to 2% of
your portfolio, no one trade can bring your entire portfolio down.
The way you grow and stay in the game is by limiting the possibility
of debilitating portfolio drawdowns, even if multiple bullish trades
go south at the same time due to a market pullback.

Rule #4: **Hedge the whole stock market in order to protect your
whole portfolio**. Most of the time, my portfolio has a significant
bias towards bullish trades. A basic risk management tool I always
employ is to use a portfolio hedge to de-risk the whole portfolio
against systemic market collapse, otherwise known simply as market
risk. You can do this easily and fairly inexpensively by taking 1%
of your portfolio and buying a few close to the money PUT options
on broad market indexes to offset your existing bullish trades. See
Section B below for a more thorough explanation of this rule with
examples. Buy puts on the S&P500 index to hedge your whole
portfolio

Rule #5: **Trade proper trade set-ups and look for trading edges
before entering each trade**. Most of these edges and set-ups put
the risk to reward ratios in your favor. Most have already been
covered earlier in this book. A summary of some of the best risk
management edges I have found over many years of investing:

- **The pre-announcement by companies of stronger than
  expected (or worse than expected) earnings is a huge
  edge.** These announcements come directly from the
  company officers and you can trade with conviction on
  them. De-risking trades often means trading on your
  expectations of future compelling news about the company.
  Pre-announcements give you the future news today and this
  is one of the best ways to reduce risk on trades. You can
  find these announcements for free on many websites. I do
  not generally trade stocks with pre-announcements that are
  not also part of my basket of stocks, unless I am very

familiar with the company. Otherwise you have not done enough homework and are essentially just trading on headlines. Remember, with this trade set-up, do not trade on this information if the next week after the pre-announcement is the week of the quarterly earnings announcement. Trading over earnings week is too volatile and unpredictable. The anticipation of future good news is the most compelling set-up for stocks. Trade when the pre-announcement of better than expected earnings is announced, then look for the date of the next earnings announcement and get out just prior to the earnings announcement.

- **Insider share buys & sells.** This edge is so powerful that some hedge funds trade entirely based on this indicator. I do not look at this alone, but if any of the stocks in my basket have strong insider buying of shares in the open market, it is a powerful bullish set-up. Trading this set-up is a great way to de-risk your trades.

- **When the names in my basket of stocks are in a bullish uptrend, and I see one or more of the names retrace to the 61.8% Fibonacci retracement line and then start back upwards – then I set my trade exit just under the likely100% extension price.** For whatever reason, swing traders make a killing off of this setup. When you can trade with 90% likelihood of a future outcome, this de-risks your trades.

- **SEC filings forecasting future stock splits** – Stock splits can be a strong indicator. You can tell that it's about to happen when a company in your basket files with the SEC requesting a shareholder proxy to authorize a large increase in the number of outstanding shares. This is typically a form 14a SEC filing in the USA. This is a telltale sign that the company is about to announce a stock split. In theory, stock splits do not by themselves add any value to the overall shares held by shareholders. Despite this, research shows that shares have a strong bias to rise leading up to a stock split and also for a few months thereafter. Another way to de-risk trades by putting the edge of good future news in your favor.

- **Use the Greeks and especially implied future sensitivity**

to volatility (Vega) to select trading strategies and strike prices. As explained in Chapter Seven, I use the Greeks also as a trade risk management set-up. Depending on my homework and resulting level of conviction, I will select different trading strategies from the six trading strategies taught in this book and aggressive or conservative strike prices.

- **My personal conviction level, based on the homework of my fundamental and technical analysis.** This will give you *personal insight and conviction*. This is a great edge and a trade set-up by itself. It can also de-risk trading. This has become harder with the prevalence of high-speed computer trading algorithms and massive institutional trading, but it still works the majority of the time. I have found that trading off of my personal conviction based on my homework works very well. About 25% of the time I get the precise timing of the rise wrong, but it usually always happens eventually if my homework says it should. If the story is intact but my timing on the move is wrong, this is where trade rollouts of expiring options and the other trade adjustments techniques taught in Chapter Eight can be employed to give me more time to be right.

Rule #6: Use limit orders (not market orders) on all trades and on the risky leg of short option trades; add an insurance protection trade to limit your downside. All trades entered have a bid price and an ask price. You can almost always get filled at a price between the bid and the ask spread by entering limit orders with a price near the midpoint between the bid and the ask prices. Never put yourself at the mercy of the market makers to fill you at any price by entering a "market order." This rule de-risks trading and will save you thousands of dollars in better fill prices over the years.

The only times I violate this rule is:
- When the market is so liquid for the stock or option that the bid / ask spread is under 3 cents. It can often be 3 cents or less on very liquid stocks like Apple. There is no sense fighting for a few pennies – just enter a market order to buy or sell.
- When it is expiration day on a losing option position and it is

within 15 minutes of the closing bell. In this situation, you need to "buy to close" an open short option obligation that you are losing on. For winning trades, you can ignore this. In this situation you will have been entering limit orders all afternoon on expiration Friday to try to roll out or close this losing option position. If you have not been filled on your limit orders and you find yourself with 15 minutes or less to the market close, change the limit order to a market order and get out. Remember, when selling options, you have an obligation. You need to close out the losing options to avoid assignment of the stock or other unintended actions that will be forced upon you if you do not close your obligation before the closing bell. At that late point, your trade has lost and it is time to convert your limit order to a market order and get out.

- The market is collapsing and you want to "go flat" with your long portfolio immediately on all bullish positions. This is very rare, but history shows there are days where the market can lose 800 points or more on the Dow or 60 points or more on the S&P. These days are painful; everything seems to be crashing. Even with insurance protection trades on your positions, you may not want to wait until your maximum allowable losses happen and stop you out at the maximum loss on each bullish position. You may want to just go flat and get out of everything- revert your portfolio to cash and regroup. It is a rare occurrence, but on the ugliest days I will sometimes use market orders to get out of my long positions only (but not hedges and trades betting for falling prices and pullbacks) immediately. This is rare but it has occurred.

Using stop-loss trade orders on your option positions is possible and recommended, just like it is with stocks. I use stop loss orders on several of my six trading strategies to limit my option losses to my target exit price. All online trading platforms have these order entry features. I use TD Ameritrade (Think or Swim), Schwab and Interactive Brokers. Many options trading experts say that with proper trade adjustments you never need to enter stop-loss orders. I have found that I still like them in certain situations, especially when I am not around watching the markets all day to put on potential trade adjustments. Stop loss orders give me a peace of mind.

Rule #7: **Only trade highly liquid stocks, options and markets**. You should ensure that everything you select for your basket of stocks is liquid. There are over 1,000 stocks with daily trading volume above 700,000 shares, and hundreds of ETFs with high liquidity and volume. There is no need to trade thin, obscure stocks with low liquidity and huge bid-ask spreads in their pricing. Unless you understand the company or know the management and are treating it as purely a speculative position with a very low percentage of your portfolio – just say no and stay with the large, highly liquid stocks to de-risk execution slippage and liquidity risk.

Rule #8: **Analyze your past trades periodically and learn from your mistakes.** This is a good risk management and learning practice. I still do this exercise once every six months. Doing so makes me a better trader and is how this book and my trading system and rules evolved. I keep a trade journal and study past trades quarterly or semiannually to minimize bad habits in the future. You can also "paper trade" by doing practice trades on most online brokerage platforms. I advise to practice any new option and stock combination strategies several times before you trade them with real money. Get comfortable with a new strategy on paper before putting real money at risk.

Rule #9: **Trade only when you are in a positive mental state.** Ensure you are putting on new trades that are well analyzed, and that you feel that you have an edge. You should be in a decisive, positive state of mind. Don't "fear trade" or "revenge trade" after a loss. You need to be in a good positive mental state to feel calm and confident to trade at your best. Occasionally, I have been in a bad mood while watching the markets, and I have seen an unexpected opportunity come up. If I am feeling low and not positive and confident – I generally skip the opportunity. There will be another opportunity; they emerge every day.

Rule #10: *Take inevitable losses or put on adjustment trades quickly.* After a short time, trading, you will begin to see fairly quickly when you are on the wrong side of a trade and it has gone dramatically awry. This is not the ordinary intra-day fluctuations of a few percentage points, but rather when you place a trade and it quickly drops 20%-25% cash on cash against you. You will notice a big negative move against your trade. In these situations, it is almost always best to put on an adjustment trade or leg out and take the loss quickly and early in the trade's life. Your first loss is usually the smallest (though it won't feel like it emotionally), and therefore it is almost always the best loss you can take. On countless occasions I have just held on to the original trade without adjusting it and hoped for a recovery. Without trade adjustments, these positions rarely recover to a profit. Remember, making a trade adjustment or taking a loss when it is inevitable is not a bad thing. In fact, it is the smart, professional move. Use the rollouts and other trade recovery adjustment techniques discussed in this book. The winners take care of themselves but you must manage and control the size of losses.

Rule #11: Don't trade purely on tips, rumors, chatrooms, headlines or the daily digital ticker tape flow. Stick to your homework and your basket of stocks. Chasing headlines and tips without homework does not work. Trust in your research and homework more than you trust the latest rumor, CNBC news blurb or what 'tradeslayer123' says about a stock in an online chatroom.

Rule #12: When in doubt, get out. Sometimes all of your research points to a clear trade in a clear direction but after you place your trade, the underlying starts behaving erratically and you just feel like you have lost the understanding of what is happening to the story and the stock price. In situations when I find that I am starting to worry about the trade more than normal, my stress level is elevated and I feel confused by the action in the stock, I have found it is almost always best to get out and re-group.

Portfolio Level & Trade Level Risk Management Rules

How to build and manage your overall portfolio risk
I advocate that you manage risk using a "whole of portfolio" approach. This means looking at risk across your whole portfolio holistically. Start by taking your full portfolio balance and look at ways to hedge the entire portfolio of predominantly long, or bullish trades with a low-cost portfolio insurance trade. If your portfolio is overweight bullish trades, buy some long put options on the overall market indexes to hedge the portfolio.

For example, look at put options on the S&P 500 (ticker: **^SPX** on Yahoo Finance; or on some brokerages sites it is ticker: **$SPX**).

This is a great portfolio insurance hedge. One I like even better to hedge my aggressive long portfolio is to buy puts on the S&P100 (ticker: ^OEX on Yahoo Finance or $OEX). Buying put contracts on the overall market indexes adds a broad-based degree of insurance to your bullish portfolio. I refer to this as adding 'big insurance.'

Alternatively, you can add "small insurance" to your portfolio by buying calls on the two-times and three-times leveraged bearish market index ETF's. I tend to default to the large insurance hedge, and just buy puts on broad market indexes and avoid the ETF proxies for portfolio hedging.

If you do want to add small portfolio insurance, you can do so by buying calls on the following leveraged bearish ETF's:

DXD	3 times leveraged BEAR (short) DJIA	The ultra-short 3 times leveraged DOW ETF
SDS	3 times leveraged BEAR (short) S&P 500	The ultra-short 3 times leveraged S&P 500 ETF
QID	3 times leveraged BEAR (short) NASDAQ 100	The ultra-short 3 times leveraged NASDAQ 100 ETF
TZA	3-times leveraged BEAR (short) RUSSELL 2000	This is the inverse (short) ETF mimics the inverse of daily investment results, equal to three times the daily performance of the Russell 2000 Index.

Let's look at an example of portfolio hedging / insurance that I typically use:

Let's say that you are managing a $1 million USD portfolio of mostly long bullish positions. You have followed my portfolio strategy planning approach and broken the portfolio into the BASE portion and the BOOST portion as follows:

- $600K in BASE portfolio, fully diversified ETFs (equities and fixed income) based on your age, goals and personal risk tolerance.
- $200K in various individual stocks and bullish collar trades plus
- $50K in large unprotected Covered Calls, plus
- $50K in bull put spreads, plus
- $40K in call debit and ratio spreads
- $20K in directional butterflies
- $40K Cash (money market sweep)

You now want to hedge this portfolio. To portfolio hedge this portfolio, I would buy approximately ten contracts of the slightly out of the money **$OEX** put options (depending on the current price and implied volatility of these options). This simple move may cost around $15-$18 per contract multiplied by ten contracts ($15,000-$18,000 of your $1 million portfolio with expiration in four months). This protection trade will partially protect the whole portfolio against a large unexpected market decline while allowing all of the bullish positions to continue to work.

I don't go too far out in time with this hedge, maybe three or four months until expiration on average, for the $OEX puts. Otherwise you overpay for this portfolio insurance and I have found you usually will want to adjust the strike price to a different level after three or four months as market levels move.
This allows all of my existing bullish positions to continue to take advantage of market upswings and appreciation but partially cuts off the down side to the whole bullish part of the portfolio. Remember, you do not need to hedge the fixed income and cash portions of your portfolio – these are already diversified hedges against stocks and stock option positions. Yes, spending $15,000-$18,000 is spending 1.5%-2% of your total portfolio value on insurance. This is expensive. You only do this because your other non-cash and non-fixed income portion of your $1 million has a high probability of making you 10%-40% or more annually. By hedging your long portfolio, you have your upside potential intact if you are right plus some sleep at night protection if the market crashes. Using this portfolio insurance means that you will not wake up one day and find your $1 million dollars is now down to $750,000 because the

market corrected by over 20% (which statistically occurs every five years).

My Portfolio Crash Stop Out rule – The portfolio hedge and trade hedges provide strong risk management controls. These controls should prevent any large portfolio drawdowns. Life, however, can occasionally be more complicated. For example, the dot com crash in 2000 -2001 and the 2008 financial crisis market crashes were both worst-case scenarios. In extreme situations, I employ my portfolio crash stop out rule.

This means if your overall portfolio is ever down 20% from your all-time high for whatever reason, you should:
❖ Tighten all insurance legs on open positions to very tight parameters (meaning you cannot loss much more than you already have, but retain your potential upside gains).
❖ Go to all cash on the rest.

I have only had to use this portfolio crash rule once, during the 2008 financial crisis. Back then, I was in a lot of cash and made a bet on a market rebound after the market lost the first 20% of its value. I saw many stocks I liked at attractive prices and I loaded up on bullish positions with wide stop-loss orders and wide spreads thinking the worst of the pain was over. I was dead wrong. The market went on to lose a total of over 50% of its value. I lost my personal maximum loss of 20% in my aggressive growth portfolio (although I lost much less in the more conservative parts of my portfolio). It turned out to be the worst financial crisis since the Great Depression in 1929. How did I cut my losses to just over 20%? By using the portfolio crash stop rule. Had I not done such wide spreads and large bullish positions after the market lost 20%, I would have done much better and should have only lost around 12%. It goes to show that emotions can override your trading rules. It was a good lesson. Now I am a stickler to following the portfolio plan and rules no matter how a feel markets should perform.

People often ask, how many positions and how many trades should they have on in the BOOST portion of their portfolio targeted to growth / aggressive growth investments? The answer is that it can vary based on size of portfolio but a good rule of thumb for an individual investor is as follows:

- No more than seven to ten total positions in the BOOST portion of the portfolio.
- Five to seven trades should be in the direction of the general market trend.
- Two trades in the opposite direction of the market trend.
- One trade that is totally independent of the general market trend (usually a non-market correlated ETF).

For each trade in the BOOST portion of the portfolio, use strong risk management related questions. Here are mine (you can of course add your own):

- How much of the account am I willing to risk on this trade idea (1%-5%)?
- How much of my portfolio account is already allocated in other trades vs. how much is in cash at the present time?
- Why types of trading strategies am I currently in and what is the next logical trading strategy to diversify the active portion of my portfolio across trading strategies?
- What is the duration (to expiration) of trades am I currently in? What length would be the next logical duration to add on the next trade?
- How is the overall portfolio currently hedged / insured? How will the next trade affect portfolio risk exposure?
- What will happen to the portfolio if the S&P falls by 3%-5%? Rallies 2%-5%?

Very few individual and retail investors ask themselves these types of questions. It is very helpful in analyzing your overall portfolio risk position and you can easily add this step. This is one of the key metrics that professional risk management functions use to look at portfolio risk exposure.

SPECIFIC ADDITIONAL RISK MANAGEMENT RULES BY TRADING STRATEGY:

Let's now look at each of the six top trading strategies taught in this book from the perspective of planning your risk management rules. All of the general risk management rules covered so far in this chapter apply to each strategy. Now we will add some trade strategy specific risk management rules.

FOR COLLARS & COVERED CALL ORDERS:

Trade specific risk management rules for Collars, Covered Calls and Large Unprotected Covered Calls:

Rule #1: For Collars, Pick stocks with a good dividend yield. The income from dividend yield will offset the cost of portfolio margin or regular margin charges, as these are typically longer-term trades of three months to over one year.

Rule #2: For Collars – select the protective put strike price approximately 10% below today's stock price. This is a rule of thumb, not an exact percentage, so shop the prices as you are setting up the trade. 8% is fine on some and 13% is fine on other trades based on the cost of the puts and the risk reward. This keeps the worst-case loss contained to a reasonable level if the stock falls dramatically.

Rule 3: For Collars & Covered Calls, sell mostly In the Money('ITM') strike prices to reduce risk even further. When you want to be very aggressive you can sell ATM or OTM strike prices but a lower percentage of these will finish as winners.

Rule #4: Don't write covered calls during the week of earnings announcements – the underlying share price is too volatile and could drop fast.

Rule #5: Use stocks for Collars and Covered Calls on which you are moderately bullish and you believe will gradually go higher but not ones you think are about to move sharply higher. Select blue chips and tech companies with some volatility but not volatile momentum stocks with dramatic price swings. Your moon-shot growth stocks you do not want to cap the upside, use the uncapped stock replacement strategy for these high growth companies.

Rule #6: Make sure the combination of buying the stock and writing the covered calls against these shares does not take up more than 5% of your total portfolio for any single trade.

Rule #7: Buy the underlying stock on a dip (near the lower band of the Keltner channels) and then wait for it to rebound in price even a small amount and then sell the calls when the underlying stock is strong and rising.

<u>Rule #8</u>: *If you think the stock you own may fall in price or stay flat, sell the covered calls using in-the-money strike prices.* This generates more cash premium and gives you a greater cushion to the downside.

<u>Rule #9</u>: *When Portfolio Margin is not being used, select stocks in the $8-$40 range to buy and write calls on* as the premiums are still nearly as good as more expensive stocks. When using portfolio margin, however, use stocks with large price denominations, which generate larger premiums on a dollar basis and also tend to pay more in dividends.

<u>Rule #10</u>: *Collars, when possible sell monthly (or less) covered calls against stocks as monthly premiums will be on average nearly double the premium collected over time vs. three months out call premiums.* The risk is a greater chance of getting called out of the stock.

<u>Rule #11</u>: *Implement large unprotected covered calls on high priced stocks that you are positive on for the next year but that are highly volatile.*

<u>Rule #12</u>: *Implement large unprotected covered calls on stocks where selling the call contracts will bring in a large premium, with a significant portion of that premium being extrinsic time value.* In this variation on the covered call strategy, you should still use slightly in-the-money calls to write. The call options you want to sell MUST have a large amount of extrinsic value (time premium) built into the premium. This is key, large time value in the premium is likely all you get to keep if the stock performs as expected. Remember, when you sell in the money calls for safety, you have to give back the intrinsic part of the option premium sold unless the stock falls dramatically. So, the external, or time value is your amount to keep if the stock moves higher – this is the value to focus on.

Rule #13: **When your outlook on the stock is moderate or only slightly bullish, write covered calls using in the money strike prices.** This takes away much of your potential risk to the downside as it builds in a very large cushion of the high-flyer stock falling dramatically. You can reduce risk further by writing deep ITM calls, generating as much cash as possible. When 75% -90% of the call premium has been realized as the underlying moves up, roll out and double dip. Aim to collect at least 40% of the original cash spent in initiating your covered call portfolio in extra cash collected in selling deep in the money covered calls. This allows you to close many of your covered call trades out weeks before the four months is up and it also compounds your returns.

FOR LONG CALLS (Stock Replacement) & LONG PUT TRADES:

I love buying deep in the money long calls (stock replacement) and long puts. Their limited downside (limited to the amount spent to buy the calls or puts) and unlimited upside often gives them the best risk/reward ratio of all the trades I employ for large upward stock moves. These trades, however, will not all be winners. Here are some additional risk management related rules to follow for such trades.

Rule #1: **For long call and put buys, buy deep in the money strike prices with high deltas** – Select strike prices to buy that have a delta of at least .80 or higher (.83 to .90 is ideal) and a minimum open interest of 100.

Rule #2: **Try to limit the amount you pay for extrinsic value (time premium) to under 1% of the stock price per month until expiration** – Remember, option prices are broken into two pieces, the intrinsic value and the time premium. Check that the time premium portion is under 1% per month until the option expiration date. If it has eight months to expiration, limit the time premium to 8% of the underlying stock price today

Rule #3: **Trade in the direction of the trend** – go with the overall stock market trend and the trend of the specific stock or ETF you are researching to put on long calls or puts. The trend is your friend. You must, however, do the other fundamental and technical homework to confirm the trend.

A deliberately trending pattern looks like the following figure:

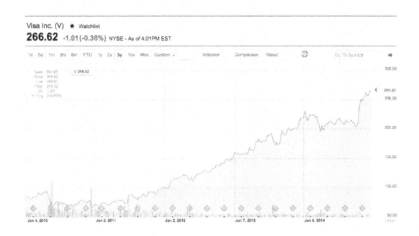

Don't trade long calls for a stock or ETF in a non-trending pattern like this:

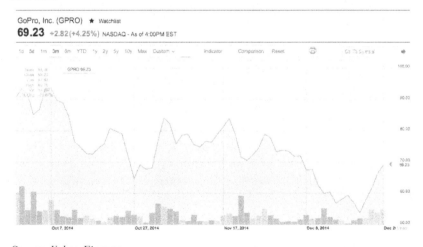

Source: Yahoo Finance

Rule #4: Trade in the direction of the stock's industry sector (bullish when there is industry sector strength or bearish when there is industry sector weakness). As we learned in Chapter Two, a large percentage of a stock's price movement is caused by what is happening with both the market overall and its industry sector (due to ETF and mutual funds buying and selling). Buy long, deep in the money calls in strong industry sectors and buy long puts in the weakest industry sectors.

Rule #5: Buy yourself enough time – more than you think you need for your thesis to play out. Your research will give you your key events, stock direction and conviction on a stock's future price movement but not the time frame in which the underlying stock will move. Buy at least six month (out to the expiration date) long call and put positions. These are highly powered / leveraged 'home-run' trades. The home run sometimes takes on a few weeks or months to materialize. They tend to take longer than you think they will. When you buy enough time, if the stock or ETF moves your way quickly, you will still win big and if it doesn't you increase your chances of winning with less time decay and more time. When your time stop hits, however, then you should exit if the long call or put has not performed as you forecast.

Rule #6: Use two types of stops – mental time stops (based on the calendar to expiration date) and actual price related stop-loss orders on every long directional option trade. Note that many options professionals do not believe in stop loss orders. They would rather just buy an insurance put or call option. However, I do use stop losses because I cannot watch the market every minute of every trading day. Sell stop orders are a bit of a blunt instrument for scaling out of a losing long option trade but they do keep you from large unexpected losses.

Let's cover mental stops first. Mental stops on longer, deep in the money directional calls or puts are typically based on time remaining to expiration date. All long option contracts are losing time value every day. At some point, you need to begin to scale out of the trade, if enough time has passed and the position has not risen as intended. I write down my intended mental time stops in my calendar on my trade log and monitor them. If they hit, then a manual sell order must be entered.

I do set actual price driven stop-loss orders as well. Generally, I scale out of long-term calls and puts. Because of this, the stop loss order that is open is generally for a percentage of my full open position at the next price trigger point. I also often set scaling price target orders for winning trades as well. It is the same principal as for losing trades; I scale out as certain upward price targets are hit.

Both the upward and loss stop orders on the same position can be set at the same time by using a 'One Cancels Other' order. OCO orders allow you to set stop loss orders and price trigger orders for your winners on one ticket. This will allow you to enter your sell prices on both the upside and the downside at the same time in one ticket. You can enter different numbers of contracts on the stop-loss side of the order vs. the winning side of the order.

Adjust your protection / stop order as the trade goes your way. When your trade thesis has been correct and your directional options trade is moving in the way you forecast, your stop loss trade will start to get wider. At no cost, you can adjust your exiting stop-loss position to bring it back to a 25% to 30% cash on cash loss from the new underlying security price. This is a trailing stop loss order but is entered manually on options.

Rule #7: *Do trade adjustments on long calls or puts when they have either a 50% gain or a 30% loss and add the adjustment trade position.*

- On winning long directional calls, if the call position has moved your way and gained 50%, add the purchase of an equal number of ATM puts (with a similar expiration date) to turn the long calls into a market neutral strangle that will put a floor under the downside, locking in your gain. Alternatively, when there is an unrealized gain of 50%, sell out of half of the position and lock in gains, letting the rest run.
- On losing long directional calls, just exit the trade or adjust into either a bearish call spread by selling nearer to the money calls if you think the underlying will continue to fall, or into a bullish call spread by selling an equal number of higher priced OTM calls with the same expiration date if you believe the stock will rise.

FOR DEBIT SPREAD ORDERS:

Like most of my favorite trading strategies, call debit spreads are designed to reduce risk. The tradeoff is that they also limit the maximum possible gain. Here are additional risk management rules to further reduce risk of loss:

Rule #1: *Place bullish call debit spreads using in-the-money strike prices for better risk management and to reduce the down side dramatically.* Remember, on debit spreads, you want to exercise the calls at maximum profit on the position at expiration. Going further in the money on stocks with excellent time premium in the option prices virtually ensures that the trade gets called out at expiration.

Rule #2: Exit debit spreads if your trade is down 30% **cash on cash** – this is the stop out price to move on from losing trades.

Rule #3: Don't trade debit spreads over earnings announcements. As with credit spreads, don't trade debit spreads over the week of a stock's earning announcement. The price swings of the underlying during earnings, and just after them, are too hard to predict.

Rule #4: **For debit spreads:** *buy call option strike prices with Deltas of .65 to .70 and sell strike prices with delta levels of .20 to .25.* This gives you an excellent 1.25 to 1 risk to reward ratio on the trade.

Rule #5: Legging into a debit spread can further reduce risk. To reduce the risk when trading debit spreads even further, leg in to the trade. Mechanically this means that you start by buying the long calls leg of the trade only. Then once the underlying rises a few dollars, leg into the debit spread by selling the OTM calls further out of the money to set up a wide spread. This gives you a wider profit range than setting both legs up at once.

FOR CREDIT SPREAD ORDERS:

These rules apply to all types of vertical credit spreads. As I described, I mostly implement the bullish put spread version of this trade (as opposed bearish call spreads). These rules apply to both versions:

Rule #1: **Hedge each vertical credit trade in the portfolio up front.** Many people will tell you to only add trade-specific hedges as adjustments on individual trades that go against you. The rationale is that spending money on insurance legs for winning trades is a waste of funds and lowers your returns. While adding insurance to winners is certainly a waste, nobody knows which of your trades will be winners and which will be losers. Because of this, you should hedge them all by entering the trade as a spread order up front. In addition, not everyone is a professional trader who can watch the market all day long. Most people have other responsibilities competing for their time that prevents them from entering perfectly timed hedges and making trade adjustments as certain trades go against you. The market can, at times, move too fast to enter good hedges. I have found that the best solution for all vertical and credit spread trades is to put on the hedging position right away.

One way to de-risk vertical credit spreads even further is to take 20% of the net credit (potential profit) on vertical spreads sold, and use it to buy extra protection in the opposite direction that I am playing on the trade. This does effectively become a variation on ratio spreads as you now have more protection if the trade goes against you than number of contracts on the risky side. You don't need to buy a large number of contracts as a risk management tool because a few long-put contracts will go a long way in hedging a bullish trade. As a rule of thumb, use no more than 20% of the net credit collected on credit spreads to buy the put protection.

This is a bullish put spread hedging example:
Stock = Apple (ticker: AAPL) is trading at $185.87 a share.
You are bullish and feel that over the next 30 days the stock will rise slightly or at least stay the same. You decide to enter a 20-contract bullish put credit spread expiring in 30 days to capture this upward move. Upon reviewing the various strike prices, implied volatility and standard deviations, you decide to sell a one strike price out the

money put credit spread as follows:

Expiration 30 days out

PUT Strike Prices selected:	# of contracts:	Bid:	Ask:
(Sell to Open) AAPL strike $180	-20	$3.25	$3.30
(Buy to Open) AAPL strike $175	+20	$1.50	$1.52

You are filled at: $3.27 - $1.51 = **net credit of $1.76**

After you are filled on this trade for a net credit of $1.76 per contract, you have:

- **A maximum profit on this trade of $3,520** ($1.76 times 2,000 shares, as you sold a 20-contract spread position).
- **A maximum loss / at risk amount of $6,480.** This is calculated as the $5 spread ($180 strike - $170 strike) multiplied by the 20 contracts ($10,000) less the credit collected on the short leg of the spread +$3,520, or total loss potential of $6,480.
- You are risking $6,480 to potentially make $3,520 (less commissions). **This is still too risky.**
- **To help mitigate this risk, take 20% of the potential maximum profit (20% of $3,520, or $704) and buy two additional long at-the-money put contracts.** I would choose the $185 strike price, and slightly longer dated than my spread (in this case, choose an expiration in six weeks). In this example, these puts cost of $3.00 (times 200 shares) = $600 plus commissions. The protection costs slightly less than $700 but it still achieves the desired hedge. If you want more protection, you could spend a little more and buy three put contracts (spending $900).

So now you have reduced the total profit you can make on this trade from $3,520 to $2,920 (which on $7,080 spent and at risk is still a potential 41% profit in 30 days) but you have added more downside protection if you are wrong. The long puts will go up quickly if the underlying stock price falls. Of course, the additional long puts do not offset all of the risk, or this would be a risk-free trade. The point is that the additional long puts help a lot in keeping your losses on spread trades smaller without dramatically reducing your profits if the trade goes your way.

In all scenarios, if the underlying stock, ETF or instruments moves as you anticipate, these small insurance costs only clip your large gains by a little but in most cases, they will reduce your losses by many multiples of the cost when you are wrong and the primary trade goes against you. In extreme cases, you can be totally wrong on the direction of the main trade and come out with a net profit on the trade as a whole when it goes dramatically against you.

__Rule #2__: Sell slightly out of the money ('OTM') strike prices when collecting time premium trades. The selection of which strike price varies slightly depending upon how far out in the future you are going until expiration, but the rule holds. Go as far OTM with the strike prices you sell as you can where it still makes your target profit on the credit you collect (this rule holds for Credit Spreads, for the covered call portion when doing a collar trades, Call & Put Ratio spreads, etc.).

__Rule #3:__ Don't spread trade on extremely expensive stocks:
This rule will be a controversial one for experienced spread traders. They will say that one of the greatest advantages to spread trading is that due to the limited risk, even very small accounts can participate in very expensive stocks they like. I used to think this too, until I got burned for over $12K, twice. I was just starting out and actually managed to lose a lot more money than was technically possible to lose on both of these trades. How did this happen? It was due to the execution leakage while exiting the trades, magnified by the huge prices of the underlying stocks.

I will give one of the two examples of my experience here:
The Trade: In 2015, I researched and liked Priceline (ticker PCLN), the online travel agency website. My research told me the stock should go higher when the stock was trading at $1,220 per share. I thought I was being very conservative and put on a 10-contract credit spread with the risky leg of the trade $100 out of the money at $1,120 for safety. Priceline would have to fall more than $100 a share in the next eight trading sessions for me to lose money on this trade. To still make a meaningful net credit I did a $10 wide-bull put

spread and took in a premium of 80 cents. I did ten contracts (for a total credit of $800 cash and the trade had a total risk of $9,200). I placed this trade with only eight days remaining until expiration and I had an 85% chance of winning when I put on the trade. Over the next six days, I watched in horror as Priceline fell $150 a share on no significant news! I was facing my maximum loss of $9200 and wondering what to do. It gets worse.

With one day until expiration and Priceline falling yet another $20 a share (it was now $1,050 a share), I was fearful that this huge expensive stock could now get put to me at any time at $1,120 a share times 1,000 shares (as that is the obligation one has when selling puts). In an attempt to prevent this, I entered an order to "buy to close" my $1,120 short puts leg of the spread to end the obligation. When the order filled, I immediately went to my positions page and started to enter the order to "sell to close" the protection leg of the trade in order to lock in the maximum potential loss of $9,200 – or so I thought.

I entered a sell to close limit order, trying to minimize the loss slightly by selecting a price to sell between the current bid and ask spread. The order did not trigger and the bid / ask spread kept moving against me every second. I kept altering my limit order, trying to get out. The bid /ask spread kept moving against me. After four limit order price adjustments by me, I finally entered a market order as I needed to get out to prevent 1,000 shares getting sold to me at $1,120. I got filled at a price that turned my 'maximum' potential loss of $9,200 into an actual realized loss of $13,000! This was magnified by the fact that I did this spread on a $1,200 stock. I ended up losing $3,800 more than was possible to lose on paper on this trade.

I could have immediately rolled-out a new credit spread on PCLN at lower strike prices to try to recover this loss. However, I was emotionally crushed, burned and afraid to put this large stock price trade on again. It would never have happened if I had collected the same 80 cent net credit on a stock like Facebook with a share price of $75 on a $4 credit spread. The bottom line – don't do large spreads on stocks with huge share prices.

Key lessons I learned from this terrible experience:
- The fear of the counterparty executing their option rights and forcing you to buy such a high-priced stock once it gets "put" to you makes it too painful to do credit put spreads on such high-priced stocks.
- The protection leg at $5 spreads is too expensive on high priced stocks to make good money. You have to do wider spreads at $10 or $15. This puts too much capital at risk for small investors. When you are wrong like I was on Priceline, it can cause losses that are too large for most non-professionals to handle.
- You can easily get the same potential gain on much cheaper stocks with tight spreads, so why take the risk of execution slippage and potential pain?
- I advise retail investors to only do $5 max spreads on stocks that are priced not more than $350 a share. The vast majority of stocks are priced under $200 a share.

By following these rules, I would have easily avoided this $13,000 loss. It would have limited my loss to about $2,500, which could have then more easily been rolled out and recovered or adjusted during the life of the trade.

Rule: #5: Don't trade right before the week of the stock's quarterly earnings announcement.

Rule #6: When rolling-out winners and losers, mechanically enter all spread trades & rollouts of spreads using the 'Spread Orders' trade entry screen. Rolling out spread orders near options expiration, or when they have hit your loss limit target, is a key tool for recovering losing spreads and compounding gains on winners. Rolling out loosing spreads takes discipline, as you sometimes lose your confidence in the underlying stock and you often have to roll a losing spread or long call three, four or even five times to get all your losses back and recover your position enough to exit at a small profit. It is often hard to stay the course emotionally when this trade has lost you money three or four times in a row. Unless the underlying news on the stock has changed dramatically, you must keep rolling out to win on the trade. If you give up, you lock in the loss. There is a way to roll and switch direction (switching the trade from a bullish put spread with a credit to a bearish call spread with a credit) and if the news has really changed, do this. If the trend is still intact and your timing just turns out to be off, keep rolling out the loosing spread until you win all of your money back plus a profit. Often rolling out (winners and losers) means rolling up or down in strike prices.

For example: Your research leads you to believe that Apple stock will go up over the next two months. You follow your pre-trade checks and you place a Bull Put credit spread as follows:

Apple share price when you placed the trade = $192

Enter a Bullish Put Credit Spread order:
- Sold to Open ten contracts of the $190 puts @ $2.90 out one week
  (& simultaneously)
- Buy to Open ten contracts of the $185 puts @ $.90 with the same expiration
- Net Credit = $2 times 1,000 shares = $2,000

However, over the next five days Apple shares fall from $192 to $187.50, which triggers your target stop loss order of around 30% loss in the trade (cash on cash). In this case I would roll out and down.

Mechanically this means I would buy back the original short leg (the $190 Puts) at a loss and sell the original long leg (the $185 puts) at a gain and then enter the new trade. The new rolled out trade would be:

Enter new credit Spread Order:
- Sold to Open ten contracts of the $187.50 puts @ $2.25 out three weeks in the future from the original order expiration date.   (& simultaneously)
- Buy to Open ten contracts of the $182.50 puts @ $.60 same new expiration date.
  Net Credit = $ 1.65 times 1,000 shares = $1,650

More aggressive traders may also double the number of contracts when rolling out a losing trade they still have strong conviction in the underlying stock. Doubling down like this is not for conservative trading.

Rule #7: *For credit spreads, do no more than $5 wide spreads and sell two strike prices OTM strike prices with low deltas for most trades to reduce risk.* When you want to be very aggressive, you can occasionally sell ATM or even one strike price ITM credit spreads – but realize that these trades have a much lower probability of finishing winners (but a much larger payoff when they do). Today's active stocks often have $1 or even 50 cent increment strike price choices on their options. With these super liquid options, I generally try to aim for spreads that are $2.50 or $3 wide when the premiums work and I can still get a net credit of at least $.75. As I typically do ten or twenty contracts this is still a minimum net credit of $750 for ten contracts and $1,500 for twenty contracts. You can often get much more – I regularly get $1,000 in net credit for ten contracts on a $3 spread at 75% probability of winning and a fairly low delta). Shop around; there are always good risk reward deals to be found. You don't have to risk $5,000 to make $1,000 deal on a credit spread. Unless you can get this extremely far OTM and a 90% + probability of winning, it isn't worth it. There are many better risk-to-reward ratio deals with a 70% to 80% probability of success.

Rule #8: *Don't pay too much for the insurance leg position on spreads. This applies to both credit spreads and debit spreads, especially if you are doing these as calendar spreads (with the protection leg much further out in the future than the short leg of the spread).* Do not overpay for the insurance leg of the spread, it takes too many winning net credits in a row just to pay back the cost of the insurance legs.

For example, I once did a bullish put calendar spread on Tesla (Ticker TSLA). My plan was to buy the put contract at three months out which was $15 out of the money as the insurance leg. It cost $7.40 and I bought ten contracts. I spent $7,400 plus commissions on the insurance protection. I was planning to sell high percentage, closer to the money puts against this insurance position to create a spread (with short expirations every two weeks for 3 months until the insurance leg expired). I had six winning trades in a row crediting ~$1,000 on each and still lost money and had big risk. On the seventh trade the stock fell $10 and I lost even more. The lesson I learned the hard way is that I paid far too much for the insurance leg of the credit spread. Even though I was right and won $1,000, six times in a row, I still lost money overall. The moral of the story, don't overpay for the protection leg of the spread trade.

The largest risk when trading vertical credit spreads is when a large move in the underlying goes against you and it happens so quickly that it blows through your short leg strike price and your long leg strike price in the same day. Sometimes the underlying stock gaps down through your put credit spread strike prices overnight; when the markets are closed, the stock opens far lower the following morning, and hence you are unable to trade out of it. These gap-downs are rare and they tend to violate the statistical norms but they do happen. When such an event occurs, take advantage of it by turning the direction of your bullish put spread trade and betting with the new fast-moving trend in the other direction. Do these by adding a trade adjustment – specifically buy short term calls or puts in the direction of the trend and let them ride as this new trend plays out. You can often more than make up your loss and even pocket a gain. For example, if you have bullish put credit spreads open and the entire market starts crashing, quickly, buy a number of long calls on the bearish inverse S&P 500 ETF (the ticker SDS, etc.). This helps defend your portfolio while giving you time to work your way out of the losing spreads.

As a final note, I like to do vertical credit spreads on stocks that are the top 50 largest hedge fund favorite stocks. These are listed for free on several public websites. This also de-risks our bullish trades a little more. This is because we do vertical credit spreads slightly out of the money for safety and if the underlying stock falls, the hedge funds are losing big money as well and they will generally step in and defend these top stocks they already own by buying more.

FOR DIRECTIONAL BUTTERFLIES & SKIP STIKE BUTTERFLY ORDERS:

As directional butterflies are entered with such a small net debit – often under $100 and that is the maximum potential loss – no further risk management rules are needed.

For skip strike butterflies, there is a potential to lose large money if the underlying makes a large, unexpected move upwards. Here are my risk management rules for skip strike (broken-wing) butterflies:

***Rule #1:** Be patient if the underlying stock price stays under the strike price of the short leg of the butterfly.* The skip strike butterfly profits from time decay but it can take a few weeks to play out. If the price of the underlying stock rises above the strike price of the short leg, close out the trade.

***Rule #2:** If you are winning and the trade is approaching expiration, take some small profits and scale out.* As the trade approaches expiration day, small fluctuations in the underlying stock price can have a significant percentage effect on the option prices in your skip-strike butterfly trade. When you have a large unrealized profit, it is best to close out half or more to lock in some profits and limit your risk. Let the rest run for maximum profits.

***Rule #3:** There is risk of early assignment of shares on the short leg of the butterfly prior to expiration.* If this happens and your short calls get assigned, then you are obligated to sell the shares short (in a call skip strike butterfly). If this happens, immediately buy to close the assigned short shares. This will usually result in a small loss but this is better than being exposed to potential further losses by having sold the stock short (through assignment). If assigned to sell the shares short, immediately buy to close the assigned portion of the position out and let your long calls (the remaining long call legs of the skip strike butterfly) run for potential future profits. The long calls in any butterfly have no risk of early assignment; the short leg does.

FOR CALL RATIO SPREAD ORDERS:

As previously mentioned, a call ratio spread is partly covered and partly uncovered. Anytime you write uncovered options, (also known as selling naked options) you expose yourself to significant loss. It can be many times greater than the cost of the option or net credit collected. The higher the ratio you write, the higher the risk potential. A 2:1 call ratio is less risky than a 3:1 ratio. Therefore, writing uncovered options is suitable only for more experienced traders who understand the risks. Cut down the risk by using the following rules:

Rule #1: Always initiate your call ratio spread for a net credit. Doing call ratio spreads for a net credit (at entry) cuts off the downside risk of the underlying stock falling. It does not eliminate the upside risk which we will handle with the other rules.

Rule #2: Call ratio spreads should only be initiated at market cycle tops or when your outlook for the stock is neutral to moderately bullish. I really like to do call ratio spreads when markets are making all-time highs, but no bearish catalysts are known. In these types of markets, the market tends to drift moderately higher but no sharp upward moves occur. That is the perfect scenario to make good money doing ratio call spreads.

Rule #3: Due to the unlimited risk of the uncovered call, buy a way out of the money protective call to limit catastrophic risk. Right after entry of a call ratio spread entered for a net credit, I like to spend just a few dollars and take away the unlimited loss potential in the trade. Remember, in this trade, loss occurs when the stock price makes a strong explosive upward move beyond the upper break-even point of the trade. After that, there is no limit to the maximum potential loss as there is in theory no limit to the price the stock can rise to. You can easily prevent this buy buying an equal number of long call contracts further out of the money just past your breakeven point. This eliminates all unlimited loss potential.

How to Position Size in Real-time to Maximize Profit in your Portfolio while Controlling Risk

As discussed earlier in this chapter, one of the best ways to manage risk in all market cycles and across all trading strategies is through the proper sizing of trades. Proper trade position sizing is one the most important ways to control how much you risk on any particular trade. Position sizing refers to how large each trade is, in dollars spent or in dollars at risk across the different positions in your portfolio. I always counsel investors to trade in equal dollar size increments spent and equal amounts at risk for each trade for the following strategies:

- Vertical credit spreads (the amount at risk).
- Debit spreads (the amount spent to enter the trade plus any extra insurance positions).
- Call ratio spreads with a credit (the amount at risk).
- Deep in the money long calls (or puts) positions.

I also do equal size trades, but with much smaller amounts at risk, for the following strategies:

- Skip strike butterflies (initial net debit or sometimes a credit).
- Directional butterflies (initial net debit).

This also applies to larger dollar trades / strategies, which by their nature in buying the underlying stock on margin require larger cash outlays:

- Collars
- Covered calls

If one or two of your trades are triple the size of the others, one big loser can wipe out all the gains in your other trades combined. Equal size trading ensures that your risk is balanced across position sizes. When I started out – I was a "$1,500 per trade guy" and I would shoot for putting on 10-12 trades at any one time. Over time I then became a '$3,000 per trade guy' across the 10-12 trades. Then I became a '$5,000 per trade guy'.

This equal trade size rule means that you will often be doing different numbers of contracts across the different trades. This is just fine. For example, it may mean you trade five contracts on Stock A; seven contracts on stock B; and three contracts on stock C, etc. Even on collars and covered calls, which as stated must be larger due to buying the underlying stock, I have found that if you use Portfolio Margin (discussed in detail in the next chapter – Chapter Ten) and you select fairly tight strike prices with your protective puts (the downside protection leg in a collar trade), you can still almost do equal size trades. For example, today my spread trades and long options average $7,500 to $10,000 per trade and my portfolio margin collar trades average $12,000 - $20,000 in cost for each.

*"If you don't make mistakes,
you're not working on hard enough problems.
And that's a big mistake. "*
- Frank Wilczer, 2004 Nobel Prize winner

Chapter 10

Using Leverage Effectively - Margin & Portfolio Margin

LEARNING OBJECTIVES

- **Understand the differences between margin & portfolio margin**

- **Use leverage effectively and safely**

- **The best leverage – the leverage of giving**

"It's not whether you're right or wrong that's important, but how much money you make when you're right and how much you lose when you're wrong."
- George Soros (Legendary Investor)

Leverage can substantially add to or subtract from an investor's performance. It must be handled carefully. Leverage cuts both ways. It can greatly magnify your gains or it can magnify your losses. This chapter will teach you my field-tested rules for gaining the benefits of using leverage while minimizing the downside.

I chose to place this chapter at the end of the book because it will not apply to all traders and investors. Many people will not use margin, portfolio margin or any other forms of leverage in their trading. By simply using the long ETFs, long stocks, the long call (stock replacement) strategy, covered calls or collar strategies taught in this book, you can do just fine without ever using margin leverage. Keep in mind, however, that without using account level leverage as discussed below you will likely not achieve the annual returns of

30%+ or more as discussed in my strategies in this book. Without the use of leverage, these same strategies may return 10% to 25% per year. That is still very good performance and you can handily beat the market without account level leverage. However, your returns will not be turbo-charged as they can be by careful use of leverage. If you choose to use leverage to put your account strategies into overdrive, *read on.*

Understand what margin & portfolio margin are and how to use them

Let's start with my favorite tools for the retail (non-professional) investor when it comes to wise use of leverage, margin and portfolio margin. These both can be the magic leverage enhancers for the retail investor. How is portfolio margin different than a traditional margin brokerage account?

Listed below are the key brokerage account types (from the leverage point of view) and a few edges in how to use them effectively:

- **Cash account** – no leverage at the account level but can use options to achieve leverage at the individual trade level. No margin, therefore, no margin charges.

- **Margin Accounts (also known as Reg-T Margin)**– A regulation T margin account is what 95%+ of retail investors use when they trade 'on margin' in their personal brokerage accounts. Regulation T ("Reg-T") is a collection of regulatory rules that govern how brokerages extend credit to customers for the purchase of securities. In general, the client can borrow up to 50% of the price of buying securities and the rest has to be purchased in cash. There are two types of margin accounts. The first type is called a *long margin accounts* and the other is a *short margin account.* I don't advise to ever sell stocks short (buy long puts instead if you want to bet on a stock or index going down). Due to this, you can ignore the short margin account. Broker / dealers are required to impose initial cash requirements and maintenance margin requirements. Margin accounts allow the investor to achieve leverage at both the *account level* (by borrowing money or pledging other securities as collateral to increase your trading capital) and at the trade level (by using the leverage inherent in options, LEAPS, etc.). The margin rates the brokerage firms' charges client are tied to the FED reserve interest rate levels plus a markup by the brokerage. The margin rates can vary widely and can be negotiated. You should call you brokerage and ask for the best margin rate reduction they can give you. It will be lower based on the size of your account and / or the volume of your trading activity

- **Pattern Day Trader Accounts –** I am not a day trader so this is not how I use leverage but for the sake of completeness, you should be aware of this. There is an additional type of leverage available to the retail investors who meet the definition of a pattern day trader. A day trader is someone who buys and sells the same security on the same day to try to make a profit by playing an intraday price movement. A Pattern Day Trader is a formal definition (flag on your account) which triggers automatically when you execute four (or more) day trades within a five-day business period. The minimum account size to be a pattern day trader is $25,000. If you meet these criteria, the leverage is higher than a regular Reg-T margin account. The buying power increases to approximately three to four times the maintenance margin requirement (vs. two times excess equity in a traditional Reg-T margin account).

- **Portfolio Margin Accounts -** Portfolio margin links your daily margin requirement on each trade to be equal to the maximum potential net loss possible on each trade and the account as a whole. What is portfolio margin in simple terms? It is a different way of figuring the margin requirements for your positions and overall account. In almost every case it offers the ability for retail traders to tie up substantially less cash on hold in each spread trade, collar trade and other protected trades and thus allows more leverage to the investor safely. The risk to the broker is also capped, which they like and is why they allow portfolio margin. By substantially reducing the cash tied up in each trade where you have a protective option position in place, using the strategies taught in this book, you can gain multiples of leverage just like a hedge fund.

One of my Brokerage firm service providers, Schwab, describes portfolio margin this way:

"Portfolio margin is a different way to calculate margin requirements for an account, allowing eligible investors to base margin requirements on the net risks of the eligible holdings in their accounts, typically offering more leverage and also increased potential for loss. Unlike strategy-based margin requirements, portfolio margin establishes a margin requirement equal to the greatest loss that, theoretically, would result if a gain or loss is calculated on the portfolio as a whole - at set increments on the upside and downside."

Portfolio Margin was passed and approved by the SEC in the United States for retail investors in 2008. Each brokerage firm has different minimum balance requirements for allowing retail traders to qualify to use Portfolio Margin. Generally, the minimum balance requirement ranges from $100,000 to $200,000 at different online brokers. By approval of portfolio margin, the SEC allows the margin to adjust to reflect the total reduced actual risk. So, while regular Reg-T margin is good and can add substantially to your percentage returns, portfolio margin is even better and is quite simply the best way to leverage for the retail investor that I know.

For example: If you buy a long stock (say 100 shares of Apple: AAPL) at $190 a share. You then add the purchase of a one contract protective put on Apple at a strike price of $170 a share. Technically, your downside risk is capped by the $170 strike price of the put option. In other words, as long as the protective put is open with a strike price of $170, the most you can lose on your Apple stock is the difference between what you paid for it (100 shares at $190) and 100 shares times the put strike price (one contract at $170). The maximum loss exposure is $20 times 100 shares, or - $2,000. With this structure, now you only have to tie up the amount of cash down to the protective put ($2,000) vs. 50% of the entire stock position ($9,500) in a traditional Reg-T margin account. Do you see the power? You can put on hold so much less cash and control the same upside.

The following are additional examples of trades that illustrate the power of trading with Portfolio Margin:

EXAMPLE #1: Disney stock (Ticker: DIS) is currently trading at $110 per share. You are slightly bullish and you want to buy 1,000 shares and collar it.

This means buying 1,000 shares of the DIS stock and simultaneously buying a ten-contract protective put position with a strike price of, for example, $15 a share lower than today's DIS share price. In this example that means buying a $95 strike put position with expiration out four months. To complete the collar, you then begin to sell short term ten contract covered call positions against the shares you now own to collect income. You could sell OTM covered calls expiring every three to four weeks until you get called out.

Now let's look at the trade using the leverage power of Portfolio margin. At full market value, buying 1,000 shares of Disney at a share price of $110, would cost $110,000. In a traditional margin account, your broker would require you to put up 50% or so of the full purchase price (or $55,000 cash) and then they would lend you the other $55,000 to buy the 1,000 shares. You then have to spend additional cash to buy the ten contract protective puts (approximately another $1,000). The point of showing traditional margin is that this would still cost the trader a lot of money tied up in this trade; at least $56,000 or so. There is a better way.

With Portfolio Margin, the SEC allows your broker to look at the actual maximum net risk you have of loss in this trade. In this example, the maximum loss is from the share price ($110) down to the protective put position strike price ($95) or $15 per share. Multiple this $15 maximum risk times 1,000 shares and the most you can lose in this collar trade is $15,000. With Portfolio Margin, this is now the total amount your broker will ask you to put on hold to enter this trade. The same trade that would have taken $56,000 to enter can now be entered with the exact same upside potential but for only $15,000 for the stock on hold + $1,000 to buy the protective puts. This greatly increases your leverage and magnifies potential returns when you are right.

Example #2: Chipotle Mexican Grill (ticker: CMG) is currently trading at $600 a share. At full price, buying 1,000 shares would cost $600,000. Even at the traditional 50% margin, it would cost $300,000. That is far too expensive for most small retail investors. With portfolio margin in a collar trade strategy, however, it would only tie up $40,000 for all of the same upside. It would look as follows:

Note: Enter all positions in the collar trade at the same time, using an 'All in One' order ticket:

- Buy 1,000 shares of CMG at $600.   (Total cost = $600,000)
- Buy ten contract protective puts down $40 at a strike price of $560 with an expiration date in six months for $12 (total cost $12,000).
- Sell ten contract OTM covered calls expiring in 3 weeks for ~$5.00 (with a strike price of $630).

With this trade, the broker will tie up a maximum of $40,000 (the total risk between the share price $600 and the protective put $560 times ten contracts or 1,000 shares). Some brokers will tie up even less than $40,000, reducing the margin requirement further by the amount of the covered call premium you have sold and taken in. By selling the covered calls, you bring in $5,000 every twenty days or so, or $10,000 every six weeks. In this example, you spent $40,000 one time to take in $10,000 every six weeks for six months (the length of your protective put). You can easily take in $40,000 in six months on a $40,000 cash investment if you do not get called out. This is a 100% cash on cash return in six months. Do this twice in a year (two 6-month collars) and your cash on cash return in 12 months would be 200%. Are you getting excited?

What if the Chipotle shares rise and you get called out at some point during the six months? Then you must sell the shares but at a $30 higher price than you bought them (you paid $600 and you would be forced to sell at $630 per share). Multiplied by 1,000 shares, this brings in an additional $30,000 profit less commissions and all the risk is gone. Still, a very good outcome.

The maximum risk in this trade is the same risk you would have in owning the stock if it declines to your protective put strike price ($560 / share). You have set up a maximum loss on this CMG trade at $560 a share due to the protective put part of the collar trade. But you can still lose if the shares decline from today's $600 down to that floor of $560. This loss is partially offset by the amount you take in on each of the covered call premiums over the six months, but you carry this risk as your maximum potential loss. You must be sure that you have done your homework and selected a good technically sound entry point using technical analysis to reduce your chance of the shares declining dramatically in the short term. Remember that the maximum risk is reduced with each covered call premium taken in and it disappears completely once you have collected enough to cover the maximum potential loss, which in this example is $40,000 less the first covered call of $5,000, or $35,000.

I hope these two examples illustrate why I like using portfolio margin, especially on collar trades. The power of the portfolio margin tool often allows me to earn over 50% gains in six months on a low-risk basis due to the fairly tight protective puts, and do so using exciting and expensive stocks.

Use Leverage Effectively and Safely

Many forms of leverage exist in the stock and option instruments available to the retail investor. Leverage essentially means using other people's money to enhance your profits. We do this in real estate all the time (by taking out a mortgage) but not so often in stock market investing. As we have seen in the previous examples in this chapter, leverage is a way to strategically increase your investment returns. Using other people's money in stock and options trading and investing often takes the form of your brokerage firm lending you money for buying and selling securities in the form of margin.

This concept of leverage exists across most asset classes, such as real estate, where the down payment to buy a house is essentially the same concept of leverage as buying a call option on stocks. It can be found in currency trading, commodities trading, and venture capital.

I will only cover the aspects of leverage specific to stock and options trading and investing. Leverage on other assets is beyond the scope of this book but consult with your financial advisor if they interest you. Trades can be leveraged easily by each of the following instruments:

1. The Leverage of Buying Options:

When buying call or put options (or LEAPS, which stands for Long-term Equity Anticipation Securities – essentially long-term options from nine months to three years until expiration), you want to maximize your chance of winning and minimize the amount you are spending for pure time premium. As we have learned, the best way to do this is to buy deep in the money options. This still gives the investor tremendous leverage vs. buying the stock while minimizing the down side substantially. Buying options deep in the money is the best way to battle the time decay inherent in buying options.

The main purpose of buying options instead of the underlying stock is to gain leverage on your investment. Options reduce the amount of money you initially spend to around 5%-15% of the amount you have had to spend to buy the equivalent shares of stock. You still control a magnified amount of upside or downside potential on a given underlying security.

Buying long options is available in all types of accounts – cash, margin, portfolio margin, IRA's, and corporate accounts.

2. The Leverage of Selling Options:

When selling options, you increase the odds of winning depending upon the options trade you structured. Time decay on spread trades works in favor of the options seller, especially in at the money (ATM) or out of the money (OTM) options. The downside is that you generally are collecting theta (time premium) at the expense of capping your gain potential. In other words, you have given up the upside to collect the income of the time premium when selling options.

The only money an option seller can generate on the trade is the amount received up front by selling and collecting the premium. The goal is to try to keep it as time passes and hopefully the underlying security moves in the direction you forecast.

Selling options also gives the trader a type of leverage. In fact, I have found that at least 60% of my overall trades are options selling to collect premium as opposed to option buying. The way we use options trading, with edges and risk management on every trade, substantially limits the risk and maintains tremendous leverage and potential gains in markets that are moving up, down, or trending sideways.

One of the hidden additional forms of leverage that is created when you sell options is that the net credit or premium collected can usually be used to do even more trades. This is especially true for in-the-money covered calls. I have a student who tries to buy stock and collect deep in the money covered call premium equal to 50% of the cash he spends to buy the original stock. He then uses this sold call premium to lever up again and do more covered calls. Can you see the power in that? He is using other people's money to pay for additional free trades while he waits to get called out in a few months' time. Talk about safe and brilliant compounding. His downside is protected by the deep in the money strike prices he is selling covered. Model this one out with a few deep in the money covered call trades and see how much cash you can generate and reuse in additional trades.

3. The Leverage of selling something you do not own.
The only place in the world I know that you can sell something you do not own and profit from it is the stock and options markets. This is one of the great leverage aspects - the ability to sell something that you do not own. How does this work? Selling something you do not own means selling a stock short. Don't ever short stocks unless you are a pro. If you want to bet on a stock going down, just buy a long put option (deep in-the-money) as this limits your risk to the amount paid for the put. You should buy the put if you expect a large rapid move downward in the stock. If you are only slightly bearish, an even better strategy is selling a bearish credit spread, known as a bear call vertical credit spread. This is also is selling something you do not own and getting paid to do so. This is my favorite way to use leverage when you don't own the stock – it gives you great leverage with protection and safety.

4. The Leverage of Portfolio Margin:

As discussed before, portfolio margin is a fantastic way to use leverage. Below are my rules to using portfolio margin leverage:

RULE #1: Try to do collar trades using portfolio margin on stocks that pay dividends as the quarterly dividends will in most cases pay for the margin interest that you have to pay the broker for the amounts borrowed to buy the shares.

(Note: I am conscious that Chipotle, in the earlier example, is a stock that does not currently pay a dividend, it was used illustratively to show worst case scenario where no dividend is paid. In actual trading, I select stocks that do pay dividends the majority of the time with an occasional collar on a biotech or tech stock with large premiums but not dividend).

RULE #2: Sell the covered calls on average $10-$15 or more out of the money at a strike price that is $10 or more above today's price. We do not want to get called out of the underlying shares if possible, though we profit if it happens.

RULE #3: Buy the protective puts with expiration dates between four to six months into the future.

The Best Leverage – the Leverage of Giving – the most important form of leverage of them all is to use your time and skills to help others.

This book has been about growing and protecting your wealth. I believe this is a good and noble thing to do. Not everyone does, but I do and I devote many of my waking hours teaching people strategies and managing, growing and protecting their money. I don't do it for the love of money (of which my belief says is the root of all evil) but for the ability that money has to magnify your ability to give to others (your time, money, skills, etc.).

Could you be a better person if you had more income and money? Most people would say yes to this question. Money enhances whatever you are doing. Money speeds your life up – for good or for bad. Money magnifies and enhances you on whatever journey you choose to be on. Growing money for your own security is nice and you should do that - but it is far from the most important thing.

What we learn throughout life is that it is not what we accumulate for ourselves that is most important. What really matters is how you give and share with others. By others I mean your family, your church, your friends, and even strangers through charitable giving. I believe that the principle of giving is the ultimate leverage. It leverages your time, resources and ability to allow you to leave a legacy and make a true impact with your life through helping other people.

Giving is not only a spiritual principle but a financial one. Many people who feel a lack in financial security say to me, "Sure it is easy for you to give, you have so much." The spiritual concept of giving doesn't actually work that way. You cannot 'out give' God. Be generous even if you feel lacking, help others even in a small way. If you can't give money, you can give time through volunteering, give someone a smile, advice, anything. Be generous and watch the leverage of giving be returned to you.

This book is about rules, strategies and formulas for growing prosperity and security for life. The leverage of giving is the strategy and formula for a life of happiness and meaning. I hope that gaining more will allow you to be and give more. Be principled and disciplined and work hard to grow wealth and apply it by being generous and a better you.

All the best!

"Keep away from people who try to belittle your ambitions. Small people always do that, but the really great make you feel that you, too, can become great."
- Mark Twain

APPENDIX

A. **EXPANDED TABLE OF CONTENTS:** Book Outline

B. **KEY TRADING RESOURCES:** (For Individual Traders): Key Trading Resources – websites, tools, etc.

APPENDIX A

EXPANDED TABLE OF CONTENTS:

Stock & Options Trading for Life:

The most effective stock & option trading strategies for individual investors to profit safely in all market conditions

ACKNOWLEDGMENTS

INTRODUCTION: My Story – Financial Freedom Through Stock & Options Trading for Life
- My Story
- Who This Book is Written For
- The Typical Investor
- The Bottom Line

Chapter 1: WHAT TO DO BEFORE YOU START TRADING - BUILD A FINANCIAL PLAN WITH A SET OF TRADING GOALS WITH TIMEFRAMES:

- **Completing Your Goal Based Financial Plan** – the trading strategies in this book focus on stocks and options but your overall percentage invested and risk tolerance needs to be in the context of your overall financial plan.

- **A Few Notes on Selecting a Financial Advisor** – Select a fiduciary, paid on a percentage of assets under management. Not a broker dealer representative paid either on a commission basis or one paid differently for selling different financial products.

- **Building Your Financial Plan** – An overview of the key activities in setting up your financial plan.

- **Build a Set of Investment Goals with Timeframes** – build a compelling 'why' for your trades; how much money do you need and when, how much do you have to start with, etc. Using these inputs design a plan that can achieve your short term, medium term and long-term objectives, with clear trading rules and action steps.

- **Basic Financial Planning Rules Everyone Should Follow.**

- **Understand the Psychological Aspects of Trading** – Trading psychology; getting mentally ready to trade & execute your trading plan. Doing the critical thinking and planning to best help assure your financial gains and success.

Chapter 2: DEVELOP YOUR TOP DOWN ECONOMIC WORLDVIEW AND SELECT YOUR BASKET OF STOCKS & KEY ETFs:

- **Why Should You Actively Trade a Portion of Your Portfolio, Instead of Just Buy & Hold the BOOST Portion of Your Portfolio.**

- **Create your Worldview Using News and Online Resources** - Develop a top-down global macro view of the world; the top five to ten issues affecting the stock market each trading day.

- **Rank & Prioritize Your Trade Candidates** – Only invest in the most compelling stocks, ETFs and set-ups given current market conditions.

- **Develop A Basket of Stocks You Love to Research, Follow** & Trade – Select no more than 50 stocks total and split them by key industry groups and sectors. Rank and rebalance quarterly.

- **Make Selections Across Key Industry Group and Sectors.**

- **Develop a Short List of Favorite ETFs to Trade and Hedge -** Develop a list of ETFs and leveraged ETFs to help you hedge the market, your portfolio and also trade for gains.

- **Be Careful Using leverage ETFs and ETNs.**

- **My Favorite ETFs.**

Chapter 3: FUNDAMENTAL ANALYSIS - ON THE STOCKS IN YOUR BASKET:

- **Use Fundamental Analysis to Help You Determine WHAT to buy and Sell.** Helps you determine WHAT to buy based on a bottoms-up fundamental analysis and future projections.

- **How to Complete the Homework for Fundamental Analysis.** How to do fundamentals on each of the companies in your basket of stocks.

- **Additional Fundamental Analysis Rules.**

Chapter 4: TECHNICAL ANALYSIS ON THE STOCKS IN YOUR BASKET: Helps you to determine WHEN to buy or sell and how to match each trading strategy to various overall market conditions.

- **How to Use Technical Analysis.**

- **The Key Technical Tools –** the key indicators I use, why and when to use them.

- **My Favorite Technical Indicators and Rules That Work.**

  - **Technical Indicators – Group #1:** To help you determine the trend and the buying and selling pressure on a stock or ETF.
  - **Technical Indicators – Group #2:** To help you confirm the current trend & to measure the strength of that trend.
  - **Technical Indicators – Group #3:** To determine low risk trade entry points and exit price targets.

- **Combining Fundamental Analysis and Technical Analysis Together.**

- **A Few Additional Tips on Combining the Analysis.**

Chapter 5: DEVELOPING YOUR PERSONAL TRADING PROCESS & GENERAL TRADING RULES – Key rules to follow no matter which trading strategy you are using.

- **Understanding the Importance of Diversifying Your Trading Strategies.** After diversifying across trading strategies, then concentrate your trades within each strategy to one or two.

- **My Favorite Trading Strategies by Risk & Reward.**

- **Trade Sequencing (Also Known as Trade Progression).**

- **Options Basics.**

- **<u>When to Place Which Types of Trading Strategy.</u>**

- **<u>Setting Profit Targets & Time Frames by Strategy</u>** - selecting high probability trades and targets by trade.

- **<u>Other General Trading Rules</u>** – covering all types of trades. My top 20 list of additional trading rules to live by.

<u>Chapter 6:</u> MY FAVORITE TRADING STRATEGIES & TRADING RULES: The most effective and risk-controlled stock & option investment and trading strategies for both income trading and long-term portfolio growth

- **<u>In creating the list of my favorite trading strategies, I made the following assumptions about you.</u>**

- **<u>Favorite Trading Strategy #1: Collars, Covered Calls & Large Unprotected Covered Calls</u>** – All three are variations on the same strategy.
  - o **<u>The Foundation of the collar trade - the covered call</u>**
    For the collar, the in the money covered call and the large unprotected covered call are variations on the basic covered call trade.
  - o **<u>Variation #1: The Collar Strategy</u>** – The safest variation of the covered call and my bread and butter strategy. Adds a protective put leg onto the bottom of the covered call.
  - o **<u>Variation #2: Writing in the Money Covered Calls.</u>**
  - o **<u>Variation #3: Writing large priced, unprotected covered calls</u>** – On expensive stocks with large call premiums four to seven months to expiration.

- **Favorite Trading Strategy #2: Stock Replacement. Buying Deep in the Money Call Options (or buying Deep In the Money Put Options When Bearish) With Long Term Expiration Dates** On stocks & industry sector ETFs (with 30% stop losses & adjusting winners to market neutral strangles).
  - o **My Method to do 'Stock Replacement' buying call options.**
  - o **My Rules for Stock Replacement (the Long Call Buying Strategy)**

- **Favorite Trading Strategy #3: In the Money Call Debit Spreads** (also known as vertical debit spreads or bullish call spreads).

- **Favorite Trading Strategy #4: Selling Vertical Credit Spreads (also known as Bullish Put Spreads and Bearish Call Spreads)** (including iron condors – selling both a bull put spread and a bear call spread at the same time on the same underlying security).
  - o **My Rules for Trading Vertical Credit Spreads:**
    - ▪ *Variation #1*: Writing Weekly Vertical Credit Spreads
    - ▪ *Variation #2:* Iron Condors – writing both a bullish put spread and a bearish call spread together.
  - o **My Rules for Iron Condors**
  - o **KEY BONUS STRATEGY: Writing Cash Backed Puts (with Protection)** – When you want to buy a stock you don't currently own but at a reduces price and get paid to do so. Don't sell cash-backed puts alone, it is safer to do a bull put spread.

- **Favorite Trading Strategy #5: Buying Directional (Out of the Money) Butterflies &**

<u>Skip Strike (Broken Wing) Butterflies</u> –
Directional butterfly spreads placed with strike
prices out of the money.
- o **My Strategy Variation #1**: A directional
  out of the money butterfly.
- o **My Strategy Variation #2**: A broken wing
  (also known as a Skip-Strike) butterfly.

- **<u>Favorite Trading Strategy #6: Call Ratio
  Spreads</u>** - with a net credit at trade entry.
  - o **<u>My Rules for Trading Call (& Put) Ratio
    Spreads</u>**

<u>Chapter 7</u>: TRADE SELECTION & THE GREEKS:

Use Probabilities for trade selection. How to use statistical
probabilities and the 'Greeks' to select trade strike process and
expiration dates.

- **<u>The Key 'Greeks' to Use & the Current Levels -</u>**
  What are the Greeks and how do we use them
  easily
  - o **<u>Understanding Delta</u>**
  - o **<u>Understanding Vega</u>**
  - o **<u>Understanding Theta</u>**

- **<u>The Statistical Probabilities of Trade Success -</u>**
  Use Probabilities for Selection. Use 1+ standard
  deviations for high probability trades
  - o **<u>My Trade Rules</u> –** for the best statistical
    probabilities of success.

- **<u>Determine you Target Exits Before Entering
  Trades</u>** – winning & losing before entering trades.

- **<u>Use a strategy of Trade Progression vs. Going
  All-in with one Strategy.</u>**
  - o My Favorite trade progression strategies.

- **<u>Pre-trade Checklist & order Placement</u>**

<u>Enhancers</u> – the page to have next to you and
check off right before placing trades by trading
strategy.

<u>Chapter 8</u>: **TRADE ADJUSTMENTS – WHAT TO DO WHEN
TRADES GO WRONG:** what to do when trades go against you –
the key difference between pros and amateurs.

- **<u>How to Decide if and when to adjust a losing trade
  position.</u>**

- **<u>Executing trade adjustments</u>** -what to do when things go
  wrong on an individual trade.

- **<u>My Favorite trade adjustments for each of the six
  trading strategies taught in Ch. 6:</u>**
    - **<u>Trade Adjustments for Losing Covered Calls /
      Collar Trades</u>**
    - **<u>Trade Adjustments for Losing Long Calls / Put
      Trades</u>**
    - **<u>Trade Adjustments for Losing Call Debit
      Spread Trades</u>**
    - **<u>Trade Adjustments for Losing Vertical Credit
      Spread Trades</u>**
    - **<u>Trade Adjustments for Losing Skip-Strike or
      Directional Butterfly Trades</u>**
    - **<u>Trade Adjustments for Losing Call Ratio
      Spreads with a New Credit.</u>**

- Handling losses trades that go against you is the key
  difference between pros and amateurs.

<u>Chapter 9</u>: **RISK MANAGEMENT RULES:**

- **<u>Understand the Importance of Risk Management and
  Following General Risk Management Rules.</u>**
    - *The Over-Complicated School of Risk
      Management.*

- o *The Over-Simplified School of Risk Management.*

- **The high percentage winner does not always make money.**

- **Risk Management – your most important job in trading & investing.**

- **General Risk Management Rules.**

- **Portfolio Level & Trade Level Risk Management Rules.**
  - o *My Portfolio Crash Stop Out rule*

- **Specific Additional Risk Management Rules by Trading Strategy.**

Chapter 10: USING LEVERAGE EFFECTIVELY & PORTFOLIO MARGIN: Using Options and portfolio margin to safely lever up where appropriate and maximize potential returns given your risk tolerance.

- **Understand the differences between margin & portfolio margin**

- **Use leverage effectively and safely**

- **The best leverage – the leverage of giving**

APPENDIX B

KEY TRADING RESOURCES (For Individual Nonprofessional Traders):
Key Trading Resources, Websites, Tools, etc.

I use all of the following websites and recommend the following online resources:

Online broker sites (with good stock and options tools):

Broker Name:	Website URL:	Key notes:
Charles Schwab	schwab.com or the one I use: Street Smart Central: www.streetsmartcentral.com	For options trading use the Street Smart Central trading platform at Schwab. My overall favorite for spreads and long call / put trades. Great walk limit tools, easy and clear to navigate and monitor positions, weak charts.
TD Ameritrade: Including both the regular website and the more advanced **Think or Swim** website. Note: you must first have an	www.tdameritrade.com and the one I use: www.thinkorswim.com	Best home professional level brokerage site. institutional level platform. Best platform for options, and short-term trading. Most professional home-

account open and funded at TD Ameritrade – then you can download the Think or Swim platform.		based traders use this but I find it overkill on many features unless you are an advanced trader.
Interactive Brokers	www.interactivebrokers.com	Nearly the lowest costs (except for a few free platforms); global market access; robust tools and market access.

News and Research sites:

Yahoo Finance	www.finance.yahoo.com	Good overall news site – look up any stock and get the current news, quote, option chain.
Investor's Business Daily (or IBD)	www.investors.com	By far the best daily newspaper in the US for investors. Wonderful site for news, IBD50, and stock checkup features are daily prep for me.
Briefing.com	www.briefing.com	Best for earnings calendars, economic events affecting overall markets and company specific events.
Stockcharts	www.stockcharts.com	My favorite chart and technical indicator site. Best place to overlay an Ichimoku cloud. Free version is great but I also like the paid version for seasonality by stock.
ETF Screen	etfscreen.com	Best ETF site – great

		filters and screeners.
FINVIZ	Finviz.com	Great simple to use but advanced screening tools – for free. If you are looking for the best pure screening tools – this is the place to start.
iViolatility	www.ivolatility.com	A great data service to help with your pre-trade analysis. Professional options traders use implied volatility as the #1 Greek and analysis metric in evaluating trades. This website has the best volatility analysis tools, and resources.

Options Market Industry & Government Websites:

Chicago Board Options Exchange	www.cboe.com	The largest options & futures exchange in the US. The website has great options and futures education resources (videos, etc.), data, statistics and put /call volume.
SEC.gov/ EDGAR	www.sec.gov/edgar	Best for company reports and regulatory filings. 10K (annual reports); 10Q (quarterly reports
Options Clearing Corporation	www.theocc.com	Clearance & settlement for 15+ exchanges. Market

		data, risk management.

Good Sites for Entrepreneurs

(Remember – you are running your trading as a business. This makes you an Entrepreneur):

Great General Resources	Great startup and entrepreneurial resources if you are setting up your trading as a business (vs. just for your own private trading):
Entrepreneur .com	500hats.com
Forbes.com	Quora.com
Inc.com	Onevest.com
SCORE.org	Audiencebloom.com
ForEntrepreneurs.com	Crunchbase.com
AllthingsD.com	Startupcompanylawyer.com
SBA.Gov	Epiclaunch.com
TED.com	Businessownerstoolkit.com
Allbusiness.com	Fiverr.com